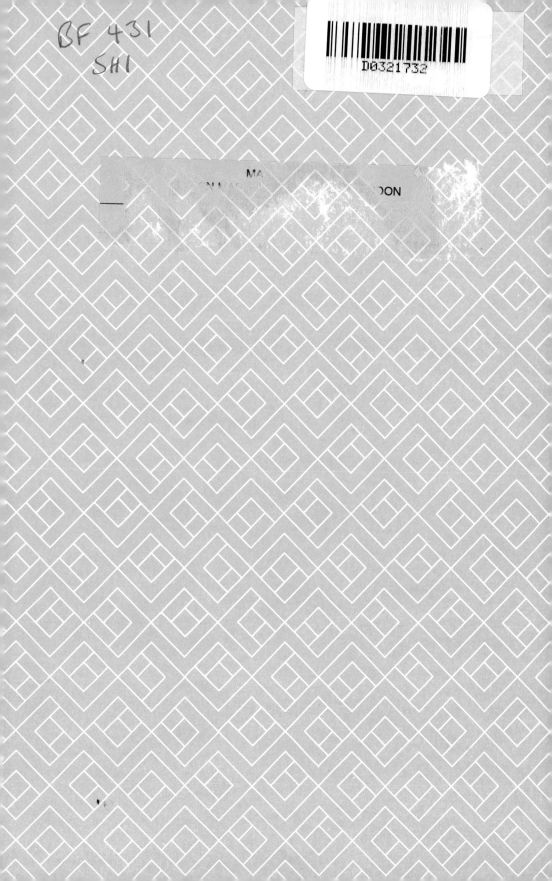

Intersensory origin of mind

In *Intersensory Origin of Mind* Thorne Shipley proposes a fundamental revision of the core of modern psychology. With a serious respect for the history of science, Shipley shows the profound limits of linear, mechanistic and naively reductionistic accounts of the mind, and proposes instead a sensory rationalist position which builds upon the principles of emergent evolution. In this way, also, he begins the construction of a scientific foundation for the psychotherapeutic process.

Combining several diverse perspectives, from the physiological optics of Helmholtz, the perceptual science of Köhler, the visual electrophysiology of Hubel/Wiesel to the theories of Dewey, Polanyi, Cassirer, Chomsky, Freud and Piaget, *Intersensory Origin of Mind* is an ambitious humanistic synthesis of sensory science. It will need to be read by anyone with an interest in philosophical psychology, the nature of human consciousness and the origin of mind.

Thorne Shipley is Emeritus Professor in Vision Sciences, Psychology and Theoretical Neuroscience at the University of Miami Medical School. He is the founder of the journal *Vision Research* and is the author of such books as *Sensory Integration in Children* (1980) and *The Theory of Intelligence* (1990).

Intersensory origin of mind

A revisit to emergent evolution

Thorne Shipley

London and New York

First published 1995
by Routledge
11 New Fetter Lane, London EC4P 4EE

Simultaneously published in the USA and Canada
by Routledge
29 West 35th Street, New York, NY 10001

© 1995 Thorne Shipley

Typeset in Times Ten 10/12 by
Florencetype Ltd, Stoodleigh, Devon

Printed and bound in Great Britain by
Biddles Ltd, Guildford and King's Lynn

British Library Cataloguing in Publication Data
A catalogue record for this book is available from the
British Library

Library of Congress Cataloguing in Publication Data
A catalogue record for this book is available from the
Library of Congress

ISBN 0–415–12003–9

To Virginia

'The mind is like a ...'

In the history of ideas, the mind has been taken to be any sort of machine, usually the most complex of the day. This lovely illustration was drawn for me by Ms Laura Sartucci. Its full exposition is given in Chapter 10.

Contents

Dynamics of mind parallels dynamics of the senses
Evidence from clinical neuropsychology
Removal of the mind from the senses allows purpose
Brain damage and a deficit in gestalt formation
Henry Head vs. stiff-necked anatomists
Vigilance: a sub-cortical alertness
Multiple personalities: psychiatric not neurological
Cognitive unity and plasticity
The denial of symptoms: sightlessness, limblessness
Intersensory processing single brain cells

Loss of claws in crabs
Inversion of newts' and frogs' eyes
Optical inversion of images in man
One-trial learning-modelling
Regeneration of sense-energy ingestion surfaces
Environment modelling vs. culture modelling
Loss of variance-processing capacity bears on sensory-rational intelligence
Cats reared seeing only vertical stripes
Seafarers and signers
Genetic geometry vs. environmental geometry

Illustrations

Preface

Sometimes, in writing a work of this nature, one is tempted to over-write. And I am very aware of that danger.

But the task that I have set myself is not simple, and I have not yet the skill to handle it with the precision that I might wish. It is in the expectation that I cannot say these things better, and that others may fail to say them at all, that I write now as I do.

As the senses all communicate to reason, so I believe that reason must not entirely leave its place of birth. What 'revealed' truth illuminates for so many of my fellows, even today, it does not illuminate for me. But even in the austere and restrained corridors of science there must still be room for the carpets of intuition and the sharp corners of imagination. And what one writes must count, also, as ethical and aesthetic truth. This is why, despite the power of reason and the often surprising rightness of science, we must recognize that other things are right as well and in equally surprising ways. And when some of the most earnestly religious among us assert with utter sincerity and confidence that there is that of God in every person, this assertion cannot but help to move us, at the same time that it raises in our minds queries as to the character of that godliness; and as to whether somewhere in nature that special presence ceases abruptly or gradually leaves off.

None the less, puzzled as we may be, we move ahead both with passion and with caution: passion, because otherwise we would not dare to go at all; caution, because we know that our passage is bound to cause some tension, especially in those who believe that they absolutely know. Or feel that they do, as feelings persist when abstract experience and belief are not yet sufficiently precise. The central question of our time is not to show that absolute knowledge exists, it does; but rather to demonstrate how to perceive or to recognize that subset of knowledge which may be universally experienced as being valid for all of time, in contrast to the perhaps more common sort of knowledge that has claim only to a momentary ontology. If this present work leaves any trails, and entices others along them, I hope that this will be in part because it aids them in finding a path to transcendental rather than to transient truth.

Growing up in Greenwich Village, in New York City, during the last throes of the great depression, the early throes of the discovery of the brutalities of Stalin in the Soviet Union, of the Japanese in China and of the atrocities of the Germans in their Nazi years, and struggling with the meaning of evolution in the light of that view of human civilization, in the centre of the radical movement in the United States while surrounded by a family and school culture embodying Quaker ideals of unanimity and pacifism and secular Jewish ones of utopian and altruistic socialism, it was natural for me to become a sort of peripatetic and somewhat muddled village philosopher, concentrating on the problem of how we know. Later on, I chose to study adult spatial vision and then colour vision to give some empirical foundation to my philosophy. The international science journal that I founded then, *Vision Research*, was actually intended by me to cover vision only primarily, and secondarily to entice in broader views of how other senses co-ordinated with sight.[1] For contingent reasons, however, the journal stayed wholly within the study of vision, so I then shifted some of my experimental energies to empirical studies on intersensory processes and on sensory-cognitive development in children, which I had come to realize were essential to give direction to my view.

And now, once again moving back to philosophy, and looking anew at the probable nature of evolution and human civilization, I find that, coming full circle, I may now have some answers to my youthful questions that will also interest professional philosophers and biologists. So, perhaps in this conjunction, there will be some fruitful gifts back from Psyche to her original mother, Sophia.

Psychology, however, naturally confronts many serious problems that need scientific analysis and answers that may be slightly more than gifts. The problems of the psychological meaning of liberty without responsibility, of exploitation without recompense, and of an ecological neglect that in itself fosters a countervailing violence are all-pervasive. And it is not possible for an experimental science bereft of philosophy to address these questions. Philosophy and biology and political science and law and, let it be said in a science text, humanistic religions are all needed to understand why human dreams are always so different from human realities. Perhaps because psychology is still such a new science it has felt an excessive need to prove itself by an exclusive emphasis on laboratory methods. And this also goes along with the strangely limited US national policy on science.

It is within this context that many of my colleagues have, in recent years, asserted that the human mind is nothing but a computer. But much of my text to follow shows this to be errant nonsense, and proves this in

---

1 This view was shared fully by my first associate editor, Fred Crescitelli, and it is with much sadness that I note his recent passing.

a strong sense. That view is also dangerous because it replaces an enduring reverence for life with a momentary fascination for a gadget.

In calculus, we have the concept of least upper bound. This is an idea that permits us to come as close as we wish to some real upper bound, but not exactly touch it. That, it seems to me, is the only correct way to approach the study of the human mind: come as close to it as we can – though this is often not as close as we may wish – but not ever quite precisely reach it. As close as we get, mind steps just a little away – if only to show that it is still in charge.

It is my purpose here to bring into one place the description of the evolutionary origin of the mind, a problem that has occupied all my scientific life. As a student of psychology, vision, and intersensory perceptual science, my concern for orderings and their sources naturally carries my studies centripetally to the mind from the eye and from the ear. It is also true that the problem of the origin of mental life holds a natural inherent fascination for many people and that its study does not need special justification. It would be presumptuous to suggest that I am the first or will be the last to undertake this task. But it does seem that, in our present state of knowledge, some synthesis can be achieved in this direction that perhaps was not possible in earlier times. An enriched phenomenology of mind is also part of what I have in my mind (wherever that may be!). Science advances more by new syntheses than by the acquisition of what some call 'new facts', precisely because it is the function of syntheses to give new meaning to those facts. Sometimes even contrary meaning. Some facts are arbitrary, and this is not always recognized; others are insistent, part of the order of the universe and its co-ordination with mental order. The fact that A usually comes before B does not have the same character as the fact that the dawn usually comes before the day. While both reflect in different ways our apprehension and comprehension of reality, the former is what we may call an invented or arbitrary fact, while the latter seems to be a discovery about how nature exists wholly apart from man. It is not arbitrary, except in the case that the day of today comes generally before the dawn of tomorrow. Man, in this view, can be considered *the arbitrary one*. But what then of one coming before two or two before many, in concrete and then in abstract form? What of the child fathering the man?

Mental life is an integration of the given with the adventitious. Indeed, the least arbitrary elements of mental life are the sensory contributions to it. But even here the perception of order within disorder is the primary event, and probabilities and non-linearities are involved.

It is not that philosophers do not have much to say on these issues. It is only that, generally, in the absence of an overall encompassing view that integrates the insights of evolution theory with those of modern sensory science, they tend to concentrate their inquiries on difficult epistemological issues that are somewhat removed from the constraints that an acquaintance with neuroscience and mental dynamics might otherwise put upon these deliberations, or at least they do upon mine. Furthermore, one can hardly make advances in this field today if one is not intimately familiar with its empirical side. Epistemology and the theory of knowledge, of oneself and of the other, while not long ago still proper subjects for largely abstract linguistic analysis in the hands of such giants as Wittgenstein and Carnap and Korzybski and Chomsky, have been transformed for psychology by other giants, such as Wertheimer and Köhler and Piaget and Hubel and Wiesel, into empirical endeavours. Sometimes advances are made in science when we learn how to investigate gently, by non-distorting or non-violating but empirical means, what previously we dared investigate only by methods intellectual and abstract. Sometimes, however, the failure to recognize the inherent limits of investigatory approaches brings us close to the end of science. There is a tightrope that responsible men and women must walk.

One place where this sort of walking has been elegantly done is in the problems of visual space. Here, Rudolf Luneburg applied the mathematics of relativity theory and non-Euclidean geometry to some, then already classical, experimental observations upon visual depth alleys or avenues (like the trees Napoleon had planted along both sides of the great rural roads of France).[2] Although there had previously been many empirical studies of visual space, few questioned its inherent metric nature or its inherent Euclidean form. Actually, no one previously had understood how it might be possible, while actually encased within that space, to make observations concerning either its metric nature or its intrinsic structure.[3] This required some advances in mathematics. What Luneburg achieved for the first time – and, unfortunately, what some researchers since have failed fully to comprehend – was (i) the application of the insight from modern differential geometry concerning the firm distinction between intrinsic and extrinsic geometry and (ii) the demonstration of how this distinction might be applied in actual empirical observations to visual space as experienced. The distinction between intrinsic and extrinsic geometry is of enormous significance in the history of mathematics, and its first application to human vision was a step of considerable importance, though naturally not of equal immensity. As we have shown elsewhere,[4] this distinction also helps us understand many other issues, a critically important one being the heredity–environment puzzle. Heredity

---

2 Luneberg, R. (1947) *Mathematical Analysis of Binocular Visual Space*. Princeton, NJ: Princeton University Press. Also Shipley, T. (1957) 'The convergence function in binocular visual space', *J. Opt. Soc. Amer.* 47: 795–821.

3 Hermann V. Helmholtz is the possible exception, as he is in so many fields. See his 'On the origin and significance of geometric axioms', *Lectures*, 2nd series, London, 1881.

4 See my book *The Theory of Intelligence* (1990). Springfield, Ill.: Thomas.

is intrinsic, it sets its own geometry; environment is extrinsic, and it sets another.[5] Each has its own variance induction and variance toleration. The resultant individual human being is thus a complex integration of these two geometries. As Einstein and others have shown, gravity can be considered the key geometric aspect of the universe, controlling the geodesics, or shortest paths for all the motions within space-time, of tiny particles of radiation (and so light) and of large particles as well at the other extreme (planets and stars and galaxies). In quite analogous fashion, the intrinsic constraints of genes set the geodesics or least energy-order-quality (EOQ) consuming paths for plant and animal development, while the extrinsic environmental constraints influence the ultimate plant or being by appropriate EOQ exchanges with the intrinsic dynamics.[6] This influence depends upon how much EOQ, and what kind, the environment can supply: if insignificant, then the intrinsic geodesics remain dominant; if significant, then the extrinsic geodesics take precedence.

Such considerations, then, and many others, lead us to novel insights concerning the origin of mind and, hopefully, to heuristically useful, if not equally novel, insights about how to examine mental function extrinsically without distorting intrinsic mental function. In this, phenomenology must play an absolutely central role.

The present work is not a history of models of the mind. While it takes account of many, and references some, it by no means intends a review of the field. That is a task that others may wish to undertake. Important

---

5 This distinction is becoming more and more crucial to our understanding of the balance that is the final organism. And this balance is significant at the levels of experience and behaviour as well as body structure, cf. Plomin, R. (1990) 'The role of inheritance in behavior science', *Science* 248: 183–8. One comment should be made on genetic behavioural research and the problem of violence. Clearly, the genetic influence on violence is profound, and cannot be gainsaid. This is shown by the fact that virtually all the social violence committed in human society today is done by males, individuals having not two X chromosomes, but only one X and one Y. Whether this propensity lies in the loss of an X or in the acquisition of a Y is moot, but all through the animal kingdom the males do most of the predation and, mostly, succeed by violence in the choosing of desirable mates. What the social persistence of these sorts of violences, among others, means is that our exosomatic cultural constraints and geodesics have not yet been quite sufficient to overcome the strong intrinsic ones. But putting findings such as the XYY male and the familial trends in social violence into this wider context may help better to direct our attentions towards enhancing the vigour of our social controls, so increasingly necessary these days with the prevalence of inter-racial and inter-religious and inter-cultural abrasiveness and conflicts.

6 EOQ, in my terminology, stands for *Energy-Order-Quality* to represent the quality of the energy expended in some process such as perceiving light or consuming food or expressing hope. Energies exist in various forms, the order of which is given by their degree of *transformability*. Thus, gravity has the highest possible order, it has an entropy of zero. It can go or be taken readily into mechanical, electrical, chemical, or thermal energy and even, under special circumstance, into molecular binding energies. On the other hand, heat is a low form of energy, i.e. from a boiling pot of water at the foot of the cataract one cannot reconstruct the falls. Protein in animal bodies is bound as a higher form of energy than is cellulose in plants. And so forth.

as it is, it is not my present task, and I do not wish to disappoint readers expecting to find herein what I cannot provide.

My effort is more modest. While it puts mechanical and computer views of mental life aside, it does show, to the contrary, that parallels between true mathematics and true phenomenology lend grace to one and conviction to the other since 'we have a direct awareness of mathematical form as an archetype'.[7] Even more than this, we are perfectly content to entertain the thought that mental life may have its own laws somewhat separate from those describing other parts of nature. In weak moments one almost hopes that they will turn up soon to help tame the raging lions within and let the rainbow warriors of the Amerindians continue on their gentle journey across the sky. Those of us trying to emulate Galileo and to elaborate on Newton, or, in this field, to advance upon William James and Sigmund Freud and Hermann V. Helmholtz, are bound to fail that high an aspiration. More modestly, one hopes only to stand with dignity in their light. Voltaire once noted wryly that a nation with many laws has many criminals, and a nation with great ignorance, many books. Time, as always, will tell. One can only accept the risk and open one's hands and let the bird fly.[8]

---

7 This generally is a task already begun by Brown, G.S. (1968) *Laws of form*. London: Allen & Unwin, p. xvi.

8 A note on style and method. This is, ultimately, a treatise in philosophical psychology and not a review of intersensory psychophysics, though that could be important. I am highly selective in the experiments that I cite, and deliberately inventive of many thought experiments, hopefully sufficiently absurd as to have a chance of being correct and setting (or upsetting) someone to do them. These take advantage of the natural parallel between mathematics and psychology.

I have used an expanded table of contents as well as an index because I think that most appropriate for a book of this sort. The footnotes are intended to be easily read, as one goes. A few are extensive, when the issue seems to warrant that.

Acknowledgements

The title of this book is chosen quite deliberately to echo long-respected traditions in bio-science. In the years since Charles Darwin published his epochal *The Origin of Species* (and Wallace his pamphlet on the same topic), in 1859, there have been a great many books discussing origins.[1] Concern for origins is so widespread because the concept is one of the many grand primal ideas, sharing with destiny the character of archetype. Each of these works has a focus, the most famous being the origin of life. My present effort is directed towards a much simpler topic, though I am aware of Einstein's admonition: 'I like things to be as simple as possible ... but not simpler.'

Mind, of course, is part of life, and it should not be at all suprising if certain Darwinian principles were found to apply. Actually, I do have a bias. My reading of Darwin in my high school years was one of the most important influences on my decision to follow the science career. I was then simply enthralled by his magnificent sense of the appropriate, his extraordinary gathering of overwhelming evidence and, although writing on a subject he knew full well would challenge major religious premises at their very core, his quiet yet earnest rejection of arrogance and contumacious debate. All this seemed to me to carry the conviction needed for genuine scientific truth. Darwin – in 'An historical sketch on the progress of opinion on the origin of species' (which appeared 'previously to the publication of the first edition of this work', i.e. previous to *The Origin of Species*) – was so circumspect that he mentioned thirty-four authors besides Wallace and himself who discussed this question and came close to the correct answer. And he was exquisitely careful to give credit to others in their anticipation of his and Wallace's ideas, especially a Dr Wells and a Mr Matthew (p. 8). On the basic conclusion, then, one

---

1 Actually, the two famous papers, one each by A.R. Wallace and C. Darwin, were read (not by either of them, as it happens) before the Linnean Society on 1 July 1858. This joining was a marvellous gesture – virtually unknown today with the DNA scandal still echoing – of sharing credit. They are listed virtually as co-authors: (1858) 'On the tendency of species to form varieties; and on the perpetuation of varieties and species by natural means of selection', *J. Proc. Linnean Soc. London* 3(9): 45–62.

may be justified in quoting this extraordinary scholar *in extensio*, both to give some indication of his gentle style and to show that, advanced as we may think we are today some 130 years later, we have not advanced all that much:

> No one ought to feel surprise at much remaining as yet unexplained in regard to the origin of species and varieties, if he make due allowance for our profound ignorance in regard to the mutual relations of the many beings which live around us. Who can explain why one species ranges widely and is very numerous, and why another allied species has a narrow range and is rare? Yet these relations are of the highest importance, *for they determine the present welfare and*, as I believe, *the future success and modification of every inhabitant of this world.* . . . Although much remains obscure, and will long remain obscure, I can entertain no doubt, after the most deliberate study and dispassionate judgement of which I am capable, that the view which most naturalists until recently entertained, and which I formerly entertained, – namely, that each species had been independently created, – is erroneous. I am fully convinced that species are not immutable; but that those belonging to what are called the same genera are lineal descendants of some other and generally extinct species, in the same manner as the acknowledged varieties of any one species are the descendants of that species. Furthermore, I am convinced that Natural Selection has been the most important, but not the exclusive, means of modification.[2] (Italics added)

It would be hard to find a more apt current view of the position on ecological evolution as espoused by the most advanced of modern biologists, or a more gracious way of making this absolutely momentous point.

My further affirmation of Darwin will be seen in my short discussion (Chapter 3) of his superb naturalistic methods, chronicling nature as she is, unsurpassed before or since, as in his *Narrative of the Surveying Voyages of H.M.S. Adventure and Beagle* (1840–3) and his later (1872) *Expressions of the Emotions in Animals and Man*.

Clearly, Darwin was not an experimentalist, and he did not do such modernly essential scientific things as test null hypotheses and falsify predictions and run correlation coefficients or analyses of variance nor did he even do curve fitting or run Chi-square or t-tests. 'Student' (that modest inventor of the t-test) was not even alive when Darwin wrote, and most of modern probability statistics remained to be developed. Non-parametric statistics had not yet been thought of. None the less, it is universally admitted that Darwin's achievement stands at the highest level in the development of biology. The facts and principles of biological

2 See *The Origin of Species by Means of Natural Selection or the Preservation of Favored Races in the Struggle for Life* (1859) New York: Modern Library Edition, pp. 13–14.

variation and evolution are accepted today by virtually all biologists every-where in substantially the form in which he (and, indeed, A.R. Wallace as well) set them out. The major factor that they missed was the role of co-operation in evolution, and this omission has long ago been set right by other biologists, including the extraordinary Russian Prince Piotr Kropotkin and the American Charles Allee in the early years of this century, and many more in recent days.[3]

The formulation of my thesis has taken several years, and has involved a variety of explorations both theoretical and experimental, and I have received encouragement from many people. I should like to note some here: Eric Gutkind, the great Jewish philosopher, was one of my earliest teachers; Arthur Lovejoy, Bentley Glass, William McElroy, William Albright, and George Boas at the Johns Hopkins University in science and in philosophy; Max Wertheimer and Wolfgang Köhler at the New School for Social Research in Gestalt Psychology; Adelbert Ames in trans-actionalism; Hans Lukas Teuber and Henri Hecaen in neuropsychology; Jean Piaget in child development; Rudolf Luneburg (posthumously) in mathematics; W. David Wright in optics at Imperial College; Michael Polanyi (the younger, primarily), and Nandor Balasz in optics and rela-tivity; and lastly George V. Bekesy in sensory interaction; after these, my students, occasionally at Dartmouth College but particularly in the Honors Program at the University of Miami which has been host to my unusual classes on these topics for some thirty years. Michael Hysen and Peter van Houten deserve special mention.

The frontispiece, as so many of the key illustrations of my ideas, was done for me by the gifted young biomedical artist Laura Sartucci. Its exposi-tion comes in Chapter 10, though its meaning surrounds this work. And I am also most grateful to Gail Horacek for transforming my illegible manuscript into some elegance.

As always, the sunshine and the dew of my days come from my wife, Virginia, and our two sons, Neal and Jesse.

---

3 Almost any modern text on evolution will discuss the role of co-operation as well as some other issues such as punctuated evolution. Social Darwinism, perhaps the most well-publicized recent concept in evolution theory, is not pertinent to the issues raised in this work, and will not be discussed here. The important post-Darwinism distinction between somatic (body) and exosomatic (or socio-cultural) evolution, however, will be much discussed in this work. Indeed, we still do not fully understand how or in what ways, if any, the advent of family-social groupings, agriculture, language, and human creative intelligence has influenced our own mental evolution (in a sort of reverbera-tion of life on life) or the evolution of plant and animal forms in nature. Such concerns form the major part of current ecologic science.

1 Some starting points for a new humanistic psychology

THE EYE OF THE IMAGINATION

The first point consists in this, that I see with the eye of the imagination those enormous fires, and the souls as it were in bodies of fire.

The second point consists in this, that I hear with the ears of the imagination the lamentations, howlings, cries, the blasphemies against Christ Our Lord and against all His Saints.

The third point consists in this that I smell with the sense of smell of the imagination the smoke, brimstone, refuse and rotting things of hell.

The fourth point consists in this, that I taste with the sense of taste of the imagination the bitter things, the tears, sorrows and the worm of conscience in hell.

The fifth point consists in feeling with the sense of touch of the imagination how these fires fasten upon and burn souls.

(Ignatius Loyola c. 1550)[1]

While these words of the founder of the Jesuits may seem ominous for beginning a humanistic psychology, they illustrate two points. The first is that mythopoesis is a crucial element in human history and, as such, provides a virtually inexhaustible supply of rich material for psychology.

One of the reasons that the scientific examination of consciousness and self-awareness is so very difficult is that the mythopoets – from the earliest days of the rise of consciousness – have anticipated much of what we might wish to say. The whole grand story of the Garden and of the expulsion from Eden refers, actually, to the sacrifice of the innocence of unawareness and the attainment of the knowledge, not of good and evil (as is said), but of the self, and, also, to the emergence of the capacity for reflexive self-awareness. How else would Adam and Eve come to recognize their own nakedness?

---

1 Fölöp–Miller, R. (1930) *The Power and Secret of the Jesuits*, trans. F.S. Flint and D.F. Tait, New York: Viking Press, especially pp. 7–8.

This is also why modern mechanistic neuroscientists who wish to sweep all such spiritual insights into the garbage heap of false facts and wrong claims – there to join terracentrism and special creation and the denial of the unconscious – commit the grave error of hubris. The truly scientific attitude is one of probability, not assertive positivistic certainty. For a scientist to stand forth in this way is to betray the calling. This is so because science deals with the order that can be found to group or to organize the 'facts' into some cohesive unity, and that task is very different from the mere accumulation of isolated truths.

It is for ever to the major credit of gestalt psychology that it demonstrated that what occur in mental life are orderings and groupings, and almost never mere summations. And that this characterizes all but the simplest of sense experiences as well as the most complex ethical, juridical, scientific, and artistic reasoning. The expression that 'the whole is more than the sum of its parts' is, in fact, *not* what the gestaltists have shown, though this is the most common description, appearing even in the technical literature. What they have shown is that the whole is *different from the sum of the parts*, which is something – now on the second level of differencing (that of a difference between differences) – that is very significantly different from *merely more*. The gestaltists have shown that truths do not 'merely add' in mental life, but integrate and cohere and, suddenly, without warning, discontinuously regroup. In the mind, if one adds up twelve apples, one might obtain a dozen; but one may also get a single pear.

It is almost as if what scientists now do or say about consciousness is anticlimactic or redundant or irrelevant, since so much has come before. And the true success of a humanistic psychology will come when it achieves something grander still: a sufficiently complete and synthesizing model of mental life that includes neuronisms and reductions at one extreme and also the mythopoets at the other. This is my task here.

Consider this idea. It is probable that some woman or set of women invented speech so as to talk to their infants and children, and then to each other (as twins often invent private languages today), and perhaps also to gain some secret advantage over men. Moreover, it is also probable that women were the first to generate in themselves the recognition of self-awareness, as emergent from the birthing process (which is also partly why men have almost always been excluded from that). Many women today do still find their best definition of themselves as mothers. In birth, what was within becomes apart, yet still remains within as the need to nurse and to suckle and to nurture. Similarly, as the ego-mind becomes apart from matter, it also remains somehow a part of matter. The question is: in what way?

And, even in this, the mythopoets were preludic, because it was Eve who gave the apple to Adam.

The first temptation, then, was certainly sexual; but it was also an immense emergent cognitive gestalt-like leap, wholly different in mind from what came before, in matter or in mind. It is, to this day.

Secondly, the very concept of the 'eye of the imagination', of the position of all the senses in the imagination, speaks directly to the fundamental theme of our present work. And – in the natural way in which the dynamics of mental life swing between opposites – the eye of the imagination and all the senses of the imagination also perceive with hope if not quite equal clarity – because most people are realists – the opposite pole of destiny from that envisaged by Loyola: heaven or utopia or, perhaps, just optimistic anticipation.

The point is that, while there has been in mythopoesis – in which, when one considers it carefully, lie the foundations of all of science – and thence in secular poetry and in the fundamental aspects of linguistic evolution a long-standing, implicit recognition that the senses of the imagination have somehow contributed to mind, there has not yet been anywhere in our science a full and convincing discussion of how this may have come about within a natural ecology of human evolution. Nor has there been an attempt to co-ordinate the form of this general insight with the more empirical sciences of the laboratory, or with modern sensory psychophysics.

This is my intention here. Consider the important issue of sensory-cognitive opposites just noted. While this is of immense interest in psychophysics and in sensory-rational psychology, it has been little discussed. We do not know why – though one can speculate – it is easier for the senses of the imagination to perceive the tortures of the damned in hell than it is to perceive the delights of the blessed in heaven. In virtually all of at least western mythopoetic literature, descriptions of hell abound, but those of heaven are almost always quite restricted and leave details largely to private imagination. In fine, the two states are not precisely cognitive opposites.

Consider some more mundane opposites, like sweet and sour. Are they precisely opposed, and in what exactly does that opposition consist? Does the middle C on the piano have any opposite? What is opposite to a square? Does cold have a precise opposite, does far, does soft? The method of after-image analysis in vision, based tightly on physiology and psychophysics, supplies us with rather neat and convincing opposites: red to blue, green to yellow and so forth. But such convenient physiologically unified foundations for the cognitive experience of opposition are not common. While loud and soft may be in opposition in the ear of the imagination, are major and minor keys in opposition in the same way? In olfaction, what are the opposites, if any? And on the skin (sharp vs. dull) or the tongue? In any thorough discussion of the origin of the concept of opposition, it is true that the senses of the imagination must be included; but it is not yet understood how it is that opposition exists in various degrees (as near as you like to being opposite, but not quite), or even that this mental concept in and of itself requires subtle and refined analysis.

The problem exists most pointedly within a given modality. Consider another example in vision. Normally, the direction in which the two eyes are looking is always the same, except for a creature like the salamander that can turn its eyes in opposite directions. Usually, the two eyes are directed to the same place, but it appears to present no difficulty at all to this small creature that sometimes it is looking rightward with its right eye and leftward with its left eye. To this day, vision scientists do not quite understand how it is making 'sense' of that necessarily dual world that it is then visually ingesting. The fact that the nerve fibres from the two eyes in the salamander cross entirely to opposite sides of its brain must surely hold a clue to this, since increasingly in the higher mammals, for example, more and more of the optic nerve fibres project back ipsilaterally to the cortex.

In contrast to this is the situation in one mutant form of the Belgian sheep dog. This rotund and intelligent and friendly creature has an optic nerve projection which is entirely ipsilateral, while in normal Belgian sheep dogs only about 30 per cent of the nerve fibres remain on the same side; the remaining 70 per cent still pass over contralaterally through the optic chiasma. The reason anyone thought to examine these dogs is that they all suffer from a congenital nystagmus: the eyes constantly jitter within their sockets. Though these animals can survive well enough in domestication and special breeding, it is sure that this would be a considerable hindrance to survival in the wild.[2]

Which is to say that the physiology of this sort of opposition – almost certainly causing the dog to receive in the brain two different or opposing images of reality at once – has direct evolutionary significance. This animal, to put it simply, must be 'seeing double', or alternating monocularly as do many humans with squint or amblyopia.

WHAT'S WRONG WITH SEEING DOUBLE?

Perhaps it is a task more for philosophers or for evolutionary psycho-biologists to tell us why life forms, primitive as well as advanced, have been able to survive at all only as they develop so as to ingest simultaneously one unitary model of the reality outside. One can easily speculate that because we 'have' only one body, we ought also to have only one mind. On the other hand, in a (Lewis) Carrollean mood, I can suppose that humans are sufficiently evolved that they could juggle in mind several and perhaps opposing models of reality at once. Is this not

---

2 See Dell'Osso, L.F. and Williams, R.W. (1994) 'Ocular motor abnormalities in achiasmatic mutant Belgian sheepdogs', *Vision Res.* 35: 109–16.

what satire is, and much of humour? When mythopoesis places God as all around and all pervasive, why does it also place him far away, Absconditus?

In a simple intersensory doubling, do the visual images in the famous movie *Fantasia* give the same picture of reality as do the aural or musical images? In part they do, which accounts for the great popularity of that film. But in part they do not, especially for musicians, which accounts for the dislike that many serious classical musicians have for that film.

This issue of opposition or double imaging can be brought home by noting that a fair description of mental health could be that it involves a single unified internal geometric co-ordination with external reality, and that all the several senses and the sensory-rational-cognitive information channels available to the individual cohere in this single self-same image. When this coherence fails, the mind-self or psyche is manifestly in trouble.

The central question for generations that has puzzled all of those aware of mental illness is just how this coherence is achieved in most instances, virtually without effort, while in other cases it cannot be achieved at all. And also, in what way heuristically may it be said that this coherence is achieved within some 'place' or 'location'? And the question that I now add to these is: how do the senses contribute to this unity and this emplacement?

Descartes, as is well known, maintained that the mind-soul has no extensivity, that it does not exist at all in some location. Indeed, that the whole idea of localizability cannot validly be applied to it. For Desartes, there is little doubt that even the use of the expression 'it' as applied to 'mind' would raise uneasiness and objections. Clearly, way back in the middle of the seventeenth century, he denied the possibility of any neuropsychology, a science which developed during the nineteenth century, and considerably by virtue of contributions from fellow Frenchmen.

Today, this is a flourishing science and, while we cannot yet in any convincing manner locate mind or consciousness or any of their dynamic attributes (ego, free will, memory, anticipation), it is clearly heuristic to describe self-awareness as having an intrinsic formal or geometric character, and the several senses as giving rise to this as their own geometric character becomes more evolved and more resilient and more precise. In the sensory-rational view, it is in part the clarity and precision of this internal geometry as self-perceived that helps co-ordinate the multisensory models of reality into a single harmonious whole. This, then, is what the primary dynamics of the mind is about: putting into geometric balance the various models of external reality that the senses take in, and setting all their cognitive elaboration into a coherence with the structure of the internal self, taking due account of the dynamic and fuzzy memories of previous models of that reality. Reason and self-awareness are then thrust forth as conflict resolvers, often effortlessly coherent yet continually engaging in the play of opposites along the length of the dimensions as well as at the antipodes.

THE UNVERBALIZABLE

Many important ideas now current in science have had a very long history, and often that is well described and accepted. Other ideas, however, while frequently underlying much of the thinking and experimentation, have remained largely undocumented. Perhaps because of their indistinctness they dwell unsuspected under the surface of even deliberate science; or perhaps because they are so subtle and obscure they have escaped conscious formulation. An illustration of the former is the idea of gravity which, being absolutely everywhere, remained long hidden anywhere in particular. An example of the second is the idea of emergent evolution, or of evolution itself, which grew up confronting a great amount of prejudice against any concept that challenged the mythopoetic idea of special creation.

The further some ideas are from direct sensory-rational input, the greater the socio-cultural contribution that must be devoted, indirectly or otherwise, to their emergence into awareness. And a proper science of psychology deals as much with concrete examples of these two sets or classes of ideas within its own field, as it does with the problem of the very existence of this duality. It is not simple to describe why some ideas are easy to express and others more difficult. Nor in what that difficulty consists. Many ideas lie just at the edge of thought and perhaps beyond the edge of what it is that can be expressed easily or at all in words. Words, like most socio-cultural inventions and conveniences, were devised by humans to serve largely concrete and economic and then mythopoetic ends. And it is not at all surprising that language fails us when we have other ends. As a simple example, let us ask: 'In what does the point of a joke consist?' It is pretty much without effort – indeed, in part it comes as a sudden relaxing of effort – that all normal people within a given culture can 'perceive' the point of a joke. But not even the best of critics among us has yet been able to put that 'getting the point' into other words, so as to make a viable and communicable model of humour. We just do not yet know how to describe, in a general universal sense, what this special perception is. We know to what jokes refer, we know a thousand different sorts of jokes, but we do not know why one joke is 'funny' and another not. Largely, if we set the conditions right – and we have now advanced in our physics so that we can readily do this – we can get pretty nearly all normal humans to experience 'blue' or 'sour' or 'up' or 'stereoscopic depth' or 'a C-chord of music'; but as to the point of a joke, well, obviously, there is no point yet to a science of that! While we can all perceive the possibilities for humour in just about anything, it seems clear that our science of humour need not in itself be funny ... though it may be a joke, to some. The science of red, of course, cannot in itself 'be' red, although it must give a 'good account' of red.

But what 'giving a good account' of something means, that also remains to be said. Even in such advanced sciences as physics and biology, many terms remain ambiguous and contain within them unverbalized, if not unverbalizable, aspects. In physics, for example, the meaning of the expression 'beginning' when referring to 'the universe' remains largely unelaborated. In biology, the expression 'evolution' covers an absolutely bewildering range of modifiers and qualifiers that only the most sophisticated agree upon (... and even then!). So it is that, in any science, even or perhaps necessarily, ideas rush ahead of words and only sometimes, over the generations, do words catch up; and then, not always satisfactorily.

It should not be at all surprising that there are many terms in psychology that are similarly pregnant yet mysterious: ego, gestalt, threshold, awareness, memory, hope, decision, imagination. Which is precisely why a fully rich psychology must deal with 'that which is beyond words', which escapes linguistic formulations and resides in what we can now confidently call preverbal consciousness. This is not so much a place, of course, despite the successes of neuropsychology, as it is a dynamic process that possesses (emerges with) the quality of experience: within. Such processes and complex qualities pervade the daily experiences of all humans, in no matter what society, even the most highly technological. They are not merely some vestiges of ancient and now to be discarded attributes of the human psyche – along with oracles and daemons and possessions and succubi and mares of the night that take us all frightfully riding – but are inherent in all our thinking and experiencing, even in the best of our mathematics and the most stern of our sciences. It is simply not possible to comprehend the events in any of the most rigid and, if you will, computerized human mental personalities, without invoking preverbal processes and presymbolic processes that influence thoughts and experiences and which compound sensations and sharpen acuities and distort or restructure texture, contour, shape, and form.

Indeed, the preverbal process of ego-strength, so stressed by Freud in his depth psychology, is as pertinent to a largely verbalizable event such as a visual or an olfactory threshold, as is a verbalizable touch-texture discrimination to a nonverbalizable process of transference. Naturally, in the laboratory, we try to simplify such connections, or sever them entirely, so that we can divide things up into separate sets of manipulable variables. But even in the physics laboratory, there are often too many variables and the task at hand has, mostly, the attraction of convenience. The mysterious is still the motivating factor, as we may see directly in the widespread search for 'intelligent life' elsewhere in the universe, as if the search for intelligent life here under our noses were not sufficiently entangling.

In sensory-rational psychology we are not trying to model the whole via the accumulation of a thousand differential threshold judgements, but rather by an examination of the facts of multi-threshold co-ordinations in one naturally textured ecological context as they are transformed and re-coordinated in another naturally textured ecological context. We are concerned as much with transformation dynamics as we are with static texture perception. Experience is never a thing; it is a flux, to which we strive to give moving form and shape sufficiently precise and communicable so that we can express it as a geometric motion or model. What really is: going on or coming about?

THE GEOMETRIC MENTAL SELF

It follows from this argument, in a way perhaps not previously realized, that the understanding of geometric relationships is crucial to many phases of psychology from the study of sensory science and perception to language and communication and social and depth psychology as well. It is a quirk of evolutionary determination (if perhaps not of some 'creative force') that it has come to seem that, when we think in a geometric mode, we think most clearly and most easily about the greatest number of variables. Naturally, in thinking beyond three dimensions, we emerge into the supra-sensory and abstract, but retain clarity about as long as we can retain clarity *about* being aware that we are aware that we are aware. And it is still well within the geometric mode that we come also to believe that we are able to communicate our ideas well and with least effort to interested others. To this day, the way we think when we do geometry and all the activities based upon it, architecture, engineering drawing, agriculture, and so forth, still resembles the simple act of pointing.

This may in part also explain geometry's primeval clarity. And why there exists a universal fascination with textures and designs and mosaics and patterns. We need not try to put them into words, the spatial relationships speak largely for themselves, as long as one can look ... and does.

On this basis, one helpful way to rephrase our previous description of mental health might be this: the internal possession in awareness of one's own mental self that is as geometrically congruent as is possible with the true character of one's mental self. Thus, in health one responds well to the famous admonition at Delphi: know thyself. In the formal sense of shape preservation or constancy, the intrinsic meta-geometry models well the intrinsic being. You feel that you cannot sing, and you really cannot sing. You feel that you can dance well, and you really can dance well. You feel that you are good at languages, and you really are good at languages. You feel that you are clever at geometry and you really are clever at geometry. You feel that you are seven feet tall when you really are seven feet tall. And so forth.

How then to communicate this intrinsic sense of recurring self-validity and of the enduring capacity for self-confirmation to another interested extrinsic awareness? Sometimes words help, for while it may be insufficient or poorly communicative to assert merely that 'I am now seeing red', the assertion 'I am now in deep mourning' almost always carries the proper geometric meaning across.

A NOTE ON TWO GEOMETRIES

We have, in passing, used the expressions intrinsic and extrinsic, in referring to geometries, and this duality is important to explain. Let us take as our illustration the existence of two sounding sources or objects which are perceived as two and are, for the time being, sensed as being just about equally far away from you, directly out in front. That they are perceived as two when they really are two is already an agreeable transformation from the extrinsic physical reality to the intrinsic perceptual reality. One could imagine many conditions in which the number of sounding objects (quite analogous to light-emitting objects and vision) was *not* correctly transformed into intrinsic experience, as in: how many voices are in that chorus? Suppose that we have had a bright idea (why some ideas are bright meaning novel or clever, I do not exactly know, though the intersensory message is getting through) to set the two auditory sources to be exactly matched noises, either white (all audible frequencies) or pink (select audible frequencies), and that the energy or power at each frequency is exactly matched physically; the two sounds then do, pretty much, match in loudness and in perceptible distance. A microphone placed midway between the ears would give some physical needle deflection or other which indicates to knowledgeable observers that: 'Yes, indeed, these two sources have equal energies or power' (we do not distinguish power from energy here, though this may be useful in other contexts).

Suppose that we now introduce a change in the two sound sources, but leave their relative positions equal and unchanged in extrinsic physical space and their total or overall relative energies equal and unchanged in extrinsic physical space. We, for example, shift the envelope of pink noise frequencies of one source up to the high-pitch frequency range (say 8,000 to 12,000 cycles per second) and we shift the envelope of pink noise frequencies of the other source down to the low-pitch frequency range (say 800 to 1,200 cycles per second).

A good flat physical audio-receiver would still indicate two equally loud, energetic, sound sources. And we then conclude that in extrinsic geometric space they have remained two and in the same place. In fact, if we were very clever we could have so balanced the sound emission energy spectra over frequencies that, when convoluted (multiplied) by the normal auditory sensitivity curve, the result for the two sources would still be equal neuro-aural arousal, which we experience as equal loudness. This, despite the asymmetrical fall-off in the sensitivity curve at these frequencies. And we might test for this equal loudness by matching amplitudes of brain-stem evoked electrical potentials or cortically evoked electrical potentials or even by some index, now more likely invasive, of the firing rates of the auditory or eighth cranial nerve. Maybe some day, we could determine that equal degrees of bending take place in the microcilia of the inner hair cells of the basilar membrane – and so forth, all indices showing, in conformity with the extrinsic physics, that nothing has changed.

However, intrinsically something has changed. The mind takes the source of the deeper pitch as 'being', 'existing' further away in physical space than the source of the shallower pitch. Which indicates that the intrinsic metric of the ear is not independent of frequency, as one might wish for simplicity. The transformation geometry in such a situation is thus non-Euclidean. Actually, there is good reason to believe that all the higher animals ascribe a greater physical distance on the basis of pitch to lower-pitched sounds. This is not an extra-somatic perception, though its evolutionary basis is presently speculative. The fact that differential pitch discrimination – how far apart must two pitches be physically to seem perceptually, intrinsically, equally far apart? – is not the same over the aural sensitivity range may hold some explanation. One can distinguish among high pitches with greater resolution than one can among low pitches. Furthermore, low-frequency waves are long waves, relatively speaking, and so travel for greater distances unimpeded by small natural obstacles than do high-frequency waves.

In passing, then, let it be noted that these processes also directly affect music perception, in that a certain three dimensionality is given by pitch changes, irrespective of what the stereo-acoustics may actually be. And this explains why there are thousands of solo parts for the violin, but few for the contra-bass.

Let us expand this discussion of extrinsic vs. intrinsic to the socio-cultural field, where its application is even more exciting. Suppose that in some family household there are, by all extrinsic criteria that the census-taker uses, four individuals of such and such ages and of such sexes and religions and ethnicities and schoolings and maturations and so forth, forming this or that geometry of relationships. But the intrinsic geometry in that household may be an entirely different thing: that is, the intrinsic numbers and relationships perceived may be quite non-conformal. There might, for example, 'be', in a very significant experiential sense, another person there, since the grandfather's 'presence' is always being noted, or the presence of the absence of a dead sibling, by not ever being mentioned out loud by anyone under a very big prohibition. Presences and absences in human psycho-social relationships are only distantly conformal – in the sense that the transformations are fuzzy – to physical presences and absences. And as far as the energies involved are concerned, or the power structures, these are so often not discernible by transformation from the physical as to prove the rule. The physically biggest and loudest human does not always rule the roost.

James Thurber, the great American cartoonist, once drew a picture of a husband obviously trying to sneak home undetected after an illicit night out on the town, only to find that the whole house itself is gradually taking on the shape of the face of his obviously anxious and perhaps justly recriminating wife.

The use of this distinction between intrinsic and extrinsic geometries, though expanded by me from classical mathematics, has limits, certainly. But since its use is intended primarily for heuristic purposes – to simplify, but not too much, our thinking and communicating about these matters – one need not be especially exercised if, in some instances, the distinction is unclear or not useful. Since it can be applied in many areas of socio-cultural function which have resisted our understanding in the past, it seems worth some struggle to explore. Rhythm and pace in life are also matters for geometric modelling, as in living life at the pace of rock music vs. living life at the pace of the *Pavane for a Dead Princess*. Such differences are matters of rates of change, and of rates of change of rates of change, which is a wholly different and more complex event that we term: acceleration. And this brings us directly to the crucial issues of mental dynamics. Largely, and to the greatest extent, these remain to be carefully described.

No one today can model communicably even such a seemingly simple act as a mind changing itself. What formal changes have taken place, and how regularly or abruptly have they come about? And all the while, some over-riding process, let us say the ego, remains the same. Thus, there are two geometries of interest. Perhaps there are more than two.

2 Many valid approaches to mind

VISION AS AN ENTRÉE

Just as most sensory psychologists have missed the importance of intersensory processes in their approaches to cognitive and mental function,
so also have most philosophers, scholars, neuroscientists, and others
interested in the general nature of the mind. For example, almost everyone interested in the higher cortical or cognitive processes, with the
exception of linguists, has taken vision as a starting point. While that is
naturally appealing, it is wrong to take vision as the end-point as well.[1]
Even most of vision, in the natural world, can best be understood as a
textural ecological event strongly influenced by context and intersensory
ingestions.

---

1 For a recent example, see Crick, F. (1994) *The Astonishing Hypothesis: The Scientific
Search for the Soul*, New York: Scribner's & Sons. This is an especially good case in
point, because Crick uses vision exclusively to 'model' consciousness. While his review
of vision is quite fair to many controversies, I must say that his hypothesis (that there
are only neurons there, in the brain-mind) is not astonishing at all, since it is the
most common hypothesis in all neural modelling literature today, with the annual
bibliography running at well over a hundred volumes in neuroscience, in engineering,
in computer science, and in vision research. Furthermore, he cuts with far too wide a
blade: calling psychoanalysis a cult and James Gibson a guru, though himself using two
figures (Figures 16 and 17) that certainly derive from Gibson; restricting all of science
only to the experimental; rejecting any religious insights whatsoever; and deriving
ethics from the scientific attitude, rather than the reverse. A crucial difficulty arises
when he states that 'sensory qualia may not ever be explicable by any sort of
neuronalism', because, as I am demonstrating throughout this work, consciousness and
self-awareness are, precisely, that: central sense-qualities of mind, especially as
emergent in the intersensory modes. Consequently, he excludes at the outset the
possibility of explaining what his title suggests he is trying to explain. Crick does,
however, leave the door open: 'There is always the possibility that the facts [will]
support a new, alternative way of looking at the mind–body problem that is significantly different from the rather crude materialism that many neuroscientists hold
today' (p. 262). Precisely.
   A refreshing rejoinder to Crick's materialism may be found in a recent work by a
systemic biologist: Smocovitis, B. (1994) *Unifying Biology: The Evolutionary Synthesis
and Evolutionary Biology*, Princeton, NJ: Princeton University Press.

Moreover, visual neuro-cognitive principles do not always apply, even *mutatis mutandis*, to the other modes. The tactile mode, for example, can be shown to summate over very large areas such as the whole arm or the chest, while summation in vision is a much more local event.

There is no getting around the fact that well over 80 per cent of the neural afferentation of the cerebral cortex derives from the visual system; none the less, the tactile modality is a much more widely distributed spatio-modality, and the auditory modality is a much more rapid one; and these differences are crucial not only in evolutionary terms but in ontological terms as well.

The fact that many even congenitally blind people have developed a strong sense of self and a resilient but conformal interchange between extrinsic and intrinsic geometries – such that they have been able to make firm and important contributions to politics and to poetry and to music and, as it happens, even to higher mathematics – attests to the force of that ego and the inherent orderliness of that interchange. By phone, for example, in a sensory version of the famous philosophical puzzle of the Chinese room (in which the key to the mind comes via a conversation), one cannot tell by casual conversation that one's respondent is blind unless one asks leading questions.

We conclude that the complex natural deep structural foundation for language learning and expression, upon which so much of exosomatic cultural evolution has depended, is a process that functions well virtually independently of vision and apart from the visual-sensory-rational contributions to mind.

So do many of the gnostic processes of active tactile exploration: the manual shape-recognitive and shape-expressive functions (e.g. as are needed for reading Braille and for making pottery). So do many of the gnostic processes of active vestibulo-kinaesthetic recognitive and expressive functions (e.g. as are needed for walking on narrow logs, swinging on branches, and swimming across rushing water). So do many of the gnostic processes of passive touch (e.g. as are needed to tell nettles from ice or silk).

LANGUAGE AS AN ENTRÉE

The central reason why the study of the effects of brain injury on the language process is so instructive is that it elaborates – if from tragic material – the many ways in which deep structural co-ordination, normal to all humans, can be adventitiously divided and still, to a considerable degree, retain its fundamental integrity. Some individuals may lose their ability to speak in one language but retain virtually normal speaking in another. By testing with electrode placement on the cortex during brain surgery, for example, we also know that some languages may be disrupted by small currents input to one location and others disrupted when the electrode is moved only a few millimetres away. We do not know how these regions compare, one individual to the next, but within the individual he or she may be able to respond to a visual stimulus only with its name in French, for example, with the electrode in one location, but only with its name in English with the electrode in another.

Some individuals after brain injury may have increased difficulty expressing the idea of the 'past', others in comprehending adverbial or conjunctival function (no 'ifs, ands, or buts'). Some individuals may be able to write with some skill, say their own name, but be unable to read what they have just a moment ago written.

Yet, interesting and scientifically enlightening as this catalogue of post-brain-trauma symptoms may be, and no matter how carefully expanded it may become, it is not something that can throw any light upon the extraordinary ability of some individuals to learn multiple languages well, in both the receptive and expressive modes. Competence in four or five languages is well-known, though there are specially trained individuals who have become competent in ten, twenty, and thirty languages. And there was at least one professor at Harvard in the early years of this century who had trained himself to become competent in well over 100 natural languages.

The study of the higher cortical symptoms due to brain injury, important as this may be in devising treatment regimens for these patients, does not inform us of the reaches and co-ordinations and limit conditions of the normal function of the brain. Such injuries are known to reduce our abilities in mathematics in various ways, although these have not been studied as thoroughly as have language losses. But such studies cannot inform us of the normal reaches of mathematical skill, which sometimes enables a rare few of us to carry as many as thirty or more pages of a proof in our heads all at the same time.

Creative skills and energies are lost, especially with onslaughts against frontal lobe function, so that poems and novels cannot be understood or invented or written, nor can paintings be appreciated or conceived or executed. Brain-injury symptoms do single out for us some startling distortions of the sensory-rational process, the many well-known visual agnosias being most instructive: loss of colour recognition, of facial recognition, of inanimate object recognition, polyopsias and metamorphopsias, and so forth. And it is true that, often enough, specific brain regions can be implicated in such losses.

But no one should forget the fact that this method, at one extreme – and the study of single cortical cell processing, at the other extreme – are fundamentally unnaturally divisive and, as such, are not intended to inform us about the integrated and cohesive function of the normal human brain. As a personal student and then colleague of two of the leaders in world neuropsychology in this century, Hans-Lukas Teuber (in the USA) and

Henri Hécaen (in France),[2] I can assert that they would be wholly in agreement with my contention that what one finds in studies in neuropsychology are the losses of integrative receptive/expressive function and of the abilities in all modes to focus attention sharply. Post-injury experience and function is characterized generally by a loss of gestalt-formative processes and, in my terms, by the loss of a well-constructed ego and a reverberative consciousness. Consequently, if one wishes to study the co-ordinative functions of the normal human mind, one must do that directly and not try to infer them from the abnormal functions highlighted in neuropsychology.

This is a very strong statement of principle, but I have no doubt also that it is fully in keeping with the whole tradition of neuropsychology, as developed over the last century in England, France, and Germany, American researchers being relatively new to this field.

This is to say, returning once again to the visual entrée, that fascinating though the visual agnosias may be (that one can recognize a moving animal, for example, but not the same animal standing still, or the horse pulling the wagon but not the wagon), their study does not give us understanding of the limits and ranges of normal visual prowess. To recognize that this colour is the same as one that you have seen only once before, some twenty years ago on a visit to Barcelona, is a rare but not unknown occurrence; to pick out one familiar face in a field of thousands; to recall the shapes and patterns of a landscape seen only through the window of a passing train, and to be able to reproduce this weeks later so convincingly as to astound the rest of normal humanity; to trace, with some newly invented pigment on a pallet knife, the outline of one's left hand held up against the rock wall of a cave, in a frighteningly dark interior lit only dimly by many small fires, and then to draw antelopes and pregnant women and archers and spearsmen, a skill learned by humans some 30,000 years ago; and for the littlest of our children to learn to recognize and to recall shapes and colours and to make representational drawings wholly preludic to any conscious awareness of the idea of representation . . . all this is to exhibit highly organized and extraordinarily complex visual skills that are emergent from the cellular anatomy and from the gross anatomy and which can be modelled heuristically and sufficiently well for communication to others *only* on their own level, in their own terms. Deeply respectful as I am of the great insights that the science of neuropsychology has brought to us, I am convinced that the insights of the gestalt psychology are overriding and that to study organization well one must address that organization at its own level.

---

2 Hécaen, H. (1972) *Introduction à la neuropsychologie.* Paris: Larousse, among his twenty-odd books in this field; Teuber, H.-L., Battersby, W.S. and Bender, M.B. (1960) *Visual Field Defects after Penetrating Missile Wounds of the Brain*, Cambridge, Massachusetts: Commonwealth Fund/Harvard University Press.

Consequently, in my view, it is always crucial to determine what that level is and, prior to this, how levels in general are to be established or understood.

POETRY'S FIRST REJECTION OF THE SENSES

> You cannot reach the spirit through the senses. The creation of beauty is a spiritual act. It is only by the complete domination of the senses that you can ever reach wisdom, truth, human dignity.
>
> (Thomas Mann *A Death in Venice*)

Let us be frank. Psychology has as much to learn from the study of the paintings in the caves at Lascaux as it does from poetry and from mathematics. Equally, neuroscience contributes, but so do philosophy and music and literature. It is important, for a correct view of the history of our science, to recognize that influences have come in from many other fields.

As an example, consider one of the lesser-known influences of psychiatric factors on vision in ophthalmology. Some years ago, several dozen women from Cambodia were brought to America for the treatment of their blindness, which was thought to be due to some mysterious unidentified physical ailment. Upon arrival, however, they were found to have been made hysterically blind by virtue of the mental and physical tortures that they had been forced to witness, and so had come to seem to themselves to have, perhaps guiltily, participated in, during brutal wars in their native land. No glasses or surgery could help with that since guilt and fear are not physical events, nor could any medicines. Similarly, ear-trumpets and audio-amplifiers do not help those who, psychologically, are not able to hear ... or choose not to listen.

Nothing is static in psychology, and with sources of relevant insights coming into our field from so many regions of conscious deliberations, we must constantly be alert; not to be overwhelmed – as, for example, when cybernetics first came in, every next paper and book in psychology had to deal with it or be considered old hat – but to be alert that special selective care must be taken. Since our subject matter is the highly complex self-aware self-awareness, we know that all human experience can speak to it, but that not all human experience can give us insights into its reaches and limits and the laws of dynamic transformation.

MODELS OF NATURE

As Einstein was often marvelling, it is a wonder that the human mind has evolved in such a way that it can comprehend nature. But, with all due respect, that process is the absolute central core of how life achieved its evolution within nature and yet apart from nature. All plants and, especially, all animals, in fine, all forms of organism, evolved from nature by modelling in most economical ways those components of nature that were crucial to their survival. As the senses were evolved to make models of appropriate energy distributions found around the organism in its ecological niche, so the integration of the senses was evolved to create overall models, singular when possible, of the sources of that energy, in order to orient to them holistically (tropistically) or to avoid them or, in any event, to take proper survival account of them.

The marvel is not that the senses and the mind model nature. The marvel is that we have achieved an awareness of doing that. Karl Popper, the historian and philosopher of science, has noted that the most important function of higher human intelligence is the function of criticism. (Theatre critics and book reviewers and other such, take note!) That is, the senses and the mind and then conscious awareness erect by emergence one or another model of nature, and the critical function then operates to oversee and to decide which model is correct, which one is the one to ascribe our experiences to and which is the one with respect to which we must plan to organize our future motions and thoughts. The bee constructs its hive, the bird its nest, the beaver its dam, the lion its pride ... all without the benefit of conscious self-awareness or criticism or understanding that there may be a better way. But, because men and women can gather themselves up mentally through several levels of removal from immediate sense arousal to assume active postures within the reverberation of consciousness, they can comprehend all these various constructions and model them all. More pointedly, they can model and understand and improve many of their own constructions. What we do not know yet, what history has not given us evidence of, is whether we can improve them all.

With all the signs of failure around us in the world – war, torture, and ecological devastation – the wonder is that we are still uncertain, and think the effort still worthy of a try.

THE ORIGIN OF SELF-AWARENESS IN INTERSENSORY CONFLICT RESOLUTION

Since the early 1970s (in my intersensory laboratory at the Mailman Center for Child Development, University of Miami, Department of Pediatrics), I have been examining this central idea: that the fundamental origin and development of consciousness and, in humans, of reverberating self-consciousness, lie within and emerge from the dynamic interaction of the senses. Leaving others to plot the plausible anatomical routes for such interactions (the bibliography is now in the hundreds),[3] I have

---

3 Stein, B.E. and Meredith, A.M. (1993) *The Merging of the Senses*, Cambridge, Massachusetts: MIT Press. See also, for a multimodal psychophysical view based upon entropy and information: Hoffman, D., Bennett, B. and Prakash, C. (1989) *Observer Dynamics: A Formal Theory of Perception*, Orlando, Florida: Academic Press.

concentrated my work at the cognitive and phenomenal levels, with some related work on the intersensorily evoked brain potentials in the early years.[4] Since the various senses are evolved to model the spatio-temporal-intensity distributions of different physical energies in nature, it is natural that they come to evoke different models of nature. The co-ordination of those differences, sometimes small and other times even contradictory in geometric import, is what the mind was evolved to do. Consequently, it is to be expected that the laws of mental process largely parallel the laws for single and multi-modal sensory process. It is one of the discoveries of psychophysics that, largely, the laws of sensory function (intensity and quality and form-texture modulation transfer functions) are similar enough across modes to give us a firm grasp upon how consciousness itself may function.

My central insight is this: as memory and consciousness and anticipation and intelligence have all emerged from sensory integration, this has come about primarily as a legacy of the resolutions of aeons of inter-sensory contrasts, rather than intersensory confirmations. It is mostly when the patterns of energy in nature that are ingested by the senses give rise to conflicting and nonconformal models of reality that the need for a central integrating and organizing monitor system, a critical ego, arises.

The ego stays fixed, while the world of the senses swirls around.

Sensory arguments ('Surely, that mouse did not really roar!') rather than sensory agreements are at issue. Ultimately, what we take for reality is some sort of compromise among the evidence of the senses, as shifted by critical reason. But if the senses had always agreed as to what is really there, conscious mind would probably not have been found necessary for survival – by nature, or our early ancestors, or by whatever processes there are in nature that may be said to be warranting 'such findings'.

If a bird is seen to be flying westerly, but its sound appears to be dimin-ishing easterly, some process overlooking the senses must 'decide' which is the true reality. Early on, the evidence suggests that even single cortical cells can co-ordinate intersensory inputs, but for reflex and minimum-choice gross motor responses, it is more probable that the colliculi at precortical brain levels serve this function. And when complex decisions need to be made, the evidence from neuropsychology suggests strongly that the frontal lobes are involved.

In sensory science we distinguish, in the analysis of the models, the 'whereness' or location of some event (known classically as 'local signa-ture', from Ewald Hering's treatment of the skin senses, published over many years in the last century) from the 'quantity' or intensity of some event, and both from the 'quality' or nature (essence) of the event. One is touched by a burning twig: where did this occur, how hot was it, and was it a twig that the wind brought from the fire? The place of

4 Shipley, T. (1980) *Sensory Integration in Children*, Springfield, Illinois: Thomas.

excitation, for example, emerges even in single cell organisms long before there is any nervous system at all. Tropisms, or whole body orientations, are the only things that such primitive creatures can do ... or have done to them. And, while some humans may seem to go tragically through much of their lives as if performing tropisms, that is not what the critical among us try to do. The necessity for decisions emerges in us, phased between the stimuli and our consideration of how to respond.

But primitive organisms respond only directly to the gradients found about them in the primal stew, of pressure-waves or nutritional or noxious molecules. There can 'be' no planning. They ingest and so register very early on, in some now solely molecular sense, the slope of these various gradients as soon as at least two molecules or quanta are absorbed at two different and resolvable times or cell/body locations. Two are needed to give the model of a slope: dx/dy. If the gradient is very steep, the organism may register this as a veritable wall or cliff, and start immediately to react (as fast as it can), as an ameoba flows away or towards some heat source as its internal viscosity changes in select fashion. And this may occur before the quality itself of the source is properly noted. Someone may throw flowers at you suddenly, and you first recoil, until you identify the object as flowers.

There is also the response of the organism to the mean average rate and flow, and the change of rate and flow, of the pressure-waves or molecules or particles in its vicinity. For single-cell creatures, some of these molecules are large enough to buffet them about; in larger animals the rate of flow, not molecular size per se, is more crucial, as when salmon swim up into rapidly moving streams but not into languid eddies. The rate of flow is important for these migrating fish. It also relates to how much oxygen there is in the water.

Suppose, for example, for some single-cell creature, we arranged that the gradient of nutriments was opposite to the gradient of radiation, so that the creature was pulled one way by one gradient and in the opposite direction by the other. Depending upon metabolic and ingestive balances not yet precisely known, the creature will move one way or the other.

Similarly, suppose that for the salmon the rate of flow was correct in one branch of the stream, but we had shifted the odour sources (and magnetic field character and taste?) of the original spawning ground to another branch – assuming that we could identify them, which is presently a moot point – the salmon would also be confronted with an intersensory challenge, and it is difficult to predict how they would solve that.

With the evolution of mammals, and then of humans, the range and type of intersensory challenges that could be ingested and cognitively resolved and met well increased enormously. But the simultaneous perception of a blue and a red butterfly in the same location would still challenge the best of us to make some unifying order out of it.

Suppose that one sees a blue berry hanging on a bush. Whether by 'innate releasing mechanisms' or via some other means, one is immediately drawn to it and picks it and puts it into one's mouth. But the taste now is bitter. In this case, the taste modality is overriding – it has been, throughout evolution, because taste ingestion is closer to survival than visual ingestion or tactile ingestion – and one spits the berry out.

THE INFANT SEARCHES FOR THE SQUARE NIPPLE

There are many other tasks, as crucial as these, the intersensory ingestive implications of which have escaped previous notice. Consider any mammalian infant, but specifically a human infant, searching for the nipple. The child, as all neonates of mammals, 'possesses at birth' (leaving aside for the moment what that sort of possession means exactly) a dynamic somatosensory need-recognition and co-ordinating capacity that results in the tendency to nuzzle and search with its face against the mother's breast until the nipple is discovered and then to suck on it until that need, the urgency of it, is satiated. But there is no doubt that it is not only the simple direct touch of face to breast that is crucial – the touching of something soft and smooth. Also of importance are the qualia of the resilience of the breast tissue as the infant presses against it, the qualia of the warmth of the mother's body, the smell of her body and of the milk, the milk's taste (rather, the child's experience of the taste qualia induced by the milk; the taste is not in the milk, though we speak this way) are all part of the intersensory experience and task of 'searching for the nipple'; also, its shape when once grasped by the lips. Naturally, at this level, on the principle of simplicity (Occam's razor), we assume only that some sensory integration takes place, not that it need reach consciousness. The infant at first sucks pretty much as it breathes, only later on does the capacity develop to be removed, ever so slightly, from the urgency of this act. But young children, even some adults, still say that they 'need' something when, or so it seems to an outsider, it is merely that they want it.

And, though we would perhaps not actually do such experiments with children, more drastic animal experiments have been made (e.g. the famous studies of Harlow) testing the limits of this sucking reflex. One can make the nipple first oval and then square or rectangular, to examine how well the infant modulates shape by its lips. One can moderate the ease of flow of the milk, and determine when the child gives up because it is too slow or too fast. One can change the taste of the milk, its temperature, its colour, fluidity, and texture, also the texture of the mother's skin and the resilience of her breast, and so forth, all in an effort to gauge the intersensory reach of the infant's intrinsic model of the breast and of the nipple and of the milk.

Clearly, such integrative intersensory co-ordinating skills are present at birth, so that it would not be surprising should they be found later on to undergird more overt and complex intersensory skills such as language development and postural control and eye–hand co-ordination. As, indeed, they do.

In short, intersensory skills are innate and remain important throughout life. During evolution, as the ecological niche narrowed, such skills had necessarily to become more and more refined to ensure survival in conditions of increasing effort and competition.

In the history of mental science, the view goes back through John Locke, the English philosopher of the seventeenth century who was its most famous exponent, and, as in so many of these views, even to Aristotle, that there is nothing in the mind which is not first in the senses. However, as Leibniz, the German mathematician and philosopher, has noted, that is 'but for the mind itself'. Which, in my terms, means at least this: the capacity to compare the models of reality ingested by each separate sense mode, and to reconcile them and to come to carry as a focus in one's thoughts a harmonious compromise emergent from these multiple intrinsic confrontations. That some forms of this have existed in higher animals, for evolutionary aeons, is certain, though it seems that only in humans has this capacity evolved so that it can, as it were, take account of itself.

Let a loud screech be heard by various animals in the jungle, including protohumans. Clearly, all animals with ears become instantly aware of that screech. And some are aroused in this way more refinedly than are the protohumans; most other mammals also recognize other animals by smell better than do the protohumans (in modern humans, olfactory gnosis remains poor); and, depending upon the illumination and ambient light conditions, a few may even see other animals better than do the protohumans.

Let these animals then variously orient to that screech, in a frank gesture of aural form-character and gnostic recognition. While many animals can better recognize other animals gnostically by their screeches than could protohumans, modern humans can become specially trained in this, so as to surpass virtually any naturally evolved aural-gnostic skill: bird watchers, for one group, or trained naturalists or hunters for others.

And, as the infant takes action when it recognizes that it is in contact with an accepting nursing mother (the stories of lactating wolves nursing human infants are not entirely mythic), so mature animals, also by means of survival intersensory co-ordinations, orient themselves appropriately with respect to the presumed source of that screech. Thus, the receptive animal establishes its orientation to that presumed source in some sort of extrinsic-intrinsic co-ordinate polar geometry, i.e. of which direction the source is in *vis-à-vis* the self. It does this virtually instantaneously. The binaural state of all higher animals helps critically with this direction-modulation ingestion (cf. Chapter 9), but also with the separate geometric determination of distance. How far away is that screech? Stereo-acoustics helps with this, but so do other things, since deep-pitched sounds travel further than high-pitched sounds, a matter of physics so universal that nature would hardly have missed evolving it into pertinent higher nervous systems.

Clearly, even so basically simple and universal an act as orienting and arousal (the sequence could be reversed) takes place via intersensory processing. Presumably, in some complex somatosensory fashion that we do not yet comprehend, the animal is 'in possession' of some image of itself and its nature and location. To what extent a snake is aware that it is a snake need not concern us, but it performs pretty consistently in a snakelike manner so as to beguile us into maintaining that, at the very least, by some intersensory means it is limited in its activities and does not try to be foxlike or to fly. But when a dog attacks a bear, is it still being only doglike, or might there not be a hint of bearness suddenly emerging?

Of course, while the dog may look up into the sky to the bird making that screech, in general it orients to it in a different fashion than it orients to the bear. While the bear, in its own way, continues to amble along totally unconcerned about screeching birds, though the attacking dog will get his attention. On the other hand, the field-mouse and the rabbit may first instantly 'freeze', and then run for their shelters, in an entirely appropriate intersensory survival response for them, being what they are – and where they are; and who that screecher is.

Indeed, when the purely sensory message has ceased, the screeching stopped, none the less, for those creatures for whom the screech carries a survival message, in a very real sense (sic), it remains 'in the air'. We term this *memory*. In primitive single-cell creatures, strong stimuli endure in the actual deformation of the body. In field-mice and rabbits we think that a lesser deformation, but a deformation none the less, persists somewhere in the higher central nervous system, perhaps the temporal lobe, and in the intrinsic geometry of synapses and neural nets exciting and inhibiting and co-ordinating in that general region. Whether this is a refractive index change, a change in chemical balance, a transmissivity change, a connectivity change, we do not really know, though much evidence abounds for all of these processes. One might equally speak of synaptic lubricities or resistances as of connectivities. But the point is that these are intersensory: the screech is heard, the body or head orients to it so that the eyes may see it, and the animal then takes all of this under advisement and acts accordingly. The mouse and the rabbit stay for a duration in their holes, in direct proportion to the loudness and proximity and object character of the sound. One would be foolish to deny the conscious gnostic character of that action.

At this stage in our knowledge of comparative cognitive psychology, one could defend the serious application of the notion of innate ideas and memories, and such, that, instantly, at birth, the best foods for survival are recognized and the most dangerous threats to survival are recognized, by a complex set of modes interacting. Or one could take a more Lockean view, and maintain that these things are learned at the nipple rather than being brought out from the womb. Depending upon which of the latest books one reads, and the subtlety of the actions, either postulate can be defended.

In any case, the key observation is the fact that memory as such comes into existence when the intersensory messages cease. Memory also retains its inherent intersensory character.

THE LAWS OF PROCESS OF THE SENSES

Thus, the rules concerning motion along sensory dimensions and between sensory dimensions and between the senses are carried over into memory as they are carried over into mind. However, as mental qualities are emergent both from memory and from sensory input, so also the laws of mind possess a distinct character of their own.

This book, as with virtually all my current projects, is an exposition on those dynamics of mind that have persisted in form from the dynamics of the senses and memory, in contradistinction to those dynamics of mind that are emergent in character and which can be approached only at the mental level.

Consider a simple intersensory-rational puzzle. Suppose that one is listening to what at first thought (co-ordination) seems to be the buzzing of a nearby mosquito. But the sound becomes louder and louder. Surely that cannot be a mosquito! Perhaps it is a plane or a train or a chain-saw or a toy buzz-bomb in a prank being played upon you by a mischievous son.

But then it gets louder still, and one becomes alarmed (*sic!*). And one pulls in memories and hypotheses and all the other senses and their residuals, and searches that implied reality as best one can for resolution, organization, and meaning. This is an active mental search, though it may be imperceptible to an outsider, especially to one who does not hear that noise. Can anything be seen of this 'buzzer' or smelled of it? Suppose that a rank odour soon also comes to fill the air, what then? Is the 'buzzing thing' now more real because we may now infer that it also stinks?

The question perpetually hides there behind the surface of such events: when does the sensory reality become of such a character as to evoke, display, be of actual survival significance? Usually, animals and humans alike have been able to decide most such questions on the basis of least-effort dynamics, which means that a single sense mode is involved and a single sensory dimension from within the set of quality dimensions mediated by that mode. But when that does not suffice, then memories and multisensory processes and reason and intelligence, although they are higher-energy-consuming activities, and also mental geodesics, as innately easiest routes to take, must be drawn in.

Certainly, it is possible that the sounding could become so loud as to crack the ear-drums and, eventually, to kill by breaking blood vessels in the brain. So survival determinations have to be made. On the other hand, one could, if the smell were to cease or turn sweet, and the sound begin to resemble the choirs of angels, come to recognize, in a leap into abstraction, that: 'God Himself is descending!'

One cannot help but wonder what it means to be 'in possession' of an idea like that.

IN POSSESSION OF ...

It is ancient wisdom to assert that psychological processes depend for their integrity upon prior body processes, and modern wisdom that these can sometimes even be 'traced down' to single cells and, lower still, to nutrients for single cells like sodium and potassium, and so forth. But it is not trivial to recognize that the dynamic processes of mental life cannot be traced back up from body processes, even in their most dynamic and energetic flux.

One result of this distance is that the mind in humans has the conscious capacity to reject the body. From this come all the wide-spread efforts of body decoration and body building. And, more profoundly, also come the concepts of the right to do with our bodies whatever we may reasonably wish, as well as some things that we may unreasonably wish.

We do not know what seems to direct (motivate would be the human word) some animals to seem to 'commit suicide', say the lemmings or beaching whales or those mysterious elephants that presumably go voluntarily to die in the valley hidden behind the waterfalls, but in all probability these behaviours do not have associated with them any clear component of reverberating self-awareness. Consequently, they cannot involve the degree of emergence that humans exhibit, nor any precise component of even simple 'oughts' much less of abstract rights.

But what is so interesting is that 'being in possession' of a self-awareness (one might argue, in some instances, that the self-awareness is in possession of us!) is the psychological foundation of the origin of the idea of rights and of psychological (as opposed to physical) possession. It is because we are unambiguously in mental possession of a vigorous reflexive self-awareness that we have been able to come to the idea of rights, in the first place, whether natural or some other; and, secondly, to the idea that we may be in possession of some.

This is a fascinating subject, to which we shall return in another place.

DYNAMIC SENSORY AND COGNITIVE REALITY

It is ironic in the history of our science that, while gestalt psychology is taught today in the texts and remembered in the histories almost exclusively because of its treatment of vision, its origin lay in the observation of Ehrenfels concerning the retention of melody despite the transposition to different keys.[5] The principles of grouping by similarity or common fate or figure-ground or closure or contour or clustering are virtually always illustrated as exclusively visual events. But it happens that there are absolutely crucial intersensory analogies, some more important than the visual.

The gestaltists themselves, and virtually all who have written on these issues since, by ignoring the original point of melody transposition, have done themselves a disservice in at least three ways. Firstly, they have forgotten to emphasize that the gestalt principles apply to all the sense modes, and to cognitive function as well. Secondly, they have used largely static visual demonstrations,[6] when the essence of the meaning of melody is its dynamic temporal coherence. And, thirdly, they have ignored the fact that most natural visual events are also dynamic, both in pre-attentive but especially in scanning forms.

GESTALT PSYCHOLOGY VS. EYE-SCAN AND SCENE-MOTION

A key factor in the evolution of the vertebrate visual system is the refined development of the six-paired muscles by which eye movements are controlled. In the fish, the eyes cannot be moved voluntarily, but the muscles function reflexively (without wilful intervention) so as to keep the eyes focused on the pursued target despite its rapid and wild escape motions and the body-head motions of the predatory pursuer. Similarly, despite sudden shifts in currents and water flow that may rock the fish's body about, the eyes are involuntarily maintained towards the point of interest. In birds, also, the eyes are *de facto* immobile, although the six pairs of muscles are present, and it is now the head of the creature which turns to keep the eyes in focus on the object of interest, despite wind currents and soarings and other violent twists and turns in flight.

A key point in the evolution of the mammalian visual system, however, and that of the reptiles and other land creatures, is the fact of the evolution of an increasingly precise fovea and of an increasing need for, and

---

5 Ehrenfels, C.V. (1890) 'Über Gestaltqualitäten', *Verteiljahresschr'. f. Philos.* 14.

6 One of the most promising gestaltists, Karl Duncker, wrote the now classical paper on induced visual motion, but this was not a recognition of the importance in vision of moving scenes in general and of moving eyes in particular. Moreover, induced motions occur in aural and tactile and vestibular and intersensory modes, and these are not mentioned seriously by him, or by most other gestaltists. See Duncker, K. (1929) 'Über induzierte Bewegung', *Psychol. Forsch.* 12: 180–250.

significance of, voluntary free movability of the eyes. And, except for the convergence movements of the eyes necessary for that special depth-perception known as stereovision, all the time that the eyes are scanning about freely, the intrinsic visual world stays put, despite the fact that its retinal image has, on simple principles of geometrical optics, to be robustly moving about. The mind, as it were, corrects for the motion of the retinal image when the eyes voluntarily scan the scene. Consequently, it is not only when patterns and textures camouflaging potential food or predators are voluntarily tracked and followed by the eyes, but it is also when the eyes voluntarily scan a fixed scene, that this process of world stabilization plays its intersensory and cognitive role. Landscape scanning and the tracking of moving aspects of the landscape, as well as the keeping of something in sight while one hotly pursues it, are all fundamental every-day occurrences in natural human vision, and for the gestaltists to so generally overlook these facts is perhaps due to the origin of gestalt psychology more in philosophy than in natural behavioural biology. In any event, the spatio-temporal modulation transfer functions of texture vision and the constancies of the visual processing of both low and high rates of change of rates of change of textures and contours, in all colours and in innumerable sets of coherent shapes, are, in the natural evolution of human vision, even more important than are the gestalts of melody transposition and constancy. Indeed, the very stability of the visual world, despite large and significant voluntary eye-scanning and head-scanning and gross body movements, is one of the crucial intersensory co-ordinations that allows mammals to forage and capture prey in the various terrains upon which they find themselves. There cannot be the slightest doubt but that, to the uninformed visual system, the world is spinning when the eyes scan. When the retinal image moves, reason takes it that a real object has moved. Unless, it is somehow (and this mecha-nism is not yet exactly known) forewarned that *this* particular retinal motion is not due to an object but due to an eye movement. That infor-mation must come from some sort of kinaesthetic-somaesthetic feedback channel. There seems no escaping that.

The refined scanning movements that are sometimes required for precise facial recognition would also not be possible without this inter-sensory co-ordination; nor would the exosomatic skills, such as reading and writing and drawing, that have developed from such skills in mankind's exosomatic cultural phase. Indeed, this is probably one of the primary constancies in perceptual psychology, and it is surprising that the gestaltists missed this fact, and the fact that there is really no visual 'thing' or 'perception' or naturally relevant sensory psychological process which is not thoroughly fused with such dynamic intersensory geometric transformations, which give stability – in their terms, constancy – to the perceptual world despite physical changes in it or in the observer.

Motion perception is so crucial to vision that the following thought experiment could well be entertained: instead of an orchestra that gives off dynamic pulses and phrases and harmonies of sound, let us imagine one in which all the 'musicians' arc in possession of flashlights and other sorts of projectors, which give off dynamic pulses and phrases and harmonies of light. Without taking this too far, into laser spotlights of violins of one sort of another, and into broad-beam cello projectors of different timbre but similar colour, one has reinvented, I suppose, abstract performance cinematography. Whether such visual orchestration would need concrete objects, as in the regular cinema, or could develop on its own in the same non-iconic fashion that music has largely developed, remains to be seen. But one could imagine some interesting concrete experiments undertaken along this line.

Wolfgang Köhler's important studies of apes solving dynamic visual problems, in fact, were a keen initial recognition of the central function of change and mobility in the gestalt approach to vision. But, in so far as I can tell, no one has previously noted that, in addition to his concepts insight and Umschlag and good errors, and the relevance of this work to general pedagogy and the comparative theory of intelligence, it also highlighted the crucial importance of dynamic vision, especially in the naturalistic ecological context.

It is clear that all these experiments would have been successful regardless of the precise shape of the boxes which the apes piled one on top of another so as to be able to climb higher, or the precise visual character of the fence from which, eventually, the dog rushed away and then around to get at the meat, or the precise size, colour, material, texture, and shape of the two sticks that the chimp Sultan put one into the other so that he could make a tool with which to reach higher. But it is absolutely certain that all those experiments would have failed had the animals not been allowed to scan the visual scene freely with eye movements.

Landscapes of one colour and tone do not benefit from a scan; similarly, a sonata in one note does not benefit from special attention. Scenes of the same shape but different colours are quite like musical patterns of the same form, melodies in different octaves or instruments. New meaning is woven in, but there is a resemblance as well. Words written in sand tell a different story from the same words written in blood, but they are the same words. A cello and a flute playing the same melody together, also play different melodies.

The more meaning changes the more it remains the same.

The point is that, even in greatly strained forms, the fact of the universal importance of dynamic temporal events in vision cannot possibly be overemphasized. No doubt, taking this to another sensory extreme, as is almost always heuristic in the thinking in any science, one also could imagine tactile symphonies played out over various distinguishable regions of the body, at various tempi and in various keys – and with various noticeably different probes: some sharp as whistles and others rounded and mellow like cellos and French horns. This thought experiment is quite odd, no doubt, because we do not have any good concept of how the audience would be gathered or addressed, but perhaps clever people could devise ways. On the other hand, since the skin is as good a pitch-modulation transformer as is the ear, it is not so fanciful after all.

In any case, it is equally true that in the tactile modality the gestalt principles apply in fully dynamic form. It is a very different recognition process, for example, that is evoked when one simply places an object in the hand to be recognized passively, in comparison to having the subject actively manipulate the object when it is in the hand. Similarly, all the self-body touches that virtually all animals engage in, when they can – the scratching of itches, the gnashing of teeth, the twisting of the hands, the shrugging of the shoulders against the weight of the greatcoat, the generalized stretching, the massaging, the caressing for comfort and for sexual love – can best be comprehended as tactile melodic trans-positions, to which all the Erhenfels principles apply. Even humans, when they cannot reach the place on the back that is itching, have been known to rub the back against a tree – though, as it happens, not all trees are equally good for that!

Others before have recognized this over-emphasis of the gestalt on static vision, if perhaps not in quite so critical a fashion, and I wish to empha-size that I am a student of the gestalt school and make these comments with the utmost respect. But Adelbert Ames, even if more in visual optics than in visual psychology, and James Gibson (following in the footsteps of his two continental mentors, Albert Michotte and Ivo Kohler) have made significant experimental inroads into the dynamics of vision, partic-ularly spatial vision, in contrast to the gestalt.

AMES AND 'THERENESS-THATNESS'[7]

It is interesting to observe that there are many aspects of the visual inges-tion of meaning that appear only when the scene is presented in dynamic form. One nice example that I have seen shows some immobile clusters of black and white blotches. As soon as motion is introduced, however, a troop of marvellous panda bears emerges . . . only to disappear entirely when once again the motion is withdrawn, despite one's 'knowing' what really *is* there. This sort of sudden emergence of meaning with motion occurs in all areas of natural vision – and with all the formal sense modes and the temporal-pitch modes as well – and it is a failure of gestalt psychology, as covered even in the advanced textbooks, to have neglected these facts all these years.

---

7 The best review of the overall work of Ames and his associates is still Kilpatrick, F.P. (1951) *Human Behavior from the Transactional Point of View*, Project No. 496(01), US Office of Naval Research.

The quirks in the history of science are no less intriguing than those in the history of other areas of human endeavour, since it is also true that Adelbert Ames fundamentally ignored the gestalt contributions and looked to other traditions for his own insights. Though his christening of the 'thereness-thatness' problem was clearly in the gestalt spirit, it was an issue of dynamic vision.

In this, a balloon is seen down at the end of a narrow dark hallway as if self-luminous. It is seen in monocular view. Then one gradually fills the balloon with air or depletes the air already in it, in systematic ways, and asks the subject what she/he perceives. For reasons not wholly understood, the assumption is made, and is difficult to alter, that one is perceiving a consistent unified and relatively fixed object that is moving towards and away from you in visual space. Since the object is a fixed 'that', it is its 'thereness' which changes. However, if one looks binocularly, one has firmer 'clues' as to the 'thereness' of this balloon, so that now one has the impression of a balloon at fixed distance changing its 'thatness'. This is the more veridical, surely, which is one reason why binocular vision developed in the natural ecology.

We now know from the work of many vision neuroscientists studying size and size-change perception, and the particular dynamics of looming visual trajectories, that both such size changes and to-and-fro motions can be mediated at one physiological level by single brain cells in the monkey's visual cortex. This finding sets up a sharp intellectual test case in point for the concept of emergence.

Because the size and the distance functions display electro-excitatory processes in two distinct and separate or non-overlapping sets of single cortical brain cells, we cannot thereby model the cognitive experience even though the form of the dynamics may be quite similar. Sometimes, for example, when the viewer is informed that he/she is perceiving a fixed balloon, the to-and-fro motion stops and only changes in size appear, even in monocular view. Perhaps the implication might be drawn that the proper ingestion of the meaning of the new instructions somehow switches the cortical processing activities from the to-and-fro neuronal modulators to the big-and-small neuronal modulators: doubtful, at best, but a tenable hypothesis.

But, regardless of how one models these experiences, however, they are sensory-rational events that occur under dynamic visual conditions, and for this reason Ames saw his work more in the tradition of the transactionalism of the American philosopher John Dewey, than in the tradition for or against the gestalt.

In another experimental thrust, this time more static and more closely related to the physiological optics that drew Ames into these experiments (though he first began as a lawyer who wanted to become a painter!), he devised a model of what he believed to be the more natural binocular world in which the mammalian eye evolved. He constructed a large rectangular framed room and covered it all inside with chicken wire. On this wire, over all the five inner surfaces, he stuck oak and maple leaves: thus, the famous 'leaf-room'. One stood and looked into this room from the other open wall, or front. In this case, one need not have anything moving, other than one's eyes, which were allowed their normal scan. What became immediately apparent was that the true physically rectangular form of the room became ambiguous, and the observer was no longer absolutely sure that she/he was looking into, and perceiving, a normally shaped room. The geometric transformation from the extrinsic space to the intrinsic or perceptual model of that space became fuzzy, which is precisely what he had hoped would happen. This allowed him to study the effects of specially designed size-distorting binocular glasses on the perception of that room. And its spatial fuzziness permitted the optically induced factors to be controlling, as opposed to the possible cognitively induced ones such as the assumption that all rooms are rectangular, therefore this one must be rectangular as well.

And, it turns out that Ames was correct, because all his binocularly introduced optical size lenses (aniseikonic lenses) induced immediate visual distortions in the apparent shape of that room. These distortions were not visible in actual normal rectangular rooms, because of the compelling contour cues, but were beautifully coherent with the predictions from optical lens theory. What was happening in this work was that the thereness-thatness assumptions, that we are always bringing with us in our transactions with carpentered rooms, were so strong as to override the effects of the geometrical optical distortions that these lenses were, without doubt, putting into the transaction. But when he employed the leaf-rooms, for which those carpentered assumptions could no longer be successfully maintained, the effect of the geometrical optical distortions became predominant. That this work also led to important insights into the clinical entity of aniseikonia as well as normal stereoscopic function should not be overlooked, though what concerns us here mostly is his insight into the use of natural texture.

THE SENSES AS PERCEPTUAL SYSTEMS

The other important researcher in those years who emphasized the importance of texture and of motion in human vision was James Gibson.[8] He began to consider these issues during World War II, while working for the US Air Force to devise better means for the promotion of pilot safety in airport landing, through visual or perceptual science.

Again, in one of the small ironies of intellectual history, although Ames' emphasis on the importance of natural texture pre-dated Gibson's by a

---

8 Gibson, J. (1966) *The Senses Considered as Perceptual Systems,* Boston, Massachusetts: Houghton Mifflin.

decade or more, Gibson does not reference Ames. Though it is unlikely that Gibson did not know of his work, Ames' work on the 'leaf-room' was published more in the literature on vision and ophthalmology, and not in that on perception, so it may have seemed somewhat obscure. In any case, Gibson's consideration of texture was more dynamic, because he was concerned with what the pilot perceives of the landing field as he comes in for a landing. What Gibson found to be so critical was the fact that the ground texture appeared to expand radially about the fixation point of vision as the pilot approached; and that the rate of expansion was a precise function of the rate of approach. For Gibson, the angle of tilt of the plane, its pitch, its yaw, and the 'point of aim' of the pilot could all be extracted by the visual system from the way in which the ground texture changed as the plane moved into the landing position. What counted was the natural texture or array in the visual field, and its dynamic changes over time.

This emphasis on textural display and its change preceded by decades the current modern emphasis on fractals and 'chaos', and in itself alerted the attention of many vision scientists to the importance of the natural dynamic ecological displays that the environment presents to us, and to all visual animals, as we move and scan about within it. This is an emphasis that has not been lost to the field, and my own work fully supports it.

The most famous single experiment to come from the Gibsonian school, completed and published by Eleanor Gibson, James Gibson's wife, is the experiment of the visual cliff. In this, as it happens, we find once again an unreferenced sequel to the work of Ames on depth perception. A large rectangular sturdy wooden box of some four feet across and some three feet high is constructed. On this is placed a thick sturdy clear glass top. A texture of one sort or another is placed immediately under the glass, for the first half of the way across. This texture is clearly visible through the glass, where it appears almost as a supporting ground. Mostly, checkerboards and the like have been used for this, rather than ecologically natural textures, but there is no doubt that grasses and pebbles and sands would do as well. (One wonders why they were not used.) At a point midway across the glass top, the texture plunges down the two or three feet to the actual floor of the box, so that the visual appearance of support is now gone. It is as if a large piece of glass projects out over a steep escarpment, hence the name: visual cliff.

Without going into details, many studies have been done with newborn animals urged by food rewards to cross out over this escarpment, and with crawling human infants coaxed over by the reassuring calls of their mothers on the other side. Responses have been obtained that are age dependent in children and in animals, and that are also species dependent. The reader is referred to that rich literature for specifics.[9]

---

9 For example, Pick, A.D. (ed.) (1979) *Perception and Its Development: A Tribute to Eleanor Gibson*, Hillsdale, NJ: Erlbaum.

What interests us here is this extraordinarily inventive use of texture for the study of depth perception in a manner that is clearly inter-sensory since it involves the kinaesthetic exploration of the conflicting visual space. Watching infant animals and the crawling children moving on this glass floor – the behavioural gestures of pause, of trial, of moving more slowly, of starting and then moving back, of arriving at the other side as a victory or a rescue – all attest to the crucial importance, in this task, of the resolution of an intersensory conflict: by vision ... the floor falls away; by active touch first ... the child at least can and does reach out with its hand to feel the glass; and then by full body kinaesthesis as the child crawls out onto the visually unsupported, unsupporting shelf ... some 'invisible and yet supporting' floor does apparently continue.

A finer experimental model of the importance of the resolution of inter-sensory conflict in the origin of consciousness and of its ultimate rever-beration would be difficult to find.

But it is important to emphasize that this is my interpretation of these experiments, and it differs somewhat from the experimenters' own. James Gibson's theoretical views developed from such demonstrations, and others, into a general theory about how sudden changes in textures in the natural environment could also pose obstacles in their own way to simple, naive first-impression models of reality. This is where camouflage in animals comes into its own, for both prey and predator, and where the need for higher and more complex considerations of textural sensory messages comes to have survival importance. He spoke of ecological optics and the optical array, trying to emphasize his belief that the study of vision by means of single isolated dots of light – the use of infinite variations of which was at the foundation of almost all of what then stood as accepted scientific knowledge in visual psychophysics and perceptual science – could give only a minimally valid and ultimately static and distorted view of what vision, as a major survival mode, was all about.

Actually, the facts are that in this field we have made a firm and now virtually century's old heuristic division between physical and geo-metrical and physiological optics, and there cannot be the slightest doubt but that the use of straightforward linear Euclidean geometrical approximations to the visual system, and to many threshold and even supra-threshold processes of vision, can very well supply us with a comprehension and understanding of vision having that refined quality universally recognized as scientific. If we wish to understand why the photoreceptive cells in all image-forming eyes are about 1 micron in diameter, physical optics points us to the wavelength of visible light which is, maximally, about 0.8 micron in size. And geometrical optics clearly explains why the retinal image is inverted by the pupil and not by the cornea or the lens, so that the problem of the need for a presumptive later-on neurological re-inversion vanishes.

Moreover, geometrical optics well explains Ames' findings in the leaf-room, and all the literally thousands of correctly functioning optical prescriptions made every day, the world over.

Restricting vision science to what can be learned via the use of tiny dots of light displayed in a large black surround can certainly be limiting, but none the less it has produced some of the greatest understanding that we have achieved in this world of how physics may relate to human experience. Optics is called the queen of the sciences precisely because of how much it tells us about the world that we see as well as the world that we do not see; and about how we must reason in accordance with these world views in order to survive in our attempts to model and to live in and to comprehend nature. Similar points had been made earlier by the great Italian optical scientist-philosopher, Vascho Ronchi,[10] but the debate between him and Gibson will occupy us only in another place because it centres neither on texture nor on intersensory processes.

Intersensory considerations are our key concern here, and the very central idiomatic expressions, such as that one may have 'sound' reasons which may throw 'light' upon these issues, already alert us to the ancient linguistic influences that such processes have had. Such idioms abound in most advanced languages.

And, just as we may have visual cliffs, so we may have auditory cliffs or walls. Suppose that, as the infant crawls over some surface, when she/he reaches the halfway point a loud screech is heard. Clearly, the crawling stops, for a hearing child. Indeed, if we continue to urge the child to cross, and we also continue to make this loud screech whenever the child reaches the halfway point, we have a pretty fair model of how to induce mental distress or illness. Such a simple intersensory conflict – and it is simple in comparison to those regularly encountered in the real world – would certainly be sufficient to cause infant animals of many species to 'freeze' (another intersensory word) into immobility. Odour and texture walls on average, perhaps, would not work so bluntly, but some clever ones might be devised. That remains to be seen ... or heard. Or smelt.

Animal tracking, for example, is often compounded by complex textural and intersensory array processing, since it is always an integration of visual and aural and olfactory and kinaesthetic and tactile messages. The mother and infant seal, for example, separated adventitiously amid thousands, seek out and recognize each other in a *mélange* of sounds and shapes and smells, by honing in largely along an olfactory trail. Vision in the infant seal is poorly developed, for the first seven to ten neonatal days.

Territorial markings in the wild are almost always achieved by urine and spoor droppings, the former exclusively olfactory. How many animals recognize other animals of the same or of different species by the geometrical optical properties of the spoor, to avoid or to pursue, we do not

---

10 Ronchi, V. (1955) *Optics: The Science of Vision,* New York: University Press.

really know. But the number is probably fairly large, even though odour is the controlling dimensionality.

As the primary *de facto* appearance of the jungle is as a visual texture to humans, so it is also an aural and an olfactory texture, especially to animals. And once physically encountered, it becomes a tactile and kinaesthetic texture as well. And survival depends exquisitely upon the proper co-ordination of all these several textural models into the perception of the sharp contours here that indicate the specific innately releasing presence of a potential predator, in comparison to the sharp contours there that indicate a specific food or a specific potential mate.

The idea of textures changing so rapidly as to indicate contours is important, and will concern us *in extensio* elsewhere. Here, we are concerned to show that the abrupt change of texture into contour is quite analogous to the earlier gestalt concept of insight, and both highlight the fact that discontinuous events occur in all modalities and in many of the interstices of reason, so that some initial comment must be made on this fact.

THE NEURO-REDUCTIONIST'S DENIAL OF SENSORY-RATIONAL PSYCHOLOGY

The active means of exploring the sensory world are by visual scanning and focus and convergence, by tilting the head so that the ears receive the maximum intensity and binaural difference and gnostic information, by doing the same for the nose and sniffing; by reaching out with the hands and touching and manipulating; and by bodily-kinaesthetically exploring the local geography. Such explorations also encounter textures and sudden changes in texture, as when the ground suddenly sinks away underneath your foot. Reflexive and protective postural movements come immediately into play to stave off instant loss of balance and control. But then, after suitable pause for physical rebalance and for mental reorganization of intention, one begins to explore once again. That animals as well as humans can do this in many ways attests to the fundamental and early evolutionary importance of this sort of intersensory conflict resolution: the ground texture looks safe to walk upon, but kinaesthetically it appears unsafe. Is it in reality unsafe? Kinaesthesis wins out over vision – as taste usually does also – and the ground seems veritably to take on a different visual appearance. The shrewd hunter searches for any minimal visual clues he can find to this novel character so that, henceforth, he can discern this by visual means from afar before he steps dangerously on it. And the system that helps with this determination of kinaesthetic safety in the face of visual indistinctiveness – or aural or olfactory – is known as reafference. This may best be considered as a complex sense mode associated with all voluntary body gestures, which consists in the virtual geometric co-ordination between the form of the intention to explore, the form of the mental plan of that exploration, the model of the actual exploration as it is executed, and an on-going comparison between all these sensory events so as to minimize the formal difference or discrepancy between the intent and what is actually effected.

We may thus understand that, even in this seemingly most simple act of voluntarily exploring, there occur enormously subtle and complex intersensory events with direct sensory-rational consequences for reason and reality testing. Furthermore, even in this usually most smoothly running of all the sensory-expressive modes, there are sudden insights and emergences and new and surprising reality formulations that are constantly assisting us in our aim to survive in the wild of tooth and claw and in our aim to survive amid the entropic disorders of modern technological intercultural urban society.

Consequently, to try to reduce these complex dynamic sensory interactions to processes occurring in one or another separate and discrete brain locus – as many in neuropsychology seem to be attempting – is to overlook the fact that it is the whole brain which is devoted to this process. The balance of inhibition and of arousal is not – in the naturally textured world and in the streets of our cities textured with crowds of people – restricted to vision alone when vision is primary, or to audition alone when audition is primary, or to kinaesthesis-reafference alone when exploration is primary, but to the complex interplay of all of them, at virtually all times. Sometimes even in the laboratory, when we try to restrict the events to one mode and to one dimension within that mode, conflicting alternative sense messages creep in despite our best attempts at control. The mere intellectual decision to respond 'yes' or 'no' takes account of multimodes. And intellectual functions, while they are founded on sensory-rational organizations and expressions, are none the less not localizable in the classical single-mode cortical sensory projection regions, however separate these may seem to be, because there is also a component of extra- or supra-sensory voluntarism in human intelligence. This latter, we try to model but most often merely cloud over with the expression 'putting one's mind to it'. (In what way is this different from 'putting someone in their place'?)

The putting of one's mind to any event can involve thinking about how best to view some event, how best to listen to it, how best to smell, taste and touch it, how best to explore it manually and bodily, and how best to consider it purely mentally in a pre-action mode. The putting of one's mind to a mathematical problem is not wholly different from the putting of one's mind to the problem of how best to smelt this metal to make a sword or how best to drill here for oil or water; or how to invent a new musical art form or a new form of democratic government.

The mind takes its nutriment not only in the form of chemicals as solids and fluids and gases, but also in the form of the *inform*ation about reality that the senses bring in. Primarily, this gauges and confirms mental expectations of the geometrical character of the distribution of the other more primary nutrients, but it also aids in planning how to search next for additional primary nutrients. And that searching, in humans, can involve the deliberate changing of one's own location in a presumably fixed external geography, or the deliberate constructional and agricultural changing of the geography of that primary nutritional geometry.

As the eye does not see or 'have' intelligence or talents – though it may be hindered at forming good geometrical images – so neither do the optic nerve, the optic radiation, the lateral geniculate, the primary visual cortex, or the now up to forty or more claimed visual protection or integration areas. And the same is true of all the senses. The anatomy does not solve sensory-rational puzzles, though it supplies nourishment for that puzzlement. The mind does that solving. And it is the mind which continues to strive to draw informational nutrition from the senses, despite peripheral and even central-cortical injuries to their anatomy. The mind is not divided by the anatomy, nor is the intelligence.

AS WE DIVIDE THE INTELLECT

The primary way in which intelligence may be heuristically divided is in accordance with the sensory-rational divisions that nature has made for us, in the evolution of the separate senses. Thereafter, subsequent divisions must be taken as derivative of these, and must retain their link to survival. As memory came, through evolution, to persist for longer and longer durations than direct sense arousal, it preserved for intelligence not only models of geography made by the eye and the ear and the nose and the skin, but also those derived from active bodily exploration in the spaces around that were suitable to be explored. Indeed, that judgement of suitability is itself a quintessential intersensory and memorial one. In this way, past experience comes to play its role in present experience. And, as hardly needs to be pointed out, while memory often does work naturally, as Ebbinghaus thought, in a fine linear way, when left 'to its own devices' it is often self-surprising, startling us with what we sometimes recall when we may not wish to recall, and by what at other times we cannot possibly bring to current mind no matter how hard we mentally try.

The widely ignored non-Ebbinghaus discontinuities of memory are as noteworthy as are the widely ignored non-Euclidean discontinuities of sensory function; and, as well, the distance of both from anatomy. To try to find these processes in some pattern of brain loci, or even in a dynamic networking of many, is to make the error of trying to model discontinuous processes by continuous ones, in addition to the error of confusing levels. The very transformation equations themselves are transforming even as we try to pin them down. The flavour of the ice-cream disappears when we talk of carbon and oxygen and protein and organic polymers.

No modern science of psychology can maintain – except in camera, perhaps – that the integrity of the brain is irrelevant to such things: that would be rank nonsense. However, no modern neurophysiology has shown, nor, I think, can ever show, that brain integrity is all that is relevant.

GENIUS LIES NOT IN THE BRAIN

To look into brain cells for the key to Einstein's conceptual geometric genius is, in a word, absurd, though some do appear to be engaged in doing just that. The brains of the major Soviet leaders were preserved for years, for the eventual purpose of trying to find therein some means to comprehend what those minds achieved. No one was around to look at the anatomy of Aristotle's brain or Mozart's or Napoleon's, to 'find' the genius therein, but this modern version of simplistic phrenology and reductionist thought has no doubt occurred to many.[11]

This error, which I am calling one of unleavened mentalism, is not confined to the bizarre mausoleums of the old Soviet Union, but appears in some of the most modern work in neuroscience. A recent reconstruction of the brain injury to Phineas Gage – a 25-year-old railroad worker in Vermont who had a three foot-long tamping rod driven entirely through his head in an accidental explosion way back in 1848 but whose skull has been preserved to this day – uses the most refined methods possible to establish the probable pathway through the brain between the entrance and exit wounds.[12] The survival of such devastating penetrating wounds to the brain is now well-known, particularly after the many survivors of missile wounds during the two world wars of this century (consider also the hundreds deliberately so wounded by prefrontal bilateral lobotomy), and the symptoms are fairly well described. But in the middle of the nineteenth century, Gage's survival was considered miraculous, and he received a good deal of notoriety. Gage made a short and tragic subsequent 'career'

---

11 A rich and enjoyable introduction to reductionism can be found in Barlow, H., Blakemore, C., and Weston–Smith, M. (1990) *Images and Understanding*, Cambridge: Cambridge University Press.

12 See Damasio, H., Grabowski, T., Frank, R., Galaburda, A.M., and Damasio, A.R. (1994) 'The return of Phineas Gage: clues about the brain from the skull of a famous patient', *Science* 264: 1102–5. In a work that I have not yet seen, A.R. Damasio extends this argument for a biology of mind, no doubt also astutely (*Descartes' Error: Emotion, Reason and the Human Brain*, New York: Putnam, in press). However, until such anatomical researchers in neuropsychology develop for us a convincing biology of the more virulent loss (than Gage's) of the ethical sense in the Nazis and some other barbarians of our century – whom, I think it safe to assume, have not suffered any ventromedial injuries to their left frontal and prefrontal brain regions – or they develop an otherwise compelling ethical dualism of their own (perhaps, this time, not biologically based?), I can only contend that the language of anatomical neuropsychology is inadequate to its own task and that, the pineal gland aside, Descartes did not make such a grave error after all.

exploiting his fame, because he was unable to hold down any regular job. He was widely observed exhibiting uncharacteristically boisterous vulgarity and became coarse and irresponsible. Many early neurologists, and others, in the ensuing decades, spoke of the loss in him of the 'ethical sense'.

In a marvellous sort of 150-year-delayed autopsy, Damasio and her colleagues not only (i) attempt to clarify the true place in the history of neuropsychology of Gage's wound and of his subsequent behaviour and also that of the physician who first analysed his injury (John Harlow, in 1868, three years after Broca's famous report), but they also (ii) appear to be looking for the location of some quite similar 'ethical sense', though expressed in the best terms and concepts that modern psychology has given to modern neuropsychology, under the 'hypothesis that emotion and its underlying neural machinery participates in decision making within the social domain and ... that the participation depends upon the ventro-medial frontal region' (p. 1104). In place of 'ethical sense' we have 'decision making within the social domain'. In their report, it is only the frontal lobes that were damaged, the left more than the right; and Broca's area and the motor areas were fully spared, which is consistent with the fact that Gage seemed to have suffered no loss in language or in motor function.

But, unfortunately, their search for the brain locus for decision making in the social domain is no less logically absurd, in my opinion, than some other forms of sophisticated phrenology, or the gestalt view of the brain as a volume conductor. The primal events of pure relational ethical perception are not static binary events, but dynamic N-ary ones, moving in mental time and in mental space.[13]

Ethics is a quality that emerges in human experience within the perception of and the acting within dynamic social relationships – often co-ordinated by intersensory perceptual organizations – and as part of the

---

13 As it happens, I plan to discuss these problems elsewhere (in *The Dynamic Human Visual Field*, a work in progress), but some points deserve noting: our methods in perceptual and cognitive neuropsychological diagnosis have not advanced much from those of Poppelreuter and others, before and during World War I: they are still largely qualitative; they take virtually no account of our advances in knowledge of middle-level cortical function in vision, or in audition or in touch; they do not make much use of our advances in psychophysical methods, as by V. Bekesy or in modulation transfer function studies or, perforce, in signal detection/decision theory; they do not touch at all on intersensory function and co-ordination; and there exist no clinical tests, good or bad, for 'decision-making' skills either within or without the social domain. Much of this lag comes from the failure to understand the dimensional aspects of human intelligence and, also, the importance of gestalt organizing principles in higher cortical function.

In any event, the intellectual challenge has been joined. But this same error of unleavened mentalism is also made by Crick (See Footnote 1 to this chapter) in his attempt to locate 'free will' in some particular region of the brain. As I am showing (see especially Chapter 12), free will is a quality of human experience and, as such, is neither neuronally explicable nor does it dwell in the brain.

complex but routine cognitive-mental processes of the normal mentally healthy individual interacting with the many surrounding natural and social environments. This is not to say that neuropsychology is wholly irrelevant to this process; but it is to say that the wrong question is being asked because of this misconception of mental life. In part, this is the fault of psychology which has not provided guidance; in part, it is the fault of the widespread and popular but nugatory philosophy that holds that science deals only with the material.

The properties of leavened mental life, its flexibilities and its illimitabilities, are emergent from the anatomy and are emergent from the physics and are emergent from the vast private matrix of self–other dualisms and, as such, do not dwell in any 'place' that our language and our philosophy and our psychology has thus far given us the capacity to think about clearly or to express well. An absolutely fundamental shift in the scientific outlook is required. Perhaps this will be one of the results of my work: to encourage the development of a new language enabling us to communicate meaningfully and in an altogether novel manner about these ancient and still burning questions.

Meanwhile, what Phineas Gage did lose, as is typical of many with similarly dramatic brain injuries, can be fairly well described: it was widespread super-egoistical inhibitory balances, normally present in all social situations, and the ability to perceive and mentally to organize complex relational emergents in the normal socialized fashion; but it was not the ability to act upon those relationships that he was still able to perceive.

While it is possible that prodigies and prodigious talents in performance skills like athleticism and violin playing and even doing figures may some day be found to have a nexus of kinaesthetic and visual and aural and related ingestive and expressive propensities, and perhaps even underlying anatomical unities, it is clear that the voluntary inventive skills necessary to creativity will not. Talents should not be confused with inventive skills, whether in humour or in music or in mathematics or in poetry or in painting or in dance or in athletics or in writing or, perforce, in science.

Indeed, most good writers find themselves limited not by the sluggishness of their mental flow but by their athleticism. Many of the writing processes – typing, scripting, and 'word-processing' – that writers can undertake are much slower than the flow and of emergence of ideas in their minds that seem worthy of being written down. One must assume also that choreographers can go much faster mentally than they can put the dance down; and mathematicians as well, and certainly inventors in mechanical or chemical fields who have an idea fully clear in their mind yet have to struggle for years to put it into practice.

The act of creativity, of getting the 'thing' in a form suitable for communication to others, is fundamentally different from the act of imagination that brought the idea clearly into mind in the first place. Discussions of creativity in the past have often confused these two distinct psychological processes.

To play a violin sonata well is one process; but to conceive an original sonata and then to write it out satisfactorily in a critical and communicable form is entirely another.

But to search for either amid brain cells and networks is a foolish and non-self-limiting task. While the empirical facts of neuronal function do suggest rational limits for modelling, there is always sufficient room to wander. Once it was known that the peripheral neural impulse was a variable-frequency fixed-amplitude spike, this lent itself neatly to the yes/no analysis of George Boole, modelling all psychophysical and cognitive changes by frequency and not by amplitude. Now that we know, however, that cortical function (as opposed to peripheral function) is dominated by gradient and analogue changes, amplitude modelling for perceptual events and experience has come back into favour. Perhaps in the near future, at some location still nearer to the Herald (that last externally measurable neural event before experience), yes/no modelling will once again be said to be permissible.

But, perhaps, at this level, the key factors will again become molecular relations, or atomic ones, as they were also at the receptive surfaces. So it seems that one can never stop, until the final tiny molecule itself is discerned, and one can point: 'There!'

It is not the ultra-structural neuro-anatomists who will have the final say, nor those who stop at the level of valence or atomic charge. The geometric shape of organic molecules is absolutely crucial to living creatures, and must also be considered. For example, an amino acid that rotates the plane of the polarization of light in one direction may be essential to life, while the amino acid of the same formula but of different shape that rotates the plane of polarization in the other direction may be an actual poison.

In fine, while we have considerable range to postulate hypothetical neurons and conceptual neurologies, we also have considerable range as to how far down into the smallest and the fastest our modelling should or must go. Strictly speaking, none of this matters critically, because Descartes was correct that the mind is not 'in' the brain. What he did not know to say or comprehend is that the mind is emergent from the brain.

Genius lies not in the brain, nor does consciousness; but in cognitive and phenomenological dynamics. It lies in the interaction of the whole human being with its present perceptual reality and with the way in which the tasks voluntarily self-set fit with that reality and seem well put. Consequently, as we shall see later on, free will is not some odd and peculiar phenomenal delusion, but another rational qualia of the mind that emerges in thought and experience when the conditions are right.

Does the blank canvas so annoy the painter that he must cover it all up? Or is she/he after another different reality altogether, that has nothing to do with canvases? Likewise, is the composer so unhappy with silence? And why does not the wood-carver leave that tree well enough alone?

In the imagination of the imagination, mankind invents gods that fill the universe, and laws of nature that seem to do the same. The two sets of inventions pervade the same spaces and the same times. But nowhere in the single brain cell or the multiple brain cells, nowhere in the single synapses or in the networks, nowhere in the sub-molecular charges or the electronic energy levels, search as we may, can we find that specially Fixed Thing that can assist us in modelling how it has come about that only mankind has taken those two great mythopoetic leaps.

It is the function of the hand to reach so as to proffer gifts, and it is also the function of the hand to receive gifts.

Sometimes it may appear that these gifts are really identical things or events. The mind can also deal with that.

While the solution of puzzles is often what even mundane mental life thrives on, and while contention with them often gives challenge and spice to the scientific life, the fact that single brain cells themselves are always balanced between arousal and inhibition, indicating an apparent dynamic geometric conformity in time and space with these other oppositions, entices us only to specious go-between models by a collapse of the many genuine scientifically modellable emergent leaps.[14]

The remainder of this work, then, will be devoted to a clarification and demonstration of this fact. Ultimately, it also addresses a puzzle that Shakespeare once put:

> ... where is fancy bred,
> Or in the heart or in the head?

---

14 Much more balanced views can be found in a wide diversity of sources: Hayek, F.A. (1952) *The Sensory Order,* Chicago: Chicago University Press; Prigogine, I. and Stengers, I. (1984) *Order out of Chaos,* Toronto: Bantam; Delbruck, M. (1986) *Mind From Matter? An Essay on Evolutionary Epistemology,* Palo Alto, Calif.: Blackwell's Scientific Publications; Critchley, M. (1979) *The Divine Bouquet of the Brain,* New York: Raven Press.

3   Introduction to the natural history of mind

THE SEQUENTIAL PLAN OF THIS BOOK

In developing the thesis that mind, in all its marvellous attributes, evolved as a survival advantage to assist in the co-ordination of sometimes coherent and sometimes incoherent intersensory messages, it is necessary to present some basic ideas of what such a thesis, or any thesis qua theory, must involve, and this chapter is devoted in part to that. It thus presents the theory of theory, or a metatheory. It also includes a discussion of parallels between sensory and cognitive function, and introduces certain neurophysiological facts concerning the existence of even single cortical cells devoted to intersensory processing. And it also reviews various insights from neuropsychology which show how the human mind, though it evolved from the senses, has now emerged from them and can persist transcendent of them. Thus, the dynamics of mental function parallel those of sensory function, not the reverse. And, as I shall try to demonstrate, the various forms of sensory interaction constitute the largest subset of animal and human experiences and the largest subset of causes for motivations and behaviour. Consequently, it is these aspects of mental function that present the greatest challenge to mathematicians and physicists and neuroscientists and other modellers seeking to describe well the underlying processes and dynamics that may 'explain' mind.

The next chapter develops some additional parallels between sensory dimensions and qualitative mental motion along sensory routes (e.g. from dark blue to light blue, from this hot spot to that cool spot, away from that noise, etc.). The point stressed is that motoric behaviour is also sensory-kinaesthetic, and the more so as it is ideational (as in a gesture of ideational prayer) and not constructive (as in a riposte or in tying a tie). This applies to virtually any real body motion along real physical pathways (as via walking, swimming, and other means) and thence to any intellectual motion along mental routes (as also on maps, and along geometric plots or graphs, and thence through imaginary landscapes and music and dance). And also, especially, along the linear arguments sometimes typical of much of mathematics. This is illustrated, in part, by proofs of the theorem of Pythagoras, and then by one of the charming sorites (or logically cascading puzzles) of Lewis Carroll. The fact that there is an infinite set of possible mental mappings of any territory – if not really an infinite set of ways actually to get around – introduces the critical challenge to behaviouristic reductionism by noting that there is, for humans, an infinite set of ways to express outwardly any inner mental state and, as well, that any given outward behaviour or gesture may have an infinite number of internal meanings or intentions. Moreover, these infinities are not often easy even to pair. Indeed, the exploration of such pairings is the point of much psychotherapy, and thence of art and literature.

Following this, comes a discussion of the multisensory nature of the qualities of our experiences of time (Chapter 5) and of space (Chapter 6). Then, in Chapter 7, ideas themselves, and our awarenesses of having them or of being in possession of them (only rarely, do they possess us), are presented as another complex set of multisensory experiential qualities, illustrated especially by the concept of mirroring and with the theory (in part, from Freud) of words which simultaneously mean their own opposites (autantonyms) as *Urworten*. The argument is then also noted that, because there exists a natural intersensory basis for onomatopoiesis, most probably it has been a crucially important factor in the origin of speech. In Chapter 8, this same concept is expanded to illustrate the fact that ideas of objects, while themselves at first as isomorphic as possible to the 'form' of the object (if not still the sound), are not things but rather an entirely different insubstantial and energetic set, and that the classical Lockean distinction between primary and secondary qualities is one which applies only to objects (and not all that well, even to these) and not to words (matching experience to gesture) nor to ideas. Further, I point out that there is a crucial set or population of our ideas which does not describe 'things' at all. Rain is not a thing, but it is also not a *no*thing; similarly, wishes, sunsets, illnesses, and routes. Consequently, the description both of intersensory and thence of cognitive experience as being, somehow, restricted to (or about) things, is shown to be in error. The key to the origin of at least human mental life is this: it derives first via the intersensory processing and co-ordination of experiences along sensory dimensions which occur not with things but, largely, with gradients. It is a natural consequence of the disorder-reduction function of language skills that they help transform these gradients easily into nouns (here is a *storm*, there is a *drizzle*), though they might well have been given a wholly different status. And, secondly, via the intersensory integration of experiences with gradients sharply enough accelerated so as to be sensed as objects, they help with naming: thunder, lightning, hail. It is the response to gradients (e.g. tropisms) which accounts for the ancient origin, in the earliest nervous system, of contralateral neuro-sensory neuro-muscular control, of which language in humans (in the left hemisphere) is the most refined and advanced and emergent asymmetry. Again, I emphasize that language behaviour has a profound sensory component: what we intend to speak is, largely, what we do indeed manage to speak and then hear ourselves doing so.

In Chapter 9, an attempt is made to relate how the various sense modes, which actually constitute a dynamic and expanding set vastly more complex than the classical Aristotelian five, integrate and co-ordinate into the development of broad abstract sensorially transcendent ideas such as causality, externality, direction, symmetry, and so forth. They are transcendent precisely because many senses are involved. Blue is less transcendent than the quality of self-awareness, for example. This is not meant to be a final or even an advanced analysis, but merely to stress how the various senses bear differently upon these several subtle intellectual experiences. Chapter 10 discusses some of the perceived and constructed analogies that have been used to model the mind, over intellectual history, and then takes note of some limitations of more recent ones such as computers and holograms and neural nets. Actually, the mind always escapes its modelling. Then we pass on (Chapter 11) to a short discussion of the neurology of regeneration in comparison to the neurology of memory, and note how an unregenerated limb injury is, in some ways, a much better model of real organismic history than is actual limb regeneration, even though the latter may aid organismic survival. In this way, the body itself models nature as well as do the senses and the mind. This analysis of the loss of an eye or an ear or a limb as the loss of variance-processing capacity gives us insights into how successful intersensory multi-rational intelligence may be in aiding organismic success. This then allows us to state in a strong sense that the mind, and sensory integration and sense-rational intelligence, are, indeed, true survival processes and not mere residuals of some other broader and more transcendent neuro-dynamic event or process. A short discourse follows on the deaf population of Martha's Vineyard (as it was up to around the early part of this century) which illustrates how the genetic failure to provide the normal intersensory plasticity to model environmental variance can, notwithstanding, be minimized in us by means of higher cultural and social orderings.

Chapter 12 then introduces a discussion of the experience of free will, as a higher and more subtle quality still of multisensory integration, that is naturally emergent in the healthy and well-nourished and well-nurtured human. And it moves on to the assertion, as a clarification of the classical psychoanalytic notion, that greater ego-strength means precisely that a wider range of social-environmental possibilities exists for that individual in which the intersensory quality of freedom can emerge. Next, Chapter 13 attempts a first-time presentation of a possible neural *anlage* for the extraordinary degree of variance-processing requisite to reflective intersensory self-awareness (somaesthetic-proprioceptive, etc.): to the awareness of being aware that one is aware. This is based upon graded (analogue) arousals in a neural complex (no doubt, a hysteretic or fuzzy net) integrating and organizing many cells and columns and modules about the hitherto wholly neglected variance-processing and modelling potential of a single cortical cell which has at least 100 (and perhaps up to 10,000) functional and independent synapses. Next, this discussion is brought together in a short and very preliminary chapter (Chapter 14) which relates some of these arguments (concerning intersensory integration and multiplicity ingestion and variance production) to how best to shape pedagogy and encourage healthy child development in an ecologically sound socio-political environment. Such a schooling, as John Dewey stressed many years ago, need not be 'correct' but it must be whimsical, dynamic, and judgemental only in the nature of pointing out alternative ways. Finally, symmetry is achieved in an Afterword (Chapter 15) that reviews some objections to the intersensory argument and to the idea of emergence and that states some of its strongest points.

Clearly, this is an overview of the task that I have set myself, and is meant only to set the stage for what follows. And, equally, it may be too much for any one person to do well. Ultimately, I can only rely upon reader generosity. On the other hand, there are many others in science today, and in philosophy and even biology and psychology, who are also trying to do such things, so perhaps I am walking in their traces. Furthermore, many writing today in engineering and in physics also leap well out of their own fields and land boldly into the realms of depth psychology and developmental psychology and even, alas, into visual perception, so it is wholly reasonable to expect that someone from the other side may try, occasionally, to leap back. As we all know, mind always conquers matter in any case, and physical and chemical reality inevitably respond to dynamic human attentions and expectations and wishes. All these things, after all, collapse as soon as we turn our back upon them. It is not only our children that are mischievous. The balance pan slips over to the lighter side; the acidic fluid gives a pH of 9 not 4; the refrigerator freezes hell; the cold-fusion heats up and unfuses; the super-collider fails, any longer, to collide; the giant artificially intelligent computer says it is tired and refuses to compute and the super conductor reverses the electrical flow. And all the highly ordered and far-from-equilibrium pretty fractal events that so intrigued us when we found them slide back towards equilibrium and disorder. The power of mind over matter is so great that all this starts to happen, even, just as we turn our minds towards home. It is then, surely, that the meek inherit.

Which goes to show that there must, in any good theory, be room for chaos: some variance set aside for the singular case; some jitter in the neurons which, itself, models, however modestly, the fascinating jitter in the mental present.

The doing of psychoneurology, and the erecting in theoretical neuroscience of postulates which attempt to demonstrate how the separate sensory models that we are forever making of the physico-chemical world (and also the social world) cohere somehow when we attend to them in that experience that we call mind, and incohere when we do not – all this seems as worthy as many other activities in science. Of course, the human mind unminds itself, even when we attend only a bit carelessly to it. At all odds, we are like an optical image way down the line carefully and earnestly trying to discern its distant object. Mind, thus, functions as arbiter between all the models of nature and of self that the senses and their history may provide. When we educate the senses, it is the mind which is learning, not they. From the time that the cell membrane evolved to protect the infant single-cell organism from being absorbed back into nature – yet gave it a consistency sufficient to elaborate enough of what that surrounding gradient nature was like for the cell body to survive – it has always been the task of organisms to be apart from nature yet to remain a part of nature. Sensory modelling itself is a preserving of the integrated self as still remaining part of original nature. So the self-conscious mind gave to humans the capacity to stand even further apart from nature, in order to recognize it and to construct a limitless set of models of it, some coherent with other models and some not, depending upon which modality was used primarily, and how much intersensory modelling was afoot, and which set of subsensory qualities was, then and there, most pertinent. The mind, the healthy present mind, selects most skilfully the most salient and most lovely and most efficacious balance. The removed skill in resolving between and then choosing among incoherent sensory-rational models of nature, and of not being overwhelmed by the conflicts, is what we mean by ego-strength: a vigorous sense of self-awareness and well-being, and a tolerance for chaos. What nature tends to muddle, the ego refines and reorders in its own special way. It is life's task to perceive order amid disorder, and to give some of that order back.

This said, let us pass to the specific arguments.

THE CARTOGRAPHY OF CHESHIRE

In developing a theory in science, then, one usually has at least five levels or classes of aspects with which one must deal effectively, and the natural history of mind is no exception. *Firstly*, there must be some specific choice concerning subject matter and the so-called 'minimum entities'. For mind, this is never easy: thoughts, perceptions, the present moment, recollections, recognitions, hunches, insights, free-will actions, and so on. (Indeed, what might mind be that we believe that it may or must have a natural, as opposed to an unnatural, history?) *Secondly*, there must be an ever-increasing collation of the facts that those scholars active in the field have come gradually to accept as at least close enough to being probably correct as to be a first major approximation to reality. In psychology, it takes a great boldness even to try to list, say: self-awareness, single-to-general evocations, logic, causality, unconsciousness, will, and so on. *Thirdly*, there must be orderings, oppositions, balances, co-ordinations, and thus a form or pattern to the facts. *Fourthly*, and these tend to be the most interesting aspects of science, there must be some descriptive specification of the laws for dynamics and change that can relate these entities in one condition or state when recognized in (or traced to) some other condition or state. These may be laws of motion or of growth or of summation or cell-division or of molecular reorganization or of psychic emergence and transformation. Essentially, this was Einstein's task in relativity: veridical geometrical communication. *Fifthly*, there are the special means, in our dealings with the subject matter of interest, by which we come to observe the things that we do observe and to know the things that we do know: introspection, communication, psychophysics, perceptual analysis, sensory rational intelligence, and so forth. Each science must embody within its province certain specific methods that may not exist in other fields or, if they do exist there, may have different connotations or functions. An experiment in mathematics, for example, is always a thought experiment by its nature, as are those in psychoanalysis. But an experiment in physics or in chemistry need not be; it can be *real*.

Albeit that, in psychoanalysis, the science is sometimes devoted exclusively to the individual case and not to general principles, one must note that the principle of the 'triple-blind' also applies to many observations in biology, chemistry, and physics. In this method, the experimenter does not know which subject or solution or cloud chamber has received the training or the chemical or the atom that is of interest. And, of course, the subject-solution-cloud chamber does not itself know. And, if the truth be known, no one knows!

This is merely to suggest at the start that many aspects of even the so-called hard sciences do not meet these ideal criteria well. Thus, in this difficult field of mental science, the reader need not fear the disappointment of being handed a whole new solution neatly aligned and summed up. Rather, what we serve up is messy and considerably hedgy. Yet that very uncertainty too – now at the second level: thinking about thinking about uncertainty – is one of the marvellous attributes of mind that makes its study so challenging and still so unendable. The reader is reminded how, whenever we get really close to mind, it leaps up and moves away . . . and returns to Carroll's Cheshire. Psychology strives for a cartography of the disappearance, a science of the act of alteration, a description by the less of the always more.

ORIGINS

There have been many discussions over the years concerning the origin of the mind but, despite their number and distinction, one still has a nagging uneasiness about virtually all of them. Since mind is part of nature, one would like to be asked to consider a naturalistic theory of its origin. Yet even today many of the proposals resemble diffuse philosophical, even theological or political, treatises rather than empirical nature-based formulations. While a directed Christian or Marxist view may well have some aesthetic and mythopoetic appeal in its own right, one hopes generally for a landscape drawn with a wider brush. In default of over-arching statements from bio-psychology, in modern times we find the field taken over, on the one hand, by physicists. This has a certain appeal because of the success of this science in other regions, but in *this* region only if one also believes the mind to be a physical and not a psychological system. And, on the other hand, by computer scientists, whose appeal is to those that believe the mind is a simple even if multi-parallel computational mechanism (cf. Chapter 10 below).

UNCOMPUTABILITY

Since, in my view, neither is true, these discourses, though sometimes beautifully reasoned and deeply pondered, will not be made much of here. In any event, no confidence has developed that a real understanding has emerged from any of them, though some do agree on focus. For example, in one of the best from classical physics we read a truly stunning attack on the simplistic notion of mind (as a Turing machine) proposed by some researchers in the field of artificial intelligence.[1]

And in one of the best in the new physics, discussing chaos theory and turbulence (processes that in their intrinsic structure begin, at long last, to really look a bit like mind), the notion of *uncomputability* has arisen which neatly parallels that of *undecidability* already there in mathematics (Gödel's theorem). 'For example, it is well known that detailed properties of turbulent flows at far-off times cannot be predicted ... even the *statistical* properties of these flows may be "uncomputable"' (see Frisch and Orszog 1990: 31).[2] This admission of uncomputability in a central field

---

1 In his recent widely publicized work, Penrose means to assert, by his echoing (but slightly misleading) title, that, like the Emperor's new clothes, not the mind as such but so-called strong artificial intelligence *models* of it are all bound to fail if we examine them in relation to the known laws of physics. I do not myself discuss artificial intelligence here, and I refer the reader to Penrose's superb analysis, especially his reply to the famous criterion of Turing (that a computer may be said to 'think' if, after five minutes of questioning, an average interrogator has only a 70 per cent chance of being correct in deciding that he/she is 'talking' to a machine or a person) and the implications of this for the related puzzle of the Chinese Room. (Penrose, R. (1990) *The Emperor's New Mind: Concerning Computers, Minds and the Laws of Physics*, New York: Oxford University Press.) On the other hand, some still do assert that a sufficiently quantized modern physics may do to model mind: cf. Lockwood, M. (1989) *Mind, Brain and the Quantum: The Compound 'I'*, Oxford: Blackwell.

2 Cf. Frisch, U. and Orszog, S.A. (1990) 'Turbulence: challenges for theory and experiment', *Physics Today* 43: 24–32. Much has been made recently in physics of turbulence
continued

of modern physics should give some comfort to those who feel that physical laws exhaust the rules for dynamics in the universe (it is easy to show that they do not, by the way, as when *in the mind* 'hot' evokes 'cold' or 'dog' or 'house' instead of a nearest neighbouring 'warmth'), and yet who find themselves puzzled by phenomenological order sometimes also emerging in mental life somehow mysteriously and uncomputably at far-off times.

One still searches amid all of these for some of those enthralling insights that galvanize whole generations of scientists and yet can pass muster before the poets. To my mind, it is clear that one of the first requirements must be to relate the origin of the mind to certain recognized principles of neuro-biology[3] and to the facts of biological evolution.

---

theory and of chaos theory, in which what appear to us to be highly ordered events (dynamic singularities) emerge from initially highly chaotic turbulent events due to the influence of very, very minor initial asymmetries (attractors), so small as often to be overlooked. In the true Heisenberg sense in some cases these may have only inferential existence. In addition to some odd sort of cortical optics (after Young) of the energy-energy interactions of mind (noted by me earlier: Shipley, T. (1989) 'When mind chooses freely to be body', *Atti, F.G. Ronchi* XLIV: 116–49), I suggest that some of the insights — about how order emerges within conglomerations of physical matter in turbulence — may also prove fruitful in comprehending how order emerges within mental flux. Consider also P. Anderson (1990, *Physics Today* 43: 9) who states: 'After all, we now know that almost all the phenomena we study, both in condensed matter and in particle theory, result from emergent processes and broken symmetries nearly as complex and evolutionary as [those in] biology.' Thus, indeed! For a more classical and contrasting determinate view of mind, see Honderich, T. (1989) *A Theory of Determinism: The Mind, Neuroscience and Life Hopes.* Oxford: Clarendon Press.

3 One must comment on the recent elegant book by the eminent immunologist Gerald M. Edelman (1990) *The Remembered Present: A Biological Theory of Consciousness*, New York: Basic Books, which presents a strong neurologically based model of those mental processes which appear *conscious*. His discussion is predicated on his previous book ((1988) *Neural Darwinism*, New York: Basic Books) and gives many insights into this difficult area. And he is correct, in my view, on several points. 1. He is treading where most academic psychologists have previously failed to tread. 2. His rejection of computer models of the mind is a long over-due criticism of some incredibly careless and slovenly psychology. 3. He seems also to accept some weak notion of levels, though he does not go quite as far in this direction as to openly support the principles of emergent evolution. 4. And he is certainly correct in his gestalt view that the subject matter of psychology is not some collection of things but some co-ordination of processes.

So it should be clear that I think his approach one of the most useful on its level. However, if he wishes, as he states, to understand consciousness and some of its products, such as poetry and imagination, he remains, in my view, on the wrong plane for that. Taking the recognition principles from molecular immunology to molecular synaptic neurology may be justified because one is not, really, moving across grand divides. But poetry and imagination occur at another level entirely from molecular processes. And the only way to understand them is to proceed on the phenomenological plane in accordance with the dynamic principles of intersensory psychophysics and perceptual recognition and expression. I myself have wondered whether parallels might not be found between the dynamics of molecular processes and, possibly, threshold sensory ones. But at threshold, vision is quantal and follows poisson laws, whereas audition and taction are pressure-mechano-receptors and are continuous above Brownian noise. In any event, one must guard carefully against assuming that parallel

continued

Secondly, one must formulate an origin, or at least an ontology, that is coherent with what modern dynamic developmental and sensory-rational psychology has to tell us about how the processes of mental life develop and take place. In these, phenomenology is of the essence and emergence is the key.

My task here is to show how it is possible to become wholly comfortable in the construction of such events.[4]

GALVANIZE THE POETS

Resolution of turbulence, far-from equilibrium coalescence[5] and the perception of order within disorder[6] are only three new members of the old multitudinous set by which we describe the *emergents* which occur in nature. That grand set certainly permits us to hold to the strong view that

---

(*3 continued*)   dynamics must be a true homology, and not a result of the fact that the scientific bias likes to model all dynamics in similar ways.

Further, Edelman does not give sufficient attention at his own molecular level to contrasting neural network models, or to chaos or turbulence theory, or to far-from-equilibrium thermodynamics. On the other hand, there is never an ending to reductionist models, and it is my view that they will all continue to miss the mark to the extent that they fail to recognize the absolutely crucial importance in mental life of non-linear phenomenology and wholly uncalculable unpredictable events. A new bio-phenomenology is required, not more models, even network ones. Or ones based on neuro-immunological recognition principles.

4 Much has been made recently of new looks in evolution, such as graded evolution or punctuated equilibrium. See especially the books by S.J. Gould (e.g. (1990) *Wonderful Life: The Burgess Shale and the Nature of History*, New York: Norton) and some others. The fundamental idea of punctuated evolution is that the process was not some sort of linear progression — though, actually, neither Darwin nor Wallace held that simplistic view — nor is it some sort of regular staircase or ziggurat leading to higher and/or more complex forms. Rather, important and significant plateaux or punctuations took place, sometimes lasting for many millennia, in which no change in species form is observed. Then, suddenly, a rapid shift occurs and a new alternative form appears. From here we may have gradualism for some thousands of years, and then another plateau. This view has the advantage that differences between the various plateaux could, in my sense, be considered emergents.

Two key directions in evolution, in fact, can be precisely stated: first is an increased cellular specialization in response to environmental energy variances. Secondly, there occurs enhanced centralization-encephalization which serves to co-ordinate these increasingly subtle texture information ingestions. But it is important to note that, while these advances ensure greater chances for self-survival and for species replication and are fully supportive of punctuated evolution, they do not support the assertions of socio-biology. Hence classical systemic biologists are in no way displaced by socio-biologists. Other balanced modern views of evolution may be found in: Poirier, F. (1990) *Understanding Human Evolution*, Englewood Cliffs, NJ: Prentice-Hall. Or Ruse, M. (1989) *The Darwinian Paradigm: Essays on its History, Philosophy, and Religious Implications*, London: Routledge. A particular fine evolutionary treatment of mind, influential on mine, is Riedl, R. (1981) *Biology of Knowledge: The Evolutionary Basis of Reason*, Chichester: Wiley, 1984.

5 Prigogine, I. and Stenger, I. (1984) *Order out of Chaos*, New York: Bantam Books.

6 Shipley, T. and Van Houten, P. (1984) 'Ranking random textures: the perception of order within disorder', *Pattern Recog.* 17: 465–73.

various emergents, i.e. noncomputable singularities, sudden reorganizations, cusps, catastrophes, insights, may even occur widely in biological organisms, governed, as they are, by the most complex physical laws imaginable, and perhaps by some others still. Indeed, because of this new recognition by physics of a dynamics sufficiently complex almost to parallel that in psychology, it has become more attractive than ever to hold that emergence lies at the foundation of our reflexive self-consciousness. Poets, of course, never doubted this. And naturally this is a view shared today more narrowly by many of the same sort of vitalist and religious biologists and mythopoets who shared in the past notions of *élan vital* and the special fluids of life – ante-dating, of course, the synthesis of urea in about 1823.[7] And while its tenor may seem to give to us all a certain antique cast, one cannot any longer scientifically reject it on that account. There is an unfolding tale.

Consider this. A derivation, mathematical or causal, consists in trying to make or construe two processes as tightly continuous as possible so that no empty unsettling cognitive steps or gaps exist between. In mathematics, the test for continuity of space, for example, is that it must be internally convex. This means that for any separation AB, a still smaller separation AB′, can always be taken in mind. And certainly this sort of continuity is an ideal in many sciences. But no one seriously tries to *derive* from the laws of physics, or even from some ideal set of such laws as it may be hypothesized for some day far in the future, any of the rules of human social life such as language syntax or jokes or social syntax or pedagogy or legal syntax or family structure or even, for that matter, the very laws of mathematics themselves, much less the rules of baseball and the recipe for the correct preparation of fancy grade maple syrup.

Why, then, do so many feel constrained to try to do this for mind? An absolutely key notion in classical biology is known as emergent evolution (cf. Morgan 1916).[8] This refers to the theoretical impossibility of establishing internally convex intellectual continuities between many of the stages in evolution. The well-established significance of sudden discrete genetic mutations is only one of many aspects of this. For example, suppose one should know all that there is to know about the atomic molecular structure and the chemical actions of oxygen and nitrogen molecules, and maybe about a few others, and about how they join together in (or make) air. Nothing therein brings us even into the vicinity of comprehending the meaning of Emily Dickinson's evocative expression: 'Inebriation of air'. It is easy to show that first-level consciousness as such exists in the higher primates and, of course, in many human pets and in some other animals

---

7 For example, Eccles, J.C. (1990) *Evolution of the Brain: Creation of the Self*, New York: Routledge.

8 Morgan, C.L. (1931) *Emergent Evolution*, New York: Holt; also Morgan, T.H. (1916) *Evolution and Genetics*, Princeton, NJ: Princeton University Press, 1925.

as well (those matched together as stern predators and as tremulous prey, especially, in whom consciousness has a tight focus). But it appears that accelerated or reflexive self-consciousness (being aware that one is aware) emerges only in the mental organization of humans. This organization is certainly not present in salt; nor is it present even in pewter. It is probably not present even 'in' gravity, though in some ways this does come close. Perhaps one might dream it to occur also in some infinite mirrorings of light. But, then again, perhaps that is what the human mind is: life's most complex and restructurable infinite mirroring of radiation and gravity, whence comes the intimate relationship of light to God, and to the ultimate source of our energy. If we seek to comprehend reflexive self-consciousness we must approach it on its own level, where it really *is*. For this, we really do need a highly sophisticated bio-phenomenology.

Actually, as one cannot have an 'almost frog' or an 'almost joke', one cannot approach mind gradually in infinitesimal cat's steps, as if trying to sneak up on it. Somewhere along the way, one has to jump and pass through no-space. One way to get almost as close as one wishes to mind, as if via an infinitesimal calculus of mental acts, is to consider the intimate character of the 'almost minds' that we already have within us, in the form of the senses. These bring us close, as we shall see.

THE MIND EVOLVED FROM YET TRANSCENDS THE SENSES

Consider the situation that one's hand is poised in the air slowly moving down to swat a fly that has landed on one's knee. Albeit that, evolutionarily speaking, this tiny creature stands relatively low, none the less, as one's hand stealthily approaches, it is sufficiently advanced to sense many things: among which are at least (i) the changing gradients in air currents, (ii) those in odours (possibly even tastes), and (iii) those in radiation shadows. There may be others. Given the event that any of these gradients changes (in the neighbourhood of the fly's sense-organs) at a rate faster than some mysterious unknown fly-steady natural state, off the fly goes instantly and escapes the brutal crush. Clearly, one cannot infer from this that the fly has some sort of highly developed survival instinct, or that the fly is aware that it has escaped some sort of a blow – particularly so because, if one's knee is really wet with perspiration, the fly comes right back for more. But one can assert that at some central ganglionic level in the nervous system of the fly, those several sensory messages have come together and been co-ordinated with sensory-expressive modes that enable (and encourage) the fly to move. We do not assert, either, that the fly has free will such that it might upon some similar occasion decide not to move. But we do observe that a co-ordinating, motion-compelling survival-promoting process is certainly taking place.

Moreover, it is not that the various changes in shadow, smell, and wind velocity merely add up like some weights on a balance-pan, and so 'automatically' occasion the pushing off of the fly into flight. No, rather there is some integral, central bio-chemical organization of the neural responses to these stimuli which, to the fly, becomes so co-ordinated that it is virtually thrust aloft by that organization. The term used classically by the gestaltist is: requiredness. Without implying that evolution has infused into such life forms 'conscious means' for their self-preservation (as if a tree were to be proud of its bark), it is absolutely correct to say that evolution has imbued all life forms with some means (surface-tension, bark, or flight) for their self-preservation. Part of what life forms do (or are) is to maintain their own 'internal milieu', to use the fine phrase of the great nineteenth-century French neuroscientist Claude Bernard. Inert matter maintains 'that' in other ways. Presumably, if some of those living-milieu-protecting methods reach into consciousness, that in itself suggests that consciousness has, on average, over many, many aeons, aided in the processes of self-preservation. Consciousness has thus evolved as a survival and mating aid. There seems to be no other conclusion possible.

Consider the other side of this event. The fly lands on your knee, which you immediately feel and mentally quite accurately and effortlessly locate in sensory-somatic space. This process in neurology is called 'local signature': the sense of the place where some sense arousal occurs. (The time, quality, and intensity dimensions will concern us later on.)[9] We now know where, not what. You turn your eyes to look upon it, but you could find it just as well in the total absence of light. Actually, typically, the fly's buzzing stops when it lands so you could also have had an auditory clue as to where it was going and have divined that it had landed on your knee from that alone (i.e. if wearing trousers). Now the fly starts a gradual march up your leg, and you have the perfect and immediate – virtually inferential, as in the mental following of a linear argument – awareness of in which direction (usually zigzag) and at what rate (usually slow) it is moving. (In arguments, when the rate is *this* slow, one says, in annoyance: 'Get to the point.') One need not look at all, actually, since the skin modalities themselves communicate this fly-creep information with considerable precision. Now, one sets oneself to swat the fly by hand. (Horses, on the other 'hand', can choose either to swat with the tail or to twitch the skin, though one doubts that the mean accuracy of either of these

---

9 While the time for such things is sometimes precise, it is as often quite imprecise. After walking through the forest, for example, one may see a scratch on one's knee but remember only vaguely that one did feel a sharp prick there sometime during the walk. As for intensity, one can pretty much tell the difference between a fly landing and a wasp or a bee, but I doubt that the precision of this is exactly known. It is known that under ideal conditions on the most sensitive glabrous surface of the thumb one can sense a difference as small as ca ± 0.1 micron. Of course, for a brick vs. a fly one has little doubt about either space or time.

gestures is 'known' even to the horse.) At that moment, one makes a deci-
sion to swat with the left or the right hand. This may even be conscious.
And one then sets out to put oneself gradually into the proper pose.
One then aims at the predicted (inferred) position and moves slowly and
gradually into the striking distance, so to speak, and suddenly plunges.
And misses.

GANGLION TO INTEGRATE SURVIVAL INFORMATION AND TO MAINTAIN THE INTERNAL MILIEU

Both for the fly and for the human, some central component of the nervous
system must have been able to achieve all these necessary sensory integrations in order to bring these experiences and gestures about. No one
has difficulty with the notion that at the level of single-cell creatures
these integrating process and their 'location' are, of course, *the mind*, and
'lie' *in* the single central-cell nucleus. But the same is true for higher
organisms.

The magnitude of the set of different complexities that are successfully
processed in some central integrating ganglion is what permits us to assert
that the fly has more than just the rudiments of mind, but that man has
or, rather, experiences (feels) mind in a vastly more complete and dynamic
form. We can, after all, imagine flies.

REFINING EDGE OF SELF-CRITICISM

Mind has evolved from the body's need to co-ordinate intersensory
messages, to make coherent order out of what otherwise would be separate and unrelated events.[10] Indeed, mind contributes to its own presence
and significance. It starts out as the 'central sympathetic ganglion' in
Freud's terms, perhaps as the thalamus in mine: the primary sensory-
somaesthetic mirror. This is why mind is also felt or experienced; it has
become for man that which experiences itself. It is thus also the refining
function of discipline and self-criticism: that which constantly sharpens the
edge on its own reflexive self-awareness. Moreover, as we shall see, when
nature herself or we in the lab distort the multisensory messages – when
these conspire to make the sound increase in one direction while the light
increases in the opposite, or the smell, or the air-flow, etc., etc. – we put
the mind into stress and we exaggerate the need (for survival) for some
central deliberate resolution of these intersensory conflicts. As deliberation increases consciousness leaps forth.

---

10 This argument can also be examined at the cellular level, as in the following article
   and in some of the references cited therein: Shaw, S.R. and Moore, D. (1989)
   'Evolutionary remodeling in a visual system through extensive changes in the synaptic
   connectivity of homologous neurons', *Visual Neuroscience* 3: 405–10.

INCREASING MULTIPLICITY IN EVOLUTION

The present thesis is this: the mind has evolved from the senses, and exists in higher animals in proportion to the increasing multiplicity and complexity of the sensory messages that may be passed through and co-ordinated. Most individuals thinking about such matters do not realize that the dynamics of mental life follow quite directly and coherently the dynamics of the senses. Where the individual senses, for example, in their physico-chemical neural transduction, generally compress the relevant external dimension into something resembling a logarithmic crunch, so also does the mind in its phenomenal experience. The whole foundation of metaphorical thought, that which Aristotle called the 'perception of similarities amidst dissimilars', stems from this rational and coherent sensuality. We say that someone is a noisy person, not meaning only that he/she shouts. If he/she is in a dark mood, it is not that he/she has turned brown. When someone is hot under the collar, the temperature is not in the day. But days, also, can somehow be sad or frivolous.

As we shall explain, the sense perception and exploration of space are preludic to the idea and imagination of space; the sense perception and exploration of objects are preludic to the idea and imagination of objects; the sense perception and exploration of time are preludic to the idea and imagination of time; the sense perception and exploration of beauty are preludic to the idea and imagination of beauty; and the sense perception and exploration of balance and harmony and comfort and reality are preludic to the ideas and imagination of balance and harmony, and also ethics and justice and love and truth.

DYNAMICS OF MIND PARALLELS DYNAMICS OF THE SENSES

This is also why poetry and mathematics and music are such parallel mental and emotional experiences and share the same noetic perfection and validity. Music is the intellectual melodic expression of the emotions. Poetry is the intellectual melodic verbalization of inner experience. And mathematics is the utter instantation of mental order. It also has a melody, which is a key to the beauty of mathematical reasoning and synaesthesia. Mathematics and poetry are forms of archetypical awarenesses whose validity and rightness are known before they are demonstrated or expressed. That is why we make the effort to prove a theorem. We know it to be correct before we start! That is why when we write poetry we actually know in advance where we are headed, and that it will be good. All these gestures are perfected in integrative fashion by the coming together of cascades of multisensory sensations and the experiences of them and of the thoughts they engender. And this includes the kinaesthetic-expressive sensations as well as the more passive-receptive ones. Over millennia upon millennia upon millennia, in the exquisition of that creature man, there arose the most variable yet viable problem solver of life's inherent challenges. These challenges are perceived better by man than by most other creatures, they are met better by man and in a greater variety of ways than by most other creatures; which is why the population explosion of humans today threatens the rest of nature's creatures as the greatest plague in all of the earth's history. It is also why however, in the recognition of this and in our engagement with the challenges of violence and pollution and social inequalities, we can still find hope.

EVIDENCE FROM CLINICAL NEUROPSYCHOLOGY

A great deal of critical evidence bearing upon this hypothesis derives from observations in neuropsychology. This science has as its subject matter the comprehension and possible amelioration of the sometimes odd and funny, often tragic, always heroic responses of human patients to brain injuries. This field is now growing faster than many and it is not at all possible to give any quick or simplistic survey. Only a few key points will be noted here.

One's first acquaintance with the extraordinary recuperative responses that many patients make to brain injury may well suggest that the mind has, somehow, an almost uncanny persistence and integrity despite the most horrendous and extensive battery imaginable to peripheral sensory function and to central higher cortical function. And this mental persistence gives rise to the conviction that there is, so to say, a mind somewhere about in man (almost?) wholly independent of the senses and largely independent, even, of much critical brain tissue.[11] Mind exists as if its job is to ignore anatomy, as Freud noted long ago *vis-à-vis* hysterical glove anaesthesia: there simply is no brain lesion that could explain that. At the extreme, there is at least one case in the literature of a hydrocephalic lad who, though apparently missing some 60 per cent of the normal internal networking tissue mass of the brain, functions well enough to do about average classroom work up at least through the eighth grade.[12]

---

11 Cf. Brown, J.W. (ed.) (1989) *Neuropsychology of Visual Perception*, Hillsdale, NJ: Erlbaum, especially his 'Essay on perception', pp. 232–55. In co-ordinating these facts Brown goes so far as to state that:

   The unity of the self, therefore, is not accomplished secondarily through an interaction or integration across the modalities, but is a unity that underlies the modalities and distributes itself into them.

   This, of course, is an ancient and most attractive concept, as I am noting. But, unfortunately, it obscures the widely accepted facts of biological evolution. The senses came first.

12 Such cases are well-known in neurology but are, apparently, not yet at all well understood. See, *inter alia*: Milhorat, T. H. (1978) *Pediatric Neurosurgery*, Philadelphia: Davis, *Contri. Neurol ser.* 16, especially Chapter 4: 'Although there is definite

continued

But the major evidence for the integrity of the mind over mere sensory-neural tissue is this:

> over the senses and over the brain, *similar brain injuries* to either cortical, cerebral or more profound brain structures in any human, of whatever race or culture or language or tradition, and over a range of age covering youth of say, 12–15, to virtually any old age, *result in almost identical cognitive neuropsychological symptoms.*

That is to say: there is an inherent geometry of human cortical and other brain processes that not only bears down identically in all humans on specific body function, but bears down identically in all humans on specific mental function as well. This common neurology is the primary and utterly inescapable truth concerning the unity of mankind. Indeed, the manifest psychological unity of the self despite such assaults, as it is experienced alike in all healthy and brain-injured adult humans, tempts one to take the mind as the veritable 'cause', if you will, of the senses. Whereas, in terms of evolution theory, the senses preceded mind at every evolutionary level, and there is no reason whatsoever to deny this sequence when one arrives at mankind. There does not seem to be any emergent bio-principle present in man that would justify our inverting these normal evolutionary directions.

The thesis of the primacy of the mind, of course, is Leibnizian, and is very attractive. It is also related to the notion of innate ideas, even to the Jeffersonian notion of inalienable rights. And, thus, it has had a most venerable and respectful following long before the Declaration.

But it simply cannot be correct. Wherever one looks in nature, there are outer membranes before there are ideas of outer membranes; and there are eyes and ears and noses and tongues before there are ideas of externality or of sounding objects (or creatures) or of stinking sources or of tasty morsels. The mind evolved from sensory integrations and interactions, not the reverse.

(12 continued) correlation between the thickness of the cerebral mantle and the eventual development of mental and motor skills ... a cerebral mantle of 2 cm or more is usually associated with a good prognosis (i.e. the patient is capable of functioning at a competitive level), and a cerebral mantle of 1 cm or less is usually associated with a poor prognosis. Ultimately, the prognosis depends upon the nature of the precipitating illness, the severity of hydrocephalus, and the effectiveness of treatment.' See also: Ishii, S. (ed.) (1986) *Hydrocephalus*, New York: Elsevier; Shapiro, K. *et al.* (ed.) (1984) *Hydrocephalus*, New York: Raven.

In a brain scan of an hydrocephalic child the ventricles are not narrow slits as in normal circumstances, but appear as large cavities. Such a scan is shown (by Lorber, J. (1980) 'Is your brain really necessary', *Science* 210: 1232–3 apparently revealing a loss of brain tissue mass of well above 60 per cent, in a 12-year-old child whose function in primary school had none the less so far been entirely normal. This is the case noted in the text.

REMOVAL OF THE MIND FROM THE SENSES ALLOWS PURPOSE

But there is none the less a key point to be drawn from neuropsychology, which is this. In man, and in all the higher mammals, *mind* as such has achieved an increasingly viable emergence from any single sense mode and even from the integration of them all. This removal of mind is a supreme survival device, it is what allows us to formulate: purpose. Moreover, in humans, the mind has achieved such independence that it can influence sensory function downwards, and in dramatic ways. One often sees (hears, feels, etc.) to a measurable degree what one expects or dreads, not what *is* actually there.[13] By *actually* we mean what most others perceive. Since mankind can formulate expectations and dreads in far richer detail than can other creatures, this downward influence is greatest in it. The principle of psychological control of sensory and body process, *of the fundamental causal importance of psychological mental states*, is now just simply too well established by the evidence from psychoanalysis and psychosomatics and other regions of experimental, perceptual, and especially social psychology (effects of attitudes and biases on perception, etc.) to be questioned any longer. And the evidence from neuropsychology points the same way.[14]

But none the less we must not mistake this direction as the evolutionarily primary one. Certainly, from the single-cell nucleus to the interneuron to the neural tube to the central ganglion to the full encephalogenesis of the brain, the direction in which the whole evolution of the nervous system has cohered is this: to give to that special central integrative-nexus greater and greater resilience and plasticity (power for homeostasis) despite more and more devastating peripheral receptive and conductive neuro-sensory injuries, and even despite many severe central cortical losses as well.

BRAIN DAMAGE AND A DEFICIT IN GESTALT FORMATION

The crucial evidence from brain-injured patients is this. From the agnosias, we find situations in which individuals can perceive an object correctly and use it correctly but not name it. From the apraxias, we find situations

---

13 Actually the gestalt psychologists fought a vain battle against this fact, holding much too strongly to the absolute primacy of sensory-cognitive perceptual order and to the balanced ineffectiveness of past experience. However much they may wish the contrary, the facts are that sometimes one does see only what one wants to see and hears only what one wants to hear. Not one's eye or ear, of course, but one's mind does this 'wanting'. As the whole is indeed always different and often more than the sum of its parts, even as we change our discernment of them, the past is also more than just the present.

14 Sperry, R.W. (1988) 'Psychology's mentalist paradigm and religion/science tension', *Amer. Psychol.* 43: 607–13 makes some of these same points with great care and power.

in which individuals can perfectly well make many of the concrete gestures of life, such as dressing and eating and even putting on a belt and tying a tie and playing a sonata, but they cannot make abstract gestures such as saluting in the absence of an officer or drinking from an empty glass or playing on an imaginary violin. From the aphasias, we find patients able to comprehend speech but unable to speak. And the reverse. From the alexias, we find patients able to write but unable to read what they have just written. There are individuals who, because of extensive (sometimes bilateral) parietal injuries (in the so-called body-image 'loci'), deny that they are blind or are deaf or cannot move a limb or that they have lost a limb (the well-known phantom limb perception). Some patients experience multiple limbs, and others experience body paraesthesias, distortions in both body size and shape, and also recurrences of visual images.

Compelling as some of this evidence seems, we cannot take it as indicating that the mind somehow was *always* supra-sensory, or that the body image has somehow now become wholly independent of the body. Breast amputations, in cancer patients, for example, do not leave a phantom breast. Limbs lost to leprosy are not phantomized. And, while phantom limbs have been reported in children as young as 5, maybe even 3, though it is difficult to determine in an infant, one must assume a role in mind of actively shaping the incredibly varied and involved kinaesthetic and somaesthetic experiences in these early years. In many of these cases (all, by the way, sensory-cognitive distortions) the sensory input remains wholly normal up to some (usually not well determined) locations in the cortex, but thereafter the *meaning* of those input sensations (primarily visual, aural, tactile, kinaesthetic, and somaesthetic) is lost. Consequently, as a set, they can no longer be integrated into a coherent higher meaning and order. What many clinical researchers (for example, Kurt Goldstein, one of the pioneers in neuropsychology) observed correctly years ago is that brain injuries induce a *deficit in gestalt formation*.[15] In my terms, this means they induce a defect in the rational interweaving that the brain is normally able to achieve with multimodal sensory threads.

HENRY HEAD VS. STIFF-NECKED ANATOMISTS

What happens in brain injury is that the patient is *forced back down into lower-level, less integratable evolutionary positions in which the rational cortical integration of sensory messages can no longer take place*, or takes place less adequately. As Henry Head put it years ago, in a now classical paper:

---

15 Goldstein, K. (1939) *The Organism*, New York: American Book.

The loss of tissue can be determined by anatomical examination and the clinical manifestations are patent to anyone who will take the trouble to observe them; but no intervening link [read: theory of the mind] is discoverable between them. Few today [and this admonition still holds] go to the length of those stiff-necked anatomists who assert that single words are localized in single cells or cell complexes; or that each psychical group of functions possesses an independent anatomical substratum, formed of certain cortical centres in combination with appropriate association paths. Yet, few have attempted to consider the steps by which a structural change evokes a physiological disorder which in turn is manifested as some defect of a special psychical process.

(Head 1923: 127)[16]

In place of the 'single-word-cell', people today are fond of talking of the hypothetical single cell in the visual system which responds only to the face of one's grandmother. At any rate, many 'stiff-necked' anatomists are still with us and one still finds serious reductionistic neurologists maintaining that holistic psychological function is derived from the summative processing of many discrete neural sub-elements or channels or modules.

But the absolutely key point about all such losses of higher cortical functions – as all the work of the giants in this field (Head, Jackson, Goldstein, Bender, Teuber, and Hécaen) and of more modern neuropsychology generally has shown – is the extraordinary level of coherence in experience that the mind of such patients is still able to extract and induce, despite major destructions in sensory-neural integrating pathways. (Psychiatric 'lesions' cause much more serious syndromes, as witness manic depressive psychoses or schizophrenia.)

The mind generally, and many of its 'named' sub-processes (no doubt, most remain unnamed) – awareness, mental focus, directed attention, motivation, apathy, curiosity, cunning – still persists in all the higher animals to a considerable extent independently of one sense, and in mankind independently of many senses. In the highest case, the human mind continually erects mirrors as mental hypotheses (reflections) to test for what is really there, even in the absence of all direct sensation. Imagination, in vision, *is* its expressive component. It is my thesis that the higher one goes in evolution, the more it is that the mind can persist in the absence of at least the inputs from the external senses, though probably not in the absence of the vestibular or kinaesthetic nor certainly the somaesthetic. The range of this is not yet known. Nor is the comparative neurology fully understood. But the specially enhanced imagination of blind poets is legendary: Homer, Milton, Borges. Indeed, in the brightest of us, imagination as expression is especially enhanced in sensory loss. Not so, of course, in animals.

---

16 Head, H. (1923) 'The conception of nervous and mental energy', *Brit. J. Psychol.* 4: 126–47.

VIGILANCE: A SUB-CORTICAL ALERTNESS

Head notes, for example: 'If we did not know that the whole brain had been removed from the cat we should say that the actions of the decerebrate animal were directed by consciousness' (1923: 133). The cat purrs correctly, flicks its ear to a touch, tilts its head to get a drop of water from its ear, licks its lips to alcohol, and altogether exhibits an enormous repertoire of coherent purposive actions. Head introduced the idea of 'vigilance' to describe this range of preconscious but co-ordinate behaviours. The decerebrate preparation in dogs and cats has been widely studied largely because of this startling vigilance. Chimps and gorillas are not that different.

In mankind, also, the common neurology also widely supports this lower-level vigilant alertness, subtly present even in a healthy conscious person. But there is a more critical alertness still. Mind remains wholly intact when there is no sight, when there is no hearing, even when both are missing. Also when there is no sensation of pain, when smell is lost, and taste.

The integrity of the human mind in the absence of these direct reality probes attests to the persistence of the imaginary reflections. Even in the absence of mobility (and all the extraordinary afferentation that that brings in via reafferent kinaesthesis), the imaginary motoric testing and rehearsal still persists, may even be enriched. Not imaginary testing, which is a new concept, but the integral behavioural and cognitive evidence (symptoms) is widely reported in clinical neurology, though perhaps best described in literature by Dalton Trumbo in his book *Johnny Got his Gun*.[17] How far this may actually go we do not know because nature, performing these brutal experiments on us, or we on ourselves in war, does none of them in a simple or a clean way. But clinicians and researchers are forever being surprised anew by the incredible resilience that patient after patient, with sensory losses and/or with brain injury integrative losses, shows in maintaining a stable inner core, remaining the same person after all, exhibiting a consistent personal awareness and personality and ego-cognition.

MULTIPLE PERSONALITIES: PSYCHIATRIC NOT NEUROLOGICAL

The so-called dual or multiple personality is a symptom of hysteria, not of brain injury. It is usually found in women who have been seriously

---

17 Trumbo, D. (1939) *Johnny Got His Gun*, New York: Bantam Books, 1970. Herein is described a man without sight or hearing or arms or legs who none the less reasons and rebuilds his reality when he reasserts control over the perception of time which he is able to calculate commencing with his sensory-rational perception of the morning sun heating the skin of his neck. That, for him, recaptured dawn.

abused as children, where serious means quite literally: exposed to murders, sexual assaults, and to physical and mental tortures. The psychopathology of this is well known. It is also known that the torture of adults, while it may bring about many other psychiatric problems, does not cause these multiple personalities.

But the key point is that multiple personalities do not result from neurological assault. Even an assault so great as to remove a whole hemisphere of the brain or to separate one hemisphere from the other (by cutting the corpus callosum, that marvellous snow-white neural radiation that unites the two halves of the brain), and so divide the sensory-motor body image in two, still leaves one mind in one mental unity. While there are neural symptoms of these separations, the crucial thing about them is that *they are so minimal.* For years it was thought that there were *no psychic sequelae at all* of the split-brain surgery. None. It took great ingenuity to find these out. Most neurological exams today would not find them. And, though this is less well known, neurological examinations of patients subjected to bilateral prefrontal lobotomies (and lobectomies) also turned up nothing. Part of the evidence in favour of these extreme surgeries – in the 1940s and 1950s when these surgeries were widely performed on schizophrenics to control violence and other destructive symptoms – was precisely this fact that it was so difficult to show genuine losses or sequelae. It is not difficult today, but that is another matter.

COGNITIVE UNITY AND PLASTICITY

Certainly cognitive unity is threatened by all these invasions, but that it survives well (mental homeostasis) such a variety of so great neurological assaults is the major insight of both classical and modern neuropsychology. Refinements of differential diagnoses are still needed, in all regions of this field. But the fact is that the extraordinary mental recovery after many significant brain injuries still strongly tests our ability to detect weaknesses and maladroitnesses and emphasizes the basic homeostatic resilience of the higher integrative cortical functions of the human nervous system. Indeed, this prodigious holistic *plasticity* of higher neural recovery is the primary aspect of mind with which all those interested in human mental-brain function must come to grips. But, while this integral plasticity transcends many exterior sense modalities, it does not survive even moderate thalamic and, especially, brain-stem assaults. All of these directly affect consciousness because they affect the lesser known but more critical *interoceptors* of the somaesthetic and vestibular modes and of kinaesthesis which are absolutely critical to voluntary motion, alertness, and awakeness. Brain-stem and/or cerebellar lesions seriously and adversely affect the centrifugal and centripetal dynamics crucial to these modes and so, largely, dissolve consciousness. These devastating effects are generally

permanent. None the less, we can state, in another of the general principles of sensory rationalism, that the transcendence of mind over at least
exteroceptive modality loss is most complete in mankind, over all other
creatures.

No doubt, maintenance of the consistency of mental self and of
body image is the primary function of the integrative actions that occur
widely throughout the central nervous system between both interoceptive
and exteroceptive neurons, as Charles Sherrington, the great British
physiologist, long ago pointed out, and in the title of his major work, *The
Integrative Action of the Nervous System*. But the many exteroceptive
processes have become especially important in humans: listening and
producing speech, for example, seeing and producing representations . . .
and then signs and symbols. The exquisite integrating functions of the
higher and most recently evolved cortical areas (occiput, but most especially the frontal lobes and also the temporal) add relation perception and
order and balance and co-ordination to all the lesser integrations characteristic of all peripheral nervous systems: reverberating, networking
synaptic potentiation, response tuning, ephaptic (or side-by-side) neural
modulation, and so on. Intersensory co-ordination is what the mind does,
not only in language learning and in ethics perception and aesthetics
appreciation, but also in the expression of these things. This is also at the
basis of that universal phenomenon called synaesthesia, widely known in
psychology for centuries. Though not widely known to lay people, it is
not at all unusual. (Some modern neurologists still seem to think it rare.)[18]
It is widely apparent in children, and is really not *odd* at all even in adults
(cf. Shipley 1980).[19] Moreover, it is a property of a great many *single*
cortical cells. Much of modern neurophysiology is devoted to finding and
exploring the properties of just such cells (cf. Fishman and Michael 1973),[20]

18 Cytowic, R.E. (1989) *Synesthesia: A Union of the Senses*, New York: Springer. The
   excellent review by L. Marks, some ten years earlier, should have put this right (1978,
   The Unity of the Senses, New York: Academic Press).

19 Shipley, T. (1980) *Sensory Integration in Children*, Springfield, Illinois: Thomas.
   As far as I know, the first and only scientific laboratory devoted exclusively to
   intersensory studies and synaesthesia in children was established by me in the 1960s
   at the Mailman Center for Child Development at the University of Miami. I ran
   this laboratory for some ten years, and the above book reports that research.
   Since funds were not then available from either state or federal sources, I disbanded
   the laboratory in the late 1970s. On the other hand, many researchers are now
   entering the field of synaesthesia and intersensory processing, and some public
   support is newly coming available. It is naturally my hope that some of the
   workers starting in this field will find of interest some of the ideas expressed in this
   book.

20 Fishman, M.C. and Michael, C.R. (1973) 'Integration of auditory information in the
   cat's visual cortex', *Vision Research* 13: 1415–19. Also, Meredith, M.A., Nemitz, J.W.,
   and Stein, B.E. (1987) 'Determinants of multisensory integration in superior colliculus
   neurons: temporal factors', *J. Neurosci.* 7: 3215–29; Innocenti, G.M. and Clarke, S.
   (1984) 'Bilateral transitory projection to visual areas from auditory cortex in kittens',

continued

and has already indicated auditory, visual, and tactile co-ordinations at many levels of the nervous system.

In fine, the fact that there is so much of the same mental person still left after extensive and massive brain injuries attests, even in the adult, to the now sensorially independent neural reality of the mind, and of the resulting self and even of the reverberating self-awareness (or ego). But we cannot let this relative remove (of mind from sensation and image) disguise the more fundamental fact that it was the peripheral senses and the need for their complex integration and disintegration which gave rise to that extraordinary co-ordinating central cephalic neurology in the first place. Indeed, in humans it has come about that, in the absence of integration between the external senses, i.e. with the loss of overt synaesthesia, the brain can still imagine its own modes and its own integration: synaesthesia *is* thus the origin of mind and thence also of our image of the physical universe.

THE DENIAL OF SYMPTOMS: SIGHTLESSNESS, LIMBLESSNESS

There is at least one important oddity in the neuro-symptomatology of the higher cortical functions which needs to be considered because it has bearing on the integrity of mind over senses. This peculiar symptom is most distressing to the patient, if instructive to the neurologist. It is this: many of the symptoms of brain damage are accompanied by their active denial. This is not the same as psychiatric denial, of hates or ambivalences or past events. It has a clear neurological basis. Actually, for the patient, the symptom is not there; it is not experienced. Something is perceived as wrong; things are not quite right; but it is not recognized/experienced exactly in what way. The most bizarre of these various denials, perhaps, is Anton's syndrome. In this syndrome, the patient has usually suffered a bilateral injury to both occipital cortices which renders him/her effectively wholly blind. He/she sees virtually nothing at all. Such cortical blindnesses result in 'no vision' not in the vision of blackness. But, in particular when the injury also extends to certain crucial parietal regions involved with body-image integrity, at least in the right hemisphere, though usually bilaterally, the patient is also made 'blind to his blindness'. That is, the patient is neurologically unaware of being blind. All blindnesses of cortical

(20 continued)   Dev. Brain Res. 14: 143–8; Newman, E.A. and Hartline, P.H. (1981) 'Integration of visual and infrared information in bimodal neurons of the rattlesnake optic tectum', *Science* 213: 789–91; Stein, B.E. (1984) 'Multimodal representation in the superior colliculus and optic tectum', in H. Vanegas (ed.) *Comparative Neurology of the Optic Tectum,* New York: Plenum, pp. 819–41; Stein, B.E., Magalhaes–Castro, B., and Kruger, L. (1976) 'Relationship between visual and tactile representations in cat superior colliculus', *Exp. Neurol.* 36: 179–96. Also, the recent review: Stein, B.E. and Meredith, M.A. (1993) *The Merging of the Senses*, Cambridge, Massachusetts: MIT Press.

origin result in what we call negative scotoma. By that we mean that the patient senses that he/she does not see well (say, to the right side) because he/she always bumps into things on that side but, as noted, he/she does not see blackness or greyness there, as he/she would in a peripherally caused blindness. (Cortical blindness resembles in some ways the experience of sightlessness that we have behind our head.) The Anton patient, moreover, denies that he does not see, because he does not 'feel' that he does not see. He confabulates about what you are wearing and about what the scene looks like out of the window and whether it is raining or sunny outside . . . and so forth. The point is this: what has been lost is precisely the brain's capacity to evaluate visual information input and to monitor what is seen and not seen and to co-ordinate this with other current (and past) experiences of visual and intersensory reality. The brain can no longer mediate an awareness of an awareness that one is (or is not) seeing. Or hearing. Or feeling. And so on.

This is a crucial example of the principle that one of the primary functions of those higher aspects of cortical function that we call mind is to *integrate sensory information* and to *control the reverberation of awareness*. In this case the senses are vision and the somaesthetic awareness of vision. Perhaps 200 cases of Anton's syndrome are known in the world's literature; and it is much rarer still in the other modalities: deaf to deafness, insensitive to skin insensitivities, and so on. Most denials of deafness are psychiatric. But that also is a sensory-integrative and cognitive deficiency.

The much better known and much more common 'phantom limb' syndrome is evidence for a related process. The limb as such is gone, usually by sudden traumatic amputation, but the brain regions remain fully intact which served (and continue to serve) to model the limb in all its sensory-integrative aspects: via touch, via skin pain, via itch, via temperature sensitivity (the missing limb often 'feels' cold), via the afferent and reafferent kinaesthetic aspects, and via the somatosensory cues (as in deep pain such as a phantom muscle cramp). These function wholly normally to preserve in the mind the experience of the limb. The healthy mind continually sends out its matching images, and the subject is unaware of his limblessness . . . unless he/she looks or reaches. And that serves only an intellectual knowing, not a phenomenological one. For a normal healthy individual veridical body-image to develop, after such amputations, the pertinent cortical regions must eventually be 'retrained'. They must lose their body-image-generating function, or change it. This sometimes takes years, so protected is the mind from some reality testings. Eventually, the subject may no longer be blind to his sightlessness (this happens more quickly) or insensitive (non-reafferent) to his limblessness. This latter is a somaesthetic-kinaesthetic persistence, and a tactile one, but it is not visual or aural. While we do not have parallel words for 'blindnesses to blindnesses' in those other modes, the analogy of Anton's syndrome is precise. Actually, subsequent brain injury to certain crucial parietal regions often has the peculiarly positive effect of 'destroying' the phantom limb.

In summary then, the significance of these very important facts from clinical neurology and neuropsychology confirms our basic premises, which are these. 1) Crucial, among the higher cortical functions are those which (i) serve to integrate throughout one's whole life the full dynamic set of multisensory experiences and yet which (ii) simultaneously generate consistent awareness of all the primary single modal events. And 2) these cortical matching-testing-imaging-imagining functions have come, advancing through evolution, to have a relatively increased persistence and inherent integrity over (and independence from) much of the set of peripheral uni-modal senses. 3) As we move higher and higher in evolution, in mankind and probably in many higher mammals as well, the mind persists to a greater and greater degree in the adult, and can normally develop in the child, in the face of increased losses of sensory input. Indeed, 4) this is precisely one of the mind's major functions: to support the integrity of the inner mental self (the I of 'I am I'), despite massive and unpredictable peripheral assaults on sensory-neural integrity.

Man's accelerated second-level mental awareness, however, is quite fragile and most neuropsychological assaults directly affect it. 5) Yet even that, and surely the first-level consciousness as well, is able to survive more of these assaults, and greater degrees of them, than is the first-level awareness of any other creature. This is precisely because evolution has brought to the mind of humans the greatest possible remove from the sense-membrane periphery that the laws of nature, so far, have allowed. 6) Mythopoesis and all the other so extraordinary flights of human fancy owe their very existence to this remove. Whether those same natural laws of physics/chemistry/biology operating during evolution (will we ever 'get' 'new' 'laws'?) will some day encourage us to a qualitatively even greater remove – a super-consciousness, so to say, forever alert and forever traversing the whole awareness regression – I dare not predict. But I can think that.

7) The central proof of the fact that the mind has not forgotten its origin is that the laws of mental function resemble so closely the laws for sensory function. For the mind and the senses to be in regular, healthy, low-cost reciprocity, such a parallel of dynamics is the ruling economic principle. And finally, 8) that even single brain cells respond simultaneously to arousals via several senses is the strongest possible demonstration of this principle.

INTERSENSORY PROCESSING SINGLE BRAIN CELLS

It may be worthwhile, therefore, to elaborate on a few of these premises, previously just informally noted. Fishman and Michael (1975),[20] for example, were among the first to identify cortical cells (in the cat) that responded both to visual stimuli from a certain location in physical space and to auditory stimuli *also located in that same region of physical space.* Other authors since have identified single brain cells that respond to sights and smells from the same region of physical space. And many authors (especially Meredith, Nemitz and Stein 1987)[20] have identified cells in thalamic ganglia, notably the superior colliculus, which integrate sensory information as long as the auditory energy-order-quality (EOQ) exchange is located spatially in approximately the same position to which the eye looks. This single-cell work is too new for us yet to have a clear idea of the precision involved, especially in higher primates, or the ranges of inter-sensory matching. But more such cells are being reported regularly in the technical literature. So it is becoming increasingly sure that the higher nervous system, the mid-brain and the cortex itself, is thoroughly perfused with single cells that have the extraordinary capacity to respond simulta-neously and successively to bimodal and perhaps even trimodal stimuli, provided that they originate from approximately the same regions of physico-sensory space-time. The subtleties of these interactions are immense, and the evocation methods present great technical challenges to the investigator who may have a natural bias *towards* finding such co-ordinations 'because they are', in Einstein's words, 'an elegant way for nature to solve its problems'.

On the other hand, by now even the sceptic has been won over. This complex single-cell intersensory physiology, taken together with the growing body of psychophysical[21] and depth psychological evidence for all the many subtle variations of sensory integration – from synaesthesia to onomatopoiesis to poetry to dreams to most gestures in life – leaves us with little doubt:

1 that much of the human brain is devoted to intersensory co-ordina-tions,
2 that these reflect the essential centripetal origin of mind, and
3 that the mind then plays this back centrifugally (imaging-imagining) in the normal development of higher sensory and intersensory or comparative rational function.

The fact that some aspects of this integration may actually take place within the single brain cell is an unexpectedly strong demonstration of the evolutionary profundity of this process, and accords well with my general thesis (discussed often in my writings) concerning the importance of synaesthetic processes in art, in language, in empathy, in communi-

---

21 A keen illustration is the motion sickness suffered by most astronauts, due to a loss of the natural intersensory coherence in the gravity-free state between kinaesthetic-vestibular and visual-tactile messages.

cation, and in reason generally. If the same thing, same event, is attested to simultaneously in two ways, this is independent corroboration of its existence and, perforce, more clearly maps out the quintessential route along which our mind is then led to perceive in the singular event the universal case.[22]

---

22 The human mind, as is natural, is perhaps the most fascinating thing-process that man recognizes in the universe, so it is also natural that much effort is expended towards its comprehension. When a new physical or mathematical idea hits the press, even before one has stopped reeling from that, someone else has put mind into its form, witness: Amit, D.J. (1989) *Modeling Brain Function: The World of Attractor Neural Networks*, New York: Cambridge University Press. The key here is the word *attractor* and its implication for the relevance of chaos theory. This trend – to be more up-to-date than anyone else – is actually all to the good, provided only that we never take the model for the real 'thing', or take the new as necessarily correct. H. Putman, for example, long a strong proponent of the notion of mind as computer, has recently given that position up: (1988) *Representation and Reality*, Cambridge, Massachusetts:, MIT-Bradford. See also 'Appendix: a short listing of some influential works'.

4 The perception of routes, methods, and linear arguments

INTERSENSORY ROUTES

We have already noted the analogy between the sensory perception of the direction of motion (say, in visual or aural or tactile space) and the direction of motion along the path of an intellectual argument.

But the truth is that this is not merely an analogy, it is an homology. They share origins. The following of a sensory argument is typically a single modal event: watching a falling star course across the sky; listening to the cries of a bird fade in the distance; perceiving the pressure of the breeze pick up; sensing the temperature of the water gradually getting colder and colder as one swims towards the spring. The following of an intellectual argument is most often multimodal, with the several sensory co-ordinations all pointing vectorially in approximately the same direction. When one perceives contradictions in an argument it is homologous to the perceiving of contradictions in the character of reality. Often these contradictions are intersensory. Thus it is wrong for the birds that seem to be flying towards one to decrease in size and for their cries to grow softer in intensity and to drop in pitch. One senses that that intersensory argument – for the presence of an approaching bird – is faulty. Actually, what we may have is some trick artificial bird contrived in the lab that really does get smaller, and softer, and drops in pitch, as it comes nearer. Sometimes nature does this as well, as when the porcupine appears to the dog by sight and by smell as a good thing to catch and to eat, and the falsity of *that* appearance is brought home directly only by the touch; similarly for the skunk, where the visual innocence is made whole by the appalling smell. For humans allergic to cats and the mango, the effect is the same: the model of reality is faulty, the various modes tell conflicting tales.

Consider the development of a route. Animals, of course, establish routes in innumerable ways, to nests and water-holes in particular, but also across valleys and over mountain passes. 'Route creating' is a universal animal intersensory-rational task that is solved mostly by simple and direct means. Ultimately, it is evolved directly from the capacity to sense the direction of a gradient. The ability, for example, to follow a hill downwards is given by many cues of which the 'pull' of gravity (kinaesthetic and also vestibular) is the major one. But there are also changes in the visuo-tactile character of the rocks and the foliage and forage, and in the smells and sounds and temperature and wind. The slope is thus a multisensory co-ordination. Even the lowest and simplest animal perceives gradients: chemical, radiant, temperature, water current flows and turbulence, electromagnetic, coriolis, and so forth. And the way in which gravity is ingested by higher animals is precisely similar. No creature has, at least as far as we know today, special receptors that indicate that gravity is now less or more, as if the bird in flight, as it soared upwards against the earth's tug, were to feel something-gravity to decrease in accordance with Newton's classical inverse square rule. Not at all, because it is also clear that the changes in gravity are much too small, under the conditions of typical animal ranging, to be taken note of by any biological sensory process. Birds soaring up in flight and fish or dolphin plunging down into the water's depth do not perceive gravitational changes but changes in pressure, which is a secondary result of gravity. To 'perceive' gravitational changes one has to pass out of the normal somatic ranges of coursing and enter into those vast exosomatic ranges achieved by man in air-flight or in satellite flight or (alas, for the vestibular system) in some amusement park rides.

The tilt of the hill, however, and its direction are felt on the animal's feet and legs, of which his neuro-muscular system takes automatic account. Some of this is under control of the vestibular (semicircular canal) system in the animal's head. That is, while diving downwards, the bird still has good sense of the position of its head as well as its body, and can twist and turn in its flight to follow bodily the frantic path of its prey as visually taken in, and even to correct for the changes in the wind. The six paired extra-ocular muscles keep its eyes steady despite the turbulence of the chase. The same with fish in water. These eye movements are involuntary. Neither the bird nor the fish can voluntarily cock its eye; but, while the bird can cock its head, the fish cocks its whole body. Similarly, the goat coming down a high mountain trail finds no difficulty in keeping its balance, in choosing the less steep and less dangerous path in preference to the more precipitous. All its senses co-ordinate in that; they evoke the same sensory-rational route. And so, of course, they do in man. (Though there is much merit in the marvellous idea of 'Pecos Bill', the American folk hero, that goats going mostly one way around the hill grow *shorter* legs on their inner side, the actual evidence for this is small!)

So, route finding and creating are not only visual, aural, tactile, and olfactory gradient trackings, but are also kinaesthetic and vestibular trackings along the gradients that gravity produces and along innumerable other physical and biological and sensorily pertinent gradients such as air pressure, oxygen density, magnetic fluxes, mean wind velocity, grass texture patterns, tree lines, water currents, mean sunlight ... and on and on: all pointing to higher densities of food, lower densities of predators.

OBJECTS AS HIGH ACCELERATIONS OF GRADIENTS

Thus, this most critical and essential task of route making – upon which, for example, the whole success of animal territoriality and primitive human neighbourhoods is founded – emerges from the simultaneous co-ordination of the perception and comprehension of a very great many sensory gradients. The more numerous the gradients and the more complex their twists and turns, the greater the demands are for processing centres (central ganglia) to compare and evaluate the multisensory information, to compare the directions of the gradients indicated by each modality separately and, as well, the slopes of the gradients and, when things get really complex, the rates of change of the slopes (or the accelerations) of the gradients. This latter is critical because, in the presence of especially high accelerations, we encounter 'objects', and in almost all sense modes. (See Chapter 8 below.) Even an ephemeral perfume reveals a rose.

INFINITE ALTERNATIVE ABSTRACT ROUTES

In giving someone directions, one can of course give them the task of choosing from an infinite (or anyway, a very large) number of equivalent gradient maps. That is to say that, in theory, there is an infinite number of equivalent ways to get from here to there ... all without any implication whatsoever about how one really ought to go. Some maps, however, do otherwise, like prayer. (A sweet one appeared in the cartoon 'Ziggy', well known in the USA. It shows two Xs on a map: one where you presently are and another indicating where you would have been had you 'listened to your mother'!)

But, of course, strict theoretical abstract neutral *multiplicity* seems hardly to characterize any real mapping, of, for example, how to get from one's home settlement to the nearby waterhole, because some routes are charged, some are secret, others royal. None the less alternatives do exist. The capacity to perceive the greatest number of alternatives, and the capacity to develop the greatest number of alternatives, and the capacity to communicate or instruct others in the greatest number of alternatives, and the capacity to pick out from among them all the best for various separate, distinct reasons (the quickest, the most beautiful, the one along which you have the best chance to. spot a deer or a lovely lady, etc.) – this capacity is precisely that which has been enhanced in the evolution of the vertebrates over other creatures, and mammals over some, and then the primates and finally humans over most others. And then, among us, it has been enhanced most in those who are the most intelligent, the most adroit, and the most successful in certain situations of their own choosing.

Much of human culture has as its aim the survival of the individual and the passing on of the individual genes to the next generation. But this does not fundamentally distinguish human culture from animal. What does that is the selection of routes for an almost unlimited set of different reasons only remotely related to survival. And many of these work to ensure co-operation, not competition, and so altruism and group survival.

Although some other route is known to be faster, one may still choose to take the slower route because it is more restful, or more challenging, or more beautiful, or more divine, or more suitable for one's present companions. The multiplicity of these reasons reveals our humanity, but not even all humans and certainly no lower animals may take note of or assume the full variety. The spider does not, we believe, build its web as it does because the web is so beautiful. One reason that we know this for sure is that there is no spider, and certainly not the one building, that can (so to say) get off its nest and step aside and look back at its web and take note of its geometry and balance. The spider, actually, is trapped on its web. Alternative routes are largely inaccessible to it; it builds precisely (we believe) as its genetic ancestors built for a thousand, a million spider generations. Though the greenery changes, the bushes and trees, the basic balance repeats with such perfection as to be a perpetual astonishment, and one of the events that we have always taken as evidence of the divine in the most humble. As it happens, the crude ommatidial eye of the spider would not allow it to 'see' its own web geometry in any case. Indeed, no animal ethologist today believes that the spider has some individual geometric (visual or even kinaesthetic) impression, much less shaped idea or unified conception of even its own just-built nest-web. There may be some crude sense of kinaesthetic sequencing. (One doubts, however, if a spider with its eyes painted black will build any nest.) But there is really no motor recall. The evidence shows that she (invariably) tracks the struggling prey by following out smell gradient codes and, especially, vibration gradient codes. A specific set of vibrations imposed on the web at a corner entices her out and to that place. Pure visual presence of an immobile fly does not. Even when it is in close confrontation and in touch with its prey, kinaesthetic and tactile and odour senses are more significant for the spider than are the visual.

But humans can see the overall geometry and note that it is so constructed that they find beauty there. We would almost certainly not, however, if such webs, even infrequently, really caught us!

Part of this sense of beauty and awe – that comes especially when we look at newly spun webs newly covered with dew – may have its origin in an unconscious appreciation of the precision required and the difficulties that would be involved were we ourselves to try to construct a similar web. More of this may have its origin in the dynamic geometry of mental processes which finds comforting parallels between the shapes that spiders weave and those balanced symmetrical shapes that we can also so easily weave, if only abstractly, in our own minds. Symmetry and circularity and radiality are geodesics of mental motion. Thus, we are mental spiders. The closer that we come to perceiving certain adventitious or created shapes in nature as congruent with those fundamental mental shape-melodies that seem easy and gentle to construe and to consider – circles, concentrics, squares, triangles, parallelograms, hexagons (beehives?), and so forth – the more we find them reassuring. We understand them easily; we recognize them; and, from within this so perfect an understanding, a special comfort emerges that we call beauty. This is why, of course, for millennia, fields, farms, villages, cities, buildings, mosaics, tiles, tapestries, and mathematics (tessellations) have above all embodied these magnificent figures in endless inner variation.[1]

In quite similar geometries, flows of natural aromas can also be beautiful, as melodies of flower perfume. And patterns of natural air vibrations can be beautiful, as choruses of bird-songs. And pressures, as breezes. And sequences of natural gravitational patterns and land-surface textures can be beautiful, as when slowly oscillating fields of pale golden blossoms are seen to fall gently away to the horizon in the far distance, and are then explored.

The establishing of routes may thus be considered as one intersensory-rational skill that animals share fully with mankind, though it is possessed by us in much higher and more complex intellectual forms.

As one passes, then, along some route, one is able to take mental note of the inner nature of the multiplicity of events, and of their normal ranges of variation and harmony. A disharmonious route, for example, is one that involves too many sudden large accelerations, too many unexpected precipitations, too many abrupt courses left or stark climbs straight up, too many intersensory conflicts or uncertainties. Such a route is usually rejected as inefficient and ugly, not one to take advisedly, etc. On the other hand, in extra-somatic evolution, humans sometimes invent obstacle courses deliberately for all sorts of reasons in which the ugliness or the hazards (the chancy aspects) of the route are, if not the sources of its beauty, at least the sources of its attractiveness and challenge. No animal creates obstacle courses except to obstruct a potential predator. Nor do they evoke Everests. Man alone creates them

---

1 There is an ancient proverbial image, in a Hebrew Midrash, of Moses striking the rock on Mt Sinai, that sparks fly off in seventy different directions. This means that there may be seventy different interpretations of all things. That, while a lovely image, is conservative. In theory, at any given moment all living humans may have discriminable interpretations of the same physical event. The senses may be single, but the mind infinite. Which is to say that there is also the opposite Midrash, that seventy rabbis separately translating the Old Testament into Greek, during the Hellenic era, came up with exactly the same translation, word for word.

and he does so virtually as often as he can whenever there exists within an exuberance of excess EOQ. Men and women always set difficult goals; that is what high creativity is all about. And we also do this quite intentionally, often taking the longer and the tougher route. Sometimes we construct mazes in the garden, with high hedges as walls, when we know perfectly well that a maze is a poor, even absurd, way to get from here to there. Imagine a small quaint neighbourhood in a big city built that way. Actually, many almost are; and these are often the most charming sections of great cities, not so much the straight streets and the elegant boulevards.

Mazes, and the whole class of challenging routes, are appealing only for exosomatic reasons. The getting from here to there in the most efficient and economical of ways, in terms of Energy-Order-Quality consumption, is a travelling that man shares fully with animals, at least in so far as we are concerned scientifically with events bearing directly upon somatic evolution. But in exosomatic social-cultural contexts great numbers of rites of passage have been erected which serve to twist or to obscure or make selective that otherwise efficient and economic travelling. Consider the universal passing from childhood to adulthood, for example. Most societies impose upon what might otherwise be thought of as a simple linear route (it is not, of course, the internal hormonal changes see to that!), various mazes and tests and obstacles all of which lend to it a special social significance and cultural meaning vastly heightened above mere biology, even as a victory or as a great new mastery. Rites running from special scarring to circumcision, spending nights alone in the desert, slaying one's first lion, passing the time of menarche in purdah, religious rituals, secularly 'coming out' are found in virtually all of human societies. The biological non-linearities of the route from maidenhood to womanhood, from youth to manhood are almost always strongly exaggerated into some highly publicized social non-linearity; not merely the passage of another year, but a special twist to that year, and a special assertion to that passing. Hereafter, one is given the admonition, the responsibility as well as the right – since one has demonstrated the inner biological maturational changes and (hopefully) the associated mental changes as well – to find one's own routes and way to self-preservation and mating. Birthdays, of course, are celebrated in many cultures, and anniversaries, and these are all little sudden accelerations that we humans impose upon the biological linearity which otherwise would characterize some of growing up and, most certainly, much of growing old.

INDIRECT ROUTES, OBSTACLES, LANGUAGE, AND GEOMETRY

And yet, on top of these extravagances, human beings also develop and explore a thousand routes to a thousand valuable and important places, only some of which secure directly or even indirectly an advance in the probability of one's own body and gene survival. As we have noted, healthy and well-nourished humans are able by neuro-metabolic means to store a greater excess EOQ – so as to have it to spend in capricious ways *not so related* – than can any other living creature. Play is this; and the erection of a challenge. Omnivorousness may have much to do with this, but, of course, the inner fluidity, efficiency, and plasticity of both digestion and the higher neural processes have much more to do with it. This is so not only because it is, in part, by virtue of this neurological (and some equivalent predigestive) flexibility that our omnivorousness has come about in the first case, but because of the abstract mental multiplicity that this can entail. We are really quite ready to try anything once, if only on a dare. No other animal is willing to do that.

From the human propensity to explore and to develop special routes to private places, we pass naturally to multiple ways to achieve other ends as well. These variances form a similar nexus, such as the ways for making shelters or fires or pots or clothes or of tracking animals or of finding berries or of constructing tools and weapons. All these, in complex holistic organization, form the essence of the human as opposed to the animal condition: vastly (emergently) increased variance processing.

And so we move still further, to the uniquely human skill: the need and wilfulness (the self-assertiveness) that leads to the 'telling' about anything to others. In this, finally, we see emerging an exclusively human prowess: not simply to pass physically along some neat, clever, beautiful, and rewarding trail, but the capacity to create that trail in total absentia for another's eyes-ears-nose-mind to ingest and comprehend – which means to imagine. If language developed to tell a story, it is a story of some event not presently unfolding. Some event that took place elsewhere elsewhen, often far, far away in mysterious sacred places and in long past times when the first men and women came stealthily forth from gods and angels. In order to evoke the mental image of even some actual recent physical exploration, one must evoke the mental image of how one first entered the situation, starting from where that special exploration actually could and did take place. That is, one evokes an organized concept of the route from *here*, composed of a more or less fanciful integration of one's visual, aural, tactile, and, above all, kinaesthetic experiences along it; also, perhaps, one's tastes and smells. But, of course, often the event which counts as such is thus really the *travelling*, not so much or even at all what occurred at its foreclosure or destiny.

It is a key contention of sensory rationalism that this capacity of sensory-mental mapping or route evoking and route taking is the origin of sequential logical reasoning and thought.

Unlike route travelling, such reasoning, as is well known, goes mostly in fits and starts, and is highly discontinuous in form, except in the most disciplined. But some route travelling along scary routes is also discontinuous: one darts from rock to rock or from tree to tree. And most ethical and legal and philosophical argument also develops in this non-differentiable way. Yet in a release from the immediacy of the present, contemplation can sometimes allow us to string the reasoning out into equal steps and into an almost linear but, in any event, sequential and accumulative form.

THE LINEAR ARGUMENTS OF PYTHAGORAS

The true inherent global discontinuity of inventive and creative thought, which proceeds by the clustering and reclustering, the balancing and rebalancing of grand diffuse imponderables, is much too complex to handle just here. I hope to discuss this elsewhere, but now I am concerned with at least the *appearance* of linearity. To illustrate this last point, let me examine one of the most important and beloved theorems in the whole of mathematics. It happens, also, to be the first. I write of the theorem of Pythagoras: that the sum of the squares of the two sides of a right triangle is equal to the square of the hypotenuse. History hides from us Pythagoras' exact route, but it does say that he slew 100 oxen in wild delight when he first 'found' his proof! And also that he swore all his followers to silence upon pain of death, when he found that the unit right triangle had so ugly and ignominious an hypotenuse as the square root of 2: $\sqrt{2}$. Surely, these can hardly be said to be calm linear events! None the less, gradients are involved, and processes rationally evolved from vision, kinaesthesis, and touch.

In arguing about the linearity – non-linearity thesis, however, it is important to remember that we are now making an intellectual journey, we are passing along a mental route towards a mental goal. But the analogy between abstract and even actual sensory journeying remains instructive: 'I can even smell the solution, I am so close!'

Consider two proofs of this theorem. In our first proof we shall be observed accepting the goal as already precisely known. In our second we shall be seen searching (in some hopefully reasonable ways) for whatever relationships between sides of triangles may turn up. Actually, as we now know, there are an infinite number of relationships between the sides of right triangles. It happens, naturally, that we have a special interest *only* in (one of) the simplest. What might this be? And how may we go about finding it?

The reader is urged concretely to consider how close this routing may actually be to an exploration of some terrain in nature *as if* to try to head someone off at the spring. And to compare that sort of kinaesthetic prowling about to this, conceived merely as an exercise in finding for right triangles one of the set of most comfortable mental rest postures.

In truth, it is more than a happy coincidence – it is an evolutionary consequence of central importance – that mental triangles are found to be related in this Pythagorean way and that, to a very fair approximation, so also are the triangles found lying about in nature. It is this fair congruency which lures us from pond to spring and entices us even to construct some triangles of our own devising. It allows even some animals to head off an escaping prey, rather than trying vainly to race it to the ground.

We now proceed. There are, as we now know, an infinite number of proofs of anything. (Pythagoras, and most mathematicians for centuries thereafter, did not know that. They thought that there was only one real proof.) Consider two.

A.   Let us take a right triangle (Q) as in Figure 4.1.[2] We already know what we want to show: $(AB)^2 + (AC)^2 = (BC)^2$. This is a little cheat; but even Pythagoras at this late date might not begrudge us this small

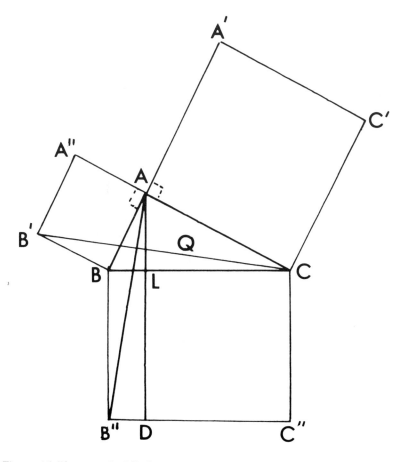

Figure 4.1 First proof of Pythagoras

---

2 A marvellous source for this and other ideas in mathematics is Davis, P.J. and Hersh, R. (1981) *The Mathematical Experience*, Boston, Massachusetts: Birkhauser.

advantage. So we erect the squares and triangles shown. By inspection triangles ABB″ and B′BC are obviously equal. (Successful inspection of this sort is another non-linearity, in that its truth leaps forth. But still, it is a mental, more than a visible, triangle that we need for this. Blind mathematicians readily follow such arguments.) But the area of triangle ABB″ is half the area of the rectangle BB″DL. And the area of triangle B′BC is half of the area of the square BB′A″A. Things equal to N times the same thing are equal to each other.

So: area BB′A″A is equal to area BB″DL. By similarities, it follows that area AA′C′C is equal to area LDC″C.

But area BB″DL + area LDC″C = square of BC, the hypotenuse.

And BB″DL = (AB)² and LDC″C = (AC)², so:

$$(AB)^2 + (AC)^2 = BC^2 \qquad\qquad \text{QED}$$

The argument has one slight subtlety: the contention that triangle ABB″ = half the area BB″DL. Consider Figure 4.2. The area of the rectangle BB″DL, of course, is: base × height. However, the area of *any* parallelogram formed by rotating two opposite sides (S) through any angle α, is still A = b × h.

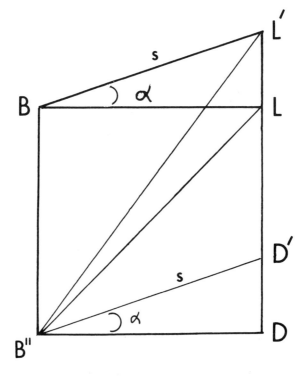

Figure 4.2 Sub-proof, to complete argument

Now, erect a triangle through opposite vertices (here B″LB or B″L′B), and the area of that triangle is still half the area of the rectangle (B″DLB) or of the parallelogram (B″D′L′B).

B. A second proof doesn't cheat at all.[3] It goes like this. Consider Figure 4.3 in which we create two smaller triangles.

Actually, we now have three similar triangles: α, the larger, and β, γ the two smaller. These triangles are similar because they have equal angles. The three right angles are, of course, equal. Angle BCA is common to both α and β. The $\angle$CBD = $\angle$BAD because the sum of the three angles of any plane Euclidean triangle is fixed, i.e. at 180°. For γ, then, the same reasoning makes $\angle$ABD = $\angle$BCD. Thus all triangles have equal angles. They are similar.

Now we proceed. In all triangles with equal angles, the ratios of all sides *in fixed relationship* to these angles (say: adjacent, opposite, and so forth) are also equal. So we have immediately that secant $\angle$ 1 equals

$$\frac{CA}{CB} = \frac{CB}{CD}$$

Then we cross multiply:

$$CA \times CD = (CB)^2 \qquad\qquad \text{Eq. 1}$$

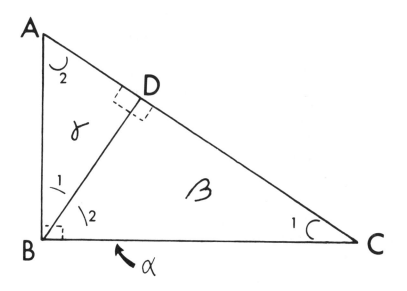

Figure 4.3 Second alternative proof of Pythagoras

---

3 I have this proof through the courtesy of Tomas Rolando, Professor in Mathematics at St Thomas University, Miami, Florida.

Next we take cosecant $\angle 1$

$$\frac{CA}{AB} = \frac{AB}{AD}$$

And cross multiply again:

$$CA \times AD = (AB)^2 \qquad\qquad \text{Eq. 2}$$

Let us add Eq. 1 and Eq. 2

$$(CA \times CD) + (CA \times AD) = (CB)^2 + (AB)^2$$

Recombining, gives

$$CA(CD + AD) = (CB)^2 + (AB)^2$$

But:

$$CD + AD = CA$$

Therefore: $CA \times CA = (CA)^2 = (CB)^2 + (AB)^2.$ QED

It happens that in this proof there is also a subtlety. This time it enters when we note that all the ratios of similar sides in similar triangles are equal. That needs to be shown. Consider any angle. Erect a vertical from the base at some point X_1 at right angles to it. Extend this to the other arm of the angle. Call this the height, h_1, of the triangle thus formed. Now, extend the base further to some point X_2 and once again erect at right angles a line which intersects the other arm of the angle. This is the height, h_2, of a second larger triangle. These two triangles, since they have the same angle at their vertex and each a right angle at their height, are similar. Consider this:

> the base X_1 times the height h_1 of triangle A_1
> divided by 2 is the area A_1.

Similarly for triangle A_2.

Putting this former into equation form we have:

$$A_1 = \frac{X_1 h_1}{2}$$

Cross multiplying and dividing gives $2A_1/X_1 = h_1$.

But we want to solve for a ratio of X/h, so let us multiply both sides of this equation by $1/X_1$.

This gives us: $2A_1/X_1^2 = h_1/X_1$

What must be shown, then, is this:

$$\frac{h_2}{X_2} = h_1 X_1$$

We know now also that:

$$\frac{2A_2}{X_2^2} = \frac{h_1}{X_1^2}$$

Substituting, we must now show that:

$$\frac{2A_2}{X_2^2} = \frac{2A_1}{X_1^2}$$

The 2s cancel, leaving us with:

$$\frac{A_2}{X_2^2} = \frac{A_1}{X_1^2}$$

For simplicity, let us suppose that our triangles are so erected that the base is equal to the height. This means that we may have a small square, A_1, and a larger square, A_2, with areas as follows:

$$A_1 = X_1^2$$

and

$$A_2 = X_2^2.$$

Thus:

$$\frac{A_1}{X_1^2} = 1 = \frac{A_2}{X_2^2} \qquad \text{QED}$$

What applies to these similar triangles, by extension, applies then to all.

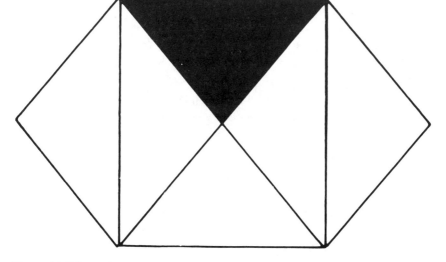

Figure 4.4 Schopenhauer's simple proof of the Pythagorean theorem for isosceles triangles, valid by inspection

Lastly, there is the simplest proof of all, which can be achieved virtually by inspection. It is found in the book by the German philosopher Arthur Schopenhauer entitled *The World as Will and Idea*. I do not know whether he is the first to give this proof. Inspection of Figure 4.4 shows immediately that the sum of the squares of the two sides equals the square on the hypotenuse. The triangle here is an isosceles triangle, with two sides precisely equal. One must make a leap, therefore, from this to other triangles which are scalene. Thus, this involves us again with such proofs as given above. No doubt, there is an infinite number of proofs, and what one accepts usually comes down to aesthetic evaluations of the intellectual route, which is precisely the whole point.

INTELLECTUAL DESTINY

In this way, it can be seen that the identifying of a real location to be abstractly reached and a theorem to be abstractly proven are both forms of intellectual destiny. One is in principle more thoroughly abstract than the other, in that no physical body movement can take a person there. But this could as well be true of real geographic journeying, as to the centre of the earth. Both capture space and time and quality-order. So also does hope. In expressing for someone else how he/she might hope to go, in some style or other, from some place not here to some other place also not here, one is first evoking that image in oneself and trying to form it into an unfolding communicable event: first this, then that, then that, and finally that. Such an unfolding is precisely the form of the unfolding that occurs when one follows out a mathematical argument and an argument in logic and, most pointedly for deeper significance in psychology, an argument in theology or in ethics or in law. If some argument has too many 'if-thens' in it, this is a precise parallel to a route which has, as one goes along, too many unsettled alternatives, intersensory or intentional.

> Well, if you wish, while en route to the spring, to pass by the village of X to see Y, then, at the third turn, you go left instead of right. If, however, after you do this you change your mind, and wish to go to the A village to see B, you can do so by taking your first left before actually coming to village X and then take the third right and the fourth left thereafter. From village A then, you must back-track three forks and then take the fourth one left, after which you head straight for about six miles to the junction of two streams, real streams not mere trickles, at which point you cross the larger of the two streams, and travel down along its opposite bank until you get to the spring at its source.

Verbal routes such as these are quintessentially abstract mental routes first, and only thereafter routes that one may actually move about in. Inductive logic functions in the same way.

There is a mountain stream. Many mountain streams start from springs. Therefore, somewhere around here there probably is a spring. Let me try to find it.

Of course one could come upon the spring by accident, in which case the route planning comes after, in trying both to wend one's way home and to do so in such a way *as if* one were to travel the route backwards, to return. This is another reason why mirroring is such an important intellectual skill. Animals, of course, do not mentally mirror; their returns are sensory tracks. Luckily, many of them can also smell the water from afar, since they possess nasal-cortical cell system-modules responsive to the humidity in the air and need merely to follow up along that gradient. Man, in the absence of such a sensation (and a requisite neurology), must follow other animals to the spring, or his reason. The mental reality of the route, its mirrored coherence and precision in mind, lends enormous support to any real kinaesthetic intersensory exploration that may ensue.

Only a fool would follow a vague route across quicksand; but, even if the route is mentally precise, most people start out with an uncanny wariness. It is always important where we step. Even the infant fears the visual cliff. Equally naturally, if the description-perception of the mental route – in however perfect, honest, and precise fashion it may have been expressed by its developer or enthusiast (some, of course, may obscure the route-instructions deliberately: we still do not know precisely how Stradivarius made his violins) – is muddled and complex and unclear beyond what one would like or has grown accustomed to, or if it strikes one as wrong or unfollowable for any number of reasons (some even that the teller of the tale may not or cannot know), we humans may reject it and go another way, or refuse the task altogether as too complex or unwieldy or distasteful. It may well also be true that you have obtained no more than a foggiest notion of the route and, while you express thanks and much gratitude, you may even admit to yourself that you probably do not and may not ever be able to comprehend that route at all, no matter how well it would be explained. Some activities have to be apprenticed to and cannot be learned even in the Nth telling: for example, skiing. Similarly, some chains of thought: for example, Carroll's sorites (see below).

MENTAL ROUTE-TRACKING SKILLS

We conclude that route exploring, route expressing, route evoking, and route comprehending are distinct intersensory-cognitive tasks in which animals and thence people differ greatly in skill, and at many levels. All these skills (map following: in space, in time, in music, in dance) form components of what we call intelligence. Routes and methods with too many twists and too great subtleties may present challenges too difficult for most of us to comprehend, much less follow (e.g. some secret codes). But one could, for example, test intersensory route-tracking skills by establishing two mental locations, here, say, and there, and then presenting N + 1 hypothetical routes between them and asking subjects to choose the best route for various reasons: which would be best for beauty, which quickest, which most easily understood? Or one could ask individuals to create, *de nouveau*, the best route for various reasons: scenery, time, distance, food, etc. This is so mundane today that even travel agents do it. And yet, of course, some of us never really can. There is the rural joke:

> A man walks up to a local farmer and asks politely, 'How do I get from here to the next town?' The farmer thinks for a moment, and then replies thoughtfully, 'Well, from here, you can't get there.'

Similar events occur in logic. From one unknown, we cannot find two, we can only approximate them. Also in empirical science: from studies of disease processes in salamanders, we cannot get to the study of disease processes in apples or in men.

In logic games, as, for example, the marvellous and delightful sorites of Lewis Carroll, the twistings may be extended virtually indefinitely yet, after only a few alternative steps, most of us are wholly at a loss as to how to proceed. (But for these logic games, there is a trick.) One of my favourites is this:

A LEWIS CARROLL SORITE

1   Whenever some of the English boys are singing 'Rule Britannia', and some not, some of the Monitors are wide-awake;
2   Whenever some of the Scottish are dancing reels, and some of the Irish fighting, some of the Welsh are eating toasted cheese;
3   Whenever all the Germans are playing chess, some of the Eleven are not oiling their bats;
4   Whenever some of the Monitors are asleep, and some not, some of the Irish are fighting;
5   Whenever some of the Germans are playing chess, and none of the Scottish are dancing reels, some of the Welsh are *not* eating;
6   Whenever some of the Scottish are *not* dancing reels, and some of the Irish *not* fighting, some of the Germans are playing chess;
7   Whenever some of the Monitors are awake, and some of the Welsh are eating toasted cheese, none of the Scottish are dancing reels;
8   Whenever some of the Germans are *not* playing chess, and some of the Welsh are *not* eating toasted cheese, none of the Irish are fighting;

9 Whenever all of the English are singing 'Rule Britannia', and some of the Scottish are *not* dancing reels, none of the Germans are playing chess;

10 Whenever some of the English are singing 'Rule Britannia', and some of the Monitors are asleep, some of the Irish are fighting;

11 Whenever some of the Monitors are awake, and some of the Eleven are *not* oiling their bats, some of the Scottish are dancing reels;

12 Whenever some of the English are singing 'Rule Britannia', and some of the Scottish are *not* dancing reels . . .?

(The solution is fun to try to work out, and I leave it to the reader.)

INFINITE ALTERNATIVE DIRECTIONS

As sensory experiences may be single or multimodal, so also may real and abstract routes be simple or complex; likewise logical arguments. In all cases part of the difficulty comes from how well the route argument may be *expressed* in the first case, which is some complex function of the precision with which it is known (by the communicator), and the skill and intent (he may well wish to deceive!) with which it is then and there elevated to his own surface awareness. Another part comes from the limited capacity of the recipient to receive the message and to ingest all the various alternatives at every stage. In theory, of course, in starting out on a voyage there are an infinite number of directions to choose from. There are many in any real case. One can, after all, perfectly well go from Boston to New York via Moscow if one wishes, and for many valid reasons. Generally, the greatest freedom is at the start. And as one progresses on the journey, the number of choices (at each discrete point) decreases in some complex fashion as a function of the number of choices already made and the number of intersections (infinite accelerations or choices) yet remaining. Ultimately, the variance converges to zero. This convergence process – in mapping, in route taking, in ceramic constructing, in war-strategy mapping, in courtship planning, in law, in logic, and, in short, in every form of directed mental dynamics – is really just precisely that: variance reduction. If there are infinite directions *in which* one may start out, then, admittedly, there are infinite directions *from which* one may take that very last step to the spring. Consider life on a sphere.

But in actual practice, along any real physical route and/or any real mental route, the whole adventure is aimed at knowing (sensing) when one is nearing the end and then reducing the number of choices, reducing the intersensory conflicts, the closer and closer one comes to that key destination. This has limits, of course, because while one can in theory pick up a circular coin from the pavement in the same way from any and all of the 360 directions, one cannot do so if half of the coin is in the fire;

or if the coin is stuck under a man hole cover; or if it lies ten feet below the pavement on the floor of a locked grate-covered subway vent. Some innovators and philosophers have felt that there was only *one* way to express a given idea perfectly (James Joyce, the Irish novelist, was one). Even if this were only approximately so, it is still true that the closer and closer one came to that perfect expression, the less numerous would be the choices that would confront one. Variance would vanish finally in the word. The truly creative among us, the geniuses, would be the ones able to travel this route most quickly and to arrive at that last single pure angle and destination with the greatest virtuosity and least cost, and with sufficient EOQ remaining to permit them to pass on to additional similar explorations with the greatest degree of mental dexterity and understanding.

When a stranger asks you to 'give directions', a typical simplification often judiciously employed is to ask the person for some landmark in the general vicinity of the goal that he/she already possesses mentally and knows how to reach, and then to describe from there the route with the least number of choice-points. One thus often sacrifices a certain loss of time and efficiency for a more probable positive result. One does the same in logic and mathematics. These are not weaknesses, but rather strengths in the mental handling of multiplicities.

A NOTE ON THE LIMITS OF BEHAVIOURISM

And so, once again with this last insight, it seems heuristic to note that it is precisely in intersensory co-ordination and evocative multiplicity modelling that the failure of behaviourism, as an explanatory principle in psychology and, perforce, for modelling the origin of mind, lies. Consideration of this antique view (as do considerations of pre-Newtonian views in modern physics) helps clarify the strengths of more modern alternatives. Behaviourism would explain logical or behavioural route following – or, presumably, might have done so had it ever, in the unlikely event, thought of this problem – by asserting that, because one had practised yes or no decisions or left and right turns in the past, one could 'somehow transfer' such decisions-turns, so to say, into the present situation (ignoring textural differences, of course) and, by rote recitation, display them one after the other in various alternations in some near random trial-and-error solo dance along the route. And by chance one might get through.

But, strictly speaking, it is a deep criticism of this view that, because one has never before expressed – much less rehearsed (re: + hearse) – yes and no decisions or left and right turns *under these precise circumstances and conditions*, the behaviourist has, consequently, to invoke the fact that one must somehow be *generalizing* (somehow thinking coherently not just behaving randomly) and inwardly expressing some species of real mental (at times frankly intersensory) sequencing of abstract yes or no decisions or left and right turns. But intersensory co-ordinations and generalizations and universalities and abstractions are just precisely those processes which the behaviourist school asserted for so many years did not really exist. Or, even if they did exist, so they maintained, they did not and should not be thought to play any causal or explanatory role in human behaviour. Consequently, logic following and route following are, for the behaviourist, wholly impossible events; also, all of mathematics; so also any coherent expressions, signing and speaking and ideational dancing foremost among them. Even pure single-modal sensory gradients cannot be tracked.

Actually, in nature, sensory gradient tracking and logic pursuing and route following are wholly common natural events. They are elevated in us by the human processes of abstraction and generalization and gestalt mental mapping, from the trail marking and territoriality indexing and route following – in the concrete *there* and *then* intersensory modes – that all higher animals perform very well indeed. Even insects follow routes, though not so complex as these. And, if we may believe in the bees' dance, some insects can 'pass on abstract mirrored instructions'. The following mentally (and then physically) of variously communicated and inferred routes and directions is a wholly natural propensity, emergent in humans from the many concrete ways that routes are sensorially found in nature (as gradients) and set out well by animals. Certainly, a good many animals do deliberately leave along the trail signs of their passing, such as urine markers and spore and even bark depletions and turned-up turf (by which we can successfully track them). But, apart from territoriality, most such signs (as broken branches and smells) are idiosyncratic and unplanned results of the passage. Other animals can certainly follow the trail blazer by tracking up the gradients, or avoid him by tracking down them. But only in a very weak sense can there be said to be an overt and deliberate communication process taking place.

INFINITE MAPPINGS OF ANY TERRITORY

The important realization is that, while many animals do construct trails both for kinaesthetic following and deliberate obscurantism, the construction is never even carefully regular. It has little sequential deliberation or syntax. And it is, numerically and in form, strictly bounded. But 'mental following' is an emergently different process, one that only people can achieve. It always has syntax (a favoured sequence), and is unlimited in numerosity. Humans, quite routinely and quite successfully, follow trails entirely abstractly to their end. Similarly, we also follow oral arguments to their (really our) conclusions. Many people, especially in pre-literate cultures, can follow a genealogy so complex and so involved as to defy normal reason. This is a trail that some 'primitive' peoples can carry out abstractly (and reliably) for over some thirty or forty generations – a feat that most westerners find completely baffling. Imagine keeping in one's head at one time a mathematical proof or a mechanical design of some thirty or forty syntactically sequential steps.

On the other hand, the concrete following of highly complex mental routes is something that western civilization (for good and evil) has brought to an especially high peak, with the development of all sorts of maps and demographic projections. These days, one can look at the same physical territory in terms of:

- how best to get around in it, for N + 1 reasons,
- how most people get around in it,
- how birds fly over it,
- how best to plant flowers in it,
- how the winds blow over it,
- where people live in it,
- where pets live in it,
- where the toilets are,
- where the AIDS cases are,
- where, in the past, dogs have howled,
- where the most likely audience for daytime TV lives,
- where the squirrels hide in it,
- what is the distribution of home equity loans,
- how large is the street by street ethnic count,
- where the sewers are,
- how whispers travel therein,
- where the natural resources in it are,
- where the most joggers are,
- where the most wine drinkers are, and the lottery buyers,
- what are the crime demographics,
- even: where are the most likely places to sell watermelon and red suspenders,
- and so on *ad infinitum*!

In short, because of human mental prowess, there can be generated an infinite number or, anyway, a small infinity of satisfactory maps and, thus, routes by which one can find one's way physically or mentally through any neighbourhood.

The complexity of the map route chosen is limited by many processes but primarily by (a) one's perceptual intersensory-cognitive skill in making fine distinctions over the field (as the distribution of tiny pale blue flowers), and by (b) that of putting them all into a coherent mental whole; next, by (c) one's regular on-demand recall of that order; then by (d) one's cognitive-intersensory skill in planning and thence carrying out those complex motions necessary to the transforming of the mental route into some sort of approximate physical reality.

Since it is necessary for some people to locate and then approach in turn every single garbage can in the city of Providence, Rhode Island, it is reassuring to know that this is achievable, both mentally and physically, with no great difficulty at all. Even so complex a *physical* mapping as that is *mentally* quite simple – provided only that one can be flexible, even then, in tolerating *locations* which are only to some degree stable because this stability varies 'all over the map' (does this mean that, if the garbage cans move too much, they no longer pin-point for us a map of Providence?), and towards tolerating *actual paths* which are also only approximately accessible, depending upon traffic conditions, tricks and pranks, the weather, natural pleasantries and disasters, and many other unforeseeable quirks and events: someone may come at you with a gun. Moreover, the touching of each can is not, in itself, wholly equivalent to the lifting of each and the dumping of its contents into the back of one's truck. For example, the *weights* of the cans may differ and N + 1 of them may be too heavy to lift at all. Or the contents of some may be smouldering, or emitting noxious fumes, and so forth. All of this affects the traverse. Even when routes are rehearsed many times, it is the normal rich human mental receptive and generative propensity always to be alert to the widest possible ranges of sensory-cognitive variance both in the route and in the elements to be found there along the way . . . even though the extreme boundaries of the variance ranges merely *may be* but never *actually are* encountered.

REAFFERENCE AND ROUTING

Strictly speaking, motoric routes are also sensory. How is this so?

The number of sensory or *a*fferent neurons found in almost all human peripheral striate musculature – the musculature controlling the body motions for standing upright, for walking, for balancing and exploring, etc. – is about four times greater than is the number of *e*fferent neurons within the same muscle or system. This means that the actual execution of most body movements is relatively four times *less* precisely guided in comparison to how refined a record is *noted* of the motion actually performed. This appears to both lead to and follow from a need, in some central location such as the intersensory cerebral cortex (frontal lobe), to index very precisely how well the motion actually *achieved* concurs with the motion actually *intended* or *planned*. This latter complex sensory-cognitive process of comparison is known as *reafference*, or self-afference. It takes place this way.

A mental (neural) model of the intended motion is established at the highest cortical level of the nervous system, perhaps posterior frontal. This neural model is then somehow divided: one epi-motion model is sent (descends) to the cerebellum to initiate the actual motion. That organ, in turn, circuits impulses both back to the cortex and down to the appropriate limbs. Another epi-motion model, known as the *efference-copy*, remains reverberating in the cortex where it is then compared to the *reafferent-copy*, which is the epi-neural model that reciprocates back up from the limb muscles in response to the actual motions themselves. This reciprocation occurs most probably to that very same cortical location wherein the efference-copy 'reverberates'. This occurs all the time the motions are actually taking place. Thereby one achieves a constant up-graded self-afferentation of what has been achieved, *in mirroric comparison* to what was intended. (This reafferent process, as it happens, was not known to the early behaviourists, or it might have modified their views. Its presence is now as well established as any such process can be in higher cortical neurophysiology.) Mental route evoking can, actually, prelude two distinct processes: one that can be purely abstract (at most, emphatic, *as if*) when the route is only contemplated or rehearsed (again, probably posterior frontal lobe) and one that can be kinaesthetic-sensory-reafferent (probably the same cortical location but now also cerebellar) if the route is actually taken. The purely mental following in logic is an identical neuro-cortical event, minus the cerebellar activation: the route traversed is constantly matched to how near to the goal it has taken us, and is then regularly up-graded. When the conclusion has been reached, we recognize that that is the one we were after. This is a mental reafference and a matching. Similarly, when we achieve a proof in mathematics: we recognize it. (That this is more likely *pre*frontal rather than posterior is wholly immaterial to the basic argument.) Moreover, the empathic cognitive-intersensory following by audience members of the route taken by a pianist playing a concerto or a jazz musician, an extemporizing dancer, poet or mime, etc., combines all these things and accounts in large part for aesthetic appeal: purpose and performance well met.

All of this should now be clear: route formations and construction details (e.g. perspective engineering drawings), manufacturing instructions and music can be communicated very well between people, wholly abstractly and with exquisite detail (concertos can be written, after all). And they can be experienced purely in the ideal and equivalently (if not identically) by another person who has never encountered that route before or that method of construction or those instructions or music, nor encountered any *actual* route objects except some only remotely resembling those actual items on the trail or those actual objects of the construction or elements of the instructions or sounds of the music (music can be read, after all, and mentally listened to). This is precisely true (not approximately so) even if he/she may, for various physical reasons, never be willing or able actually to follow the route or the designs or the instructions or the music. Such a person, moreover, in some cases of extreme mental ingestive skill and imagination, and maybe knowing the territory and the lay of the land well, just might learn the route and the methods even better than the storyteller or the originator. Thus, the student out-reaches the master. This special improvement – in certain parts of the route or method, or the whole – remains moot, of course, until he/she suggests them from the vantage point of his/her rather more perfect comprehension.

CRITICAL JUDGEMENT

This requires critical judgement, another unique human propensity. It can be exercised on hypothetical logics and imaginary routes and ideal methods (even how to make a 'holy' cake) and on melodies, on real but only intellectually known logics and routes and procedures, on mythical logics and routes and recipes and, as well, on logics and routes and proposals that one takes every day to work or to play.

The following in actuality of a river to its source is not, strictly speaking, homologous to the following of an argument to its logical conclusion. But rivers do flow directionally from spring to delta as do arguments from premise to conclusion. Moreover, the following of an imaginary or merely conceived river to its mouth is. The novelist does not, convincingly, violate nature.

This sharing of common principles – in the description of the intersensory-rational processes of the exploration and formalization of routes *for some specific conditions* and of the refining of instructions to some design or purpose and of the creation of musical and artistic patterns to some specific end – shows that they are all homologous to the intersensory-rational processes of honing one's intellectual argument, say in court or elsewhere, to some point ('Imagine what it would be like if . . .') and for some particular audience or judge or jury. For the gifted, there exists a very great number of different ways to construe the same argument and method, another small infinity. In the American folk expression, 'There are many ways to skin a cat' one assumes either that there are no ways because one never does or that there is an infinite number and that there could even be cats as big as mountains. Which route, design, method, or argument one uses at any moment depends, first of all, upon how well and differentially (emergently, insightfully) one perceives the various intersecting purposes (mentally grasps the pattern of the intents), and then upon how well one can execute them, which means also how finely one can monitor how well one is doing (does the pot throw well? are one's words well chosen?) against one's own mental image of what it is that one *ought* to be doing. So, we come again to that same big reafferent imperative, but now on a purely mental level: words, gestures, expressions, must all take on well the form of one's ideas and intents. That is, one must also perceive these well. This process of mentally monitoring as you go – in logic and in mechanics and in design and in planning and in argument and in informal language gesture and formal creation of any sort – is an absolutely central fact of human cognitive function, almost wholly overlooked in earlier descriptions of what the mind is like. Henceforth, it must take centre stage.

Arguments go right to the point, are circular, ramble about, are tenuous, are cunning, are *tours de force*; just as are designs, methods, routes, musics, and novels.

At all times, the wise and the shrewd person keeps a few alternatives at the ready, just in case: a mental sampling of simple and intricate, logical and illogical, possible and yet unexpected spatio-temporal gestural patterns. The senses all together instruct the mind in these, and the mind then instructs back.

5 Time as quality from routes as durations

As animals are conscious, so animals experience time. They do not experience that they experience time. This second-order temporal quality seems reserved for man. And even this is wholly distinct from the scientific conception of time as a physico-chemical process which includes us all as creatures in the physico-chemical universe. This distinction is critical, though psychic time forms its base, as we shall see, and it is similar to distinctions made by scientists in other areas of reality. (We may also say that science itself makes these distinctions because science is time-binding, it is deliberately constructed *as* an active process.)

AWARENESS OF AWARENESS – ACCELERATIONS OF CONSCIOUSNESS, A^2

Inherent in the concept of routing that humans have developed, and an intricate aspect of the conscious development of methods for natural object manipulation and novel object construction, is the experience of second-order time. In somatic nature, circadian and seasonal rhythms and the biorhythms of hunger and fatigue and menstruation and heartbeat and breathing and the growing of body and facial hair and of nails, and the like, are all indications of the succession of events that in themselves are or could be sufficient to give rise, in prepared and capable mental organizations, to an awareness of the awareness of time. But, in themselves, these apparently do not alone suffice. Apart from menstruation, such events occur in animals. Something additional emerged from these when that specially adroit prowess of mental energy control requisite to the *conscious* planning and developing of alternatives evolved. This accelerated or second derivative of awareness, A^2, is also at the basis of the language capacity (metalanguage, in modern terms) and the extraordinary sensory-mental imaging (visions of visions, V^2) that found its way down into dark caves and thence up on to artifically lit walls some 35,000 years ago. Language is the most noticeable expressive emergent of this special mental organization, but routing and planning and modelling and time awareness are expressive emergents as well.

SPIDERS' WEBS AND BEES' HIVES

Presumably, as the bee sets out to make its hive, it does not then 'take some stock' of the time or effort that would be involved. Nor presumably does the spider 'plan' its web; or certainly not in the way that we would have to were we to try to construct a similar web from threads of the size and 'stickiness' that we could handle. Somehow, by means of processes that the mere unfolding of pre-programmed genetic geometry does not at all adequately describe, nature has made such seemingly complex tasks, relatively speaking, quite easy for the bee and the spider. This means that they need expend very little EOQ in planning routes and in estimating times and durations and efforts, etc., in the achieving of these marvellous ends. We would have to do those things, of course, were we to try to build such structures, but not the bee or the spider. For them, these are unnecessary, and impossible in any event.

Consider another, perhaps more convincing, example of routing: the migrations of fish and especially of birds. These are fascinating to us because of the humanly dramatic distances that we know to be involved. Such distances are well beyond our own natural journeying and we would have to expend enormous EOQ in order to achieve them, most especially if they were to be of similar manifest order and precision. None the less, from comparative brain–behaviour studies, we must also assume that neither fish nor bird achieve any actual 'conception' of their routes. They migrate. They may even know that they do so, i.e. travel. But they do not know that they know that they travel.

Arctic terns, for example, are among the most intrepid migrators, covering some 5,000 miles and possibly remaining aloft all the six–eight weeks of the time that it takes for that incredible journey. In human terms, this seems an impossible achievement. As with the spiders' web making, the bees' hive building, and many other constructions that some animals achieve by means of low EOQ consumption, man is so evolved that in order to achieve even roughly similar things, he must expend vast amounts of EOQ. But then, the bee does not ever try to spin the spider's web; nor does the bird attempt to make a hive. And surely the spider does not try to migrate. Although we have all seen webs floating across spiderly-vast gaps between bushes and neighbouring trees, the spider herself does not do much 'breeze-hopping'.

> These animals do construct in space-time, and they do travel; but they have no second-order awareness that they do so. Some, like spiders, with only minimal central neural organizations, may have no first-order awareness either. But in all cases, no choices are involved.

HIGH EOQ, IF WE BUILD WEBS AND HIVES

This is the key: the fact is that the multiplicity of route planning available to mankind is of a wholly different and fundamentally emergent sort than that available to all other creatures. For us, choices almost always abound. We can plan and then build 'hives', design and construct 'webs' (and, no doubt, think hubristically to improve on those that bees and spiders build!) and, in this century at least, we can fly in some crude fashion a bit like birds and swim a bit like fish and even achieve some voyagings of similar and respectable magnitudes.

Naturally, the routings of lower animals are not as flexible as ours, maybe because their 'planning' (if that word can be allowed) has somehow already been achieved by their somatic evolution via the relatively rigid unfolding of some highly complex intrinsic genetic geometry. For them, these actions are geodesics: the shortest routes between two goals. Because that unfolding is tightly time-locked – to internal biorhythms and to circadian patterns and summer–winter cycles and the like – neither the need nor the possibility arises for spending what little excess EOQ such creatures may have. When there can be no alternatives, there need not be any special energy-order-quality costs devoted to choosing among them.

On the human level, although we can surely think of *not* breathing, generally we do not have to spend much EOQ to think *of* breathing; similarly of digesting, of heart beating, and so forth. Even for man, the propensity for the dynamic expression of a large number of the somatic sustaining processes is fully 'encoded' in genetic phosphate energy transfers and DNA-amino acid transformations and unfoldings.[1] But when these things fail us somatically, we can think up, plan, and devise methods for their artificial buttressing. This is so, first of all, because we have awarenesses of the awareness that they have failed and, secondarily but crucially, because we generally have an excess of free EOQ to devote to such thoughts. At the limit, we can (and do) even think about replacing 'brains', though whether this would be an achievement that we should ever make manifest or would be happy with is another matter.

So when we seek (note the visual implications of that word) to understand (and the kinaesthetic ones of that) the origin of the concept-experience of time, we might well attend (and the aural ones of that) to the critical central core of the phenomenal aspects of planning that routing and constructing and building and effort focusing among alternatives necessarily entails. This route is perceived as harder than that one, as more beautiful than this one, but it is also perceived as 'taking *longer*' than that. There are many ways to throw a clay pot or to scar the face and body

---

1 A recent paper suggests how the DNA molecule may seem to 'solve' complex combinatorial problems exceedingly rapidly. See Adleman (1994) 'Molecular computation of solutions to combinatorial problems', *Science* 266: 1021–4.

properly and, among all those different ways, there are some that 'will take longer than others'.

The tern, before it begins its marvellous aerial exhibition, does not, it seems quite safe to assume, consider alternatives at all and certainly not ones that are in some fashion shorter or longer than others. Nor does the bee, when beginning its hive, think of different methods to achieve the same goal, and certainly not whether one is shorter or longer than another.

THE FREEDOM OF HAVING VARIABLE GOALS

Only man does this, because he has the (second derivative) mental skill and physical prowess to consider and make multiple routes and to consider and develop different methods, and even to consider and establish variable goals. Indeed, this multiplicity is precisely what the socio-political system in the civil democracies is so strongly constructed to support. This is why there is a sound basis for democracy in the structure of the human mind. The ultimate inalienable right is to multiplicity. Time, in its exploration, is also of the essence.

In almost all free social activities, what we mean by freedom also involves time. While learning or voluntarily rehearsing – songs, violin-sonatas, plays in football, speeches, routes, mathematical proofs, science experiments, dances, or letters-to-the-editor – we control time by binding it; on a deeper psychological level, we may achieve this because we have the freedom to move within time and to parcel it out.

Time, just because of this melding of freedom and multiplicity, may appear to some as anarchical and one of the more puzzling attributes of human experience. More books in physics and philosophy have been devoted to it than almost to any other issue of the human condition, perhaps only with the exception of such things as the after-life and free will and the ultimate creation. But in the light of our present sensory-rational considerations, it does seem that some deeper comprehension of this may come forth: the key, once again, is multisensory integration.

TIME AS A QUALITY OF HUMAN EXPERIENCE

Time is first and foremost a complex multi-determined reverberated quality of human experience. It is experienced in various gradient forms via pretty nearly all of the senses and pretty nearly all of the mental processes derived from them, in a way that heat, say, or blue or $C^{\#}$ or roughness are not. While these are virtually single modal, all of the senses contribute significantly to the experiential quality of time. It unfolds with almost unfathomable multiplicity through all the dynamic external sensations (colours, sounds, smells, motions) and especially within all the integrated and internal somaesthetic ones. All these penetrate temporally to the removed conscious processes of mental life. In contrast to this, blue is largely (but not exclusively) a quality of experience of the visual mode; bitter is largely but not exclusively a quality of the gustatory mode; sharp is largely but not exclusively a quality of the olfactory mode; and warmth is a quality largely but not exclusively of the tactile mode. The 'not exclusively' means that other modes do share these qualities to some extent and that, consequently, they may also have an assisted entrance into mental processes, at the very least, in the forms of metaphorical thinking and language. Time, on the other hand, is a quality that is processed by eye, ear, tongue, nose, skin, muscles, somaesthesis, and even the vestibular modalities.[2] It enters mind in all these ways.

CONGRUENT SENSORY METRICS IN TIME

Each has its own temporal metric which means that each contributes to its own awareness of the awareness of time, T^2.

> In the healthy person, *these metrics are to a large degree congruent.* (I suggest that they may not be congruent in the schizophrenic.)

As we have many choices in how we move in or manipulate space (as evolution has given us this propensity and as democratic society helps us rehearse it in actuality), so we also have choices in the way that we move in or manipulate time. One thinks, none the less, especially in the view of the universe that much of modern physics promulgates, that at some more sophisticated and removed levels of reality, time proceeds at its own pace wholly independently of man; and, so also, we are led to believe that, at some more sophisticated and removed physical levels of reality, space exhibits its own smallness or immensity (light-years upon light-years) wholly independently of man. And, no doubt, while time and space are 'correct' (i.e. useful, heuristic) descriptions of some in-anthropomorphic real physical events, therein they are a *wholly different time* and *space.*

> The *quality* of time and the *quality* of space require *for their special presence* a quality processing and emerging process.

Par excellence, and in some truly ultimate sense, plant and thence animal creatures are the only 'quality-emerging' processes that exist in the universe. That is to say – setting aside many views of God – no non-living entities, such as rocks, airs, waters, crystals, metals, minerals, soils, etc., that appear to populate the universe together with the plants and the animals, do 'quality processing and emerging'. This is true even for any of the simple and relatively pure unimodal qualities such as pitch or sour. How much more true must this be for such complex and multiple qualities as *time*? (Or, lest anyone should miss the point: as free will and as a sense of destiny?)

---

2 The reader is referred to any standard text on sense anatomy and function.

MULTIPLE SENSORY AWARENESSES OF TIME

What I am trying to state as clearly as I can – in the hope that this brings some understanding to this fascinating but confused area of thought – is the primary fact that 'time is a quality of human experience' about which we have multiple awarenesses. It is a property of the inanimate universe *only* by extrapolation, but that extrapolation cannot also include 'quality'. Time, especially, is a key quality in which we think-experience when we are choosing between routes and methods and solutions and laws, etc. – and when we are trying to *keep* appointments and *to beat* or, at least, *to make* it. (By the way, do we 'make' time the same way we make work or shoes?)

Time in the wider nature includes ours but extends well beyond the experience. That is what is so difficult to comprehend.

In so far as our discussions of 'time' relate to it as a pure quality of human experience, then its ultimate derivation is, firstly, from the complex integration of the multiplex intersensory matrix and, secondly, from the cognitive skills we also have for multiple planning and diverse effort. This much seems now to be established. This clear and unambiguous recognition of *time as quality*, though surely not historically unique, is a particularly helpful clarification.

It (a) shows how time, as a quality of mind, arises from sensory integration, and (b) enables us to settle certain other puzzles that philosophers have, from time to time (sic!), quite justly raised.

Consider an instructive analogy: time as clock. One may, for example, study the behaviour of clocks and not the experience of time. Take them up to mountain tops and down into deep caves, bury them in hot sand in the desert and cold snow in the arctic; plunge them under miles of ocean water and send them flying way up into the stratosphere on satellites and even missiles. In this way, one can build better and better clocks if one means clocks that do not change performance under such exigencies. Indeed, one can develop what might be called the engineering science of clocks. Really, this would be the engineering of clocks, i.e. in order to make more error-free clocks we must know how clocks perform under the greatest reasonable variety of circumstances. But clocks themselves are devices used by us to measure what? Ah! here is where the science enters in.

To measure time! And to do this better, which means more openly communicably, than by relying only on our normal somaesthetic awarenesses. One would never make the error of confusing the engineering activity with clocks, no matter how bustling and productive and profitable and successful in earning gold stars and funds from various formidable government agencies, with this latter *science of time*. That is an entirely different activity. Clocks are inventions of human mental prowess (as are all of engineering and science) which have been developed through (and to enrich) an overt sensory-rational intersensory confrontation with certain dynamics of physical reality. The bio-psychological processes, however, have evoked in man a prior state: an awareness that he is aware of time. From the manifest imperfections of this came the idea of and thence the desire for clocks in the first place. And concern with that involves us with science.

This second-level awareness, as we are showing, is invariably the crucial element. It is thus an experience of an experience, a meta-phenomenology. We experience time as passing around, by, and through us. What we construct as clocks are in one sense very meagre models of that experience, but in another sense (to a degree unknown for sure) are elevated from that experience and shed the private aspects of it so as to help us in our attempts to relate more precisely with nature and to share the experience with others. 'Look', we can say, 'the clock hands now both point to 12. It must be noon already. My goodness, how time flies!'

To be active in the *science of time* one is not so much active with a given clock – although this could be a part of one's activities – one is involved with all clocks and no clocks, one is involved with the idea of time, and with the idea of the idea of time, and with the desire to construct various models of that to assist in the public communication of one's awarenesses of time and of one's ideas of time. For example, some aspects of time are experienced as continuous, therefore smooth flowing and smooth turning are good models of that. Other aspects of time appear to start and to stop, to rush forward and sometimes even to stand still. Sometimes time, contrary to our general experience, seems to go backwards. For these sorts of time, public models might better be some sorts of discontinuous devices like tick-tocks and stumbles and drips of water from icicles . . . and jokes. Other 'good' clocks might be the angles through which sunflowers occasionally tilt, the delightfully imprecise sequencing of flowers in bloom, the successive wakings of animals and insects and birds . . . or even of something that naturally grows in reverse, as did Merlyn, provided only that the apparent change is regular.

It is our ideas of our ideas of time, our abstractions from our sometimes erratic and inconsistent somaesthetic holistic sensations-experiences, that make us wish to have public models that do not always depend either upon these experiences, or the sun. Sundials are good models only in so far as it is a sunny day. If we chose to make a clock out of a collection of birds that woke up, species by species, at different hours of the day, we would have first to make sure that they did this reasonably consistently whether the sun was out or not, and whether it was winter or summer, etc. Clearly, bird wakings would not be a very good public model of our experience-idea if they changed more unpredictably than our own wakings, or even at all under these conditions. Moreover, such natural rhythms are slow and would never meet our 'needs' for indicating (talking about) very small times, such as the conscious duration of the instantaneous present, or very, very small times like lightning flashes and sudden insights. Birds, thoughtless creatures that they are, just don't seem to wake up with that degree of regularity! So, we are left to invented devices if we do need to mark minutes and sometimes even seconds. Seconds are not so much experienced as being *needed*, even by people in hi-tech environments, as they are experienced as ideas which may count. We thus have to get hold of periodic processes that march much faster and more regularly than the mere successive exaltations of larks.[3] So we turn to natural pendular vibrations or to concocted springs and other such periodic dynamics. But, as we know, even human rhythmic tappings could be a clock for a short while: good if you can see the tapping; better if you can hear it; best if you can both see *and* hear it. And this is possible only because we can create a mental image of rhythm and then reafference to it. Animals cannot produce arbitrary rhythms, or even their own natural rhythms at will. Only humans can.

Of course the day is a natural clock that we all experience; but we cannot study that in the way that we might study a wrist-watch, or the clock in some great cathedral, or even the singular Big Ben. Unlike 'days', some clocks are such that we can get hold of them, both in principle and in concrete material form. This is especially so when there are many models of them, when they are 'mass' produced. Others, like Big Ben, exist in only one manifestation. We cannot, so to say, study it except by studying that one there up in parliament. More pointedly, we cannot study the diurnal clock of nature at all, in these manipulative ways. That is, we cannot – though some day we may and today some might wish to – slow down the sun or speed up its roll across the sky. With little creatures, we can catch them and put them into rooms, and into little boxes inside rooms, and then we can make-believe that we are the sun, and we can rotate lights about and throw off heat in all sorts of 23-hour cycles, or 25-hour cycles, and thus study the natural resiliences of their biological clocks. We can even do that with ourselves: measuring how we adjust and readjust our natural biological clocks under various contrived diurnal cycles. We can even study wavelength effects: is a diurnality in blue the same as one in red, and so forth? But this is not studying the natural biological clock of the sun, or the moon, or the stars. That is another affair entirely, and requires more the abstract methods of astronomy than the concrete methods of experimental manipulation.

This means that the science of time is not the study of the mechanics of clocks, although (since clocks are our inventions) the mechanics of

---

3 One can, as it happens, 'clock' the setting of the sun and the changing colours of the evening twilight, and thence the increasing lunar hues of the night sky, by the changing species of fireflies that emerge in regular sequence to match the colour of their flashes to give best contrast to the ambient light. See Lall, A.B., Strother, G.K., Cronin, T.W., and Seliger, H.H. (1988) 'Modification of spectral sensitivities by screening pigments in the compound eyes of twilight-active fireflies', *J. Comparative Physiol. A.* 162: 23–33.

clocks would not exist without the science-experience of time. Suppose that we were a blind race and had come across a friendly race that was not blind. Eventually, after some long months of careful interactions and great lengthy deliberations – possible only because we are aware that we are aware and, consequently, *aware that there may well be many alternative ways in which to be aware* – we might come to comprehend that there was some energy process in the universe to which we were not responsive but to which it was. We would then develop – gradually, of course, since we could not see – a science of their *vision*. Indeed, we now know that there exist in bionature many energy-frequency classes and levels to which we are not responsive but to which some other creatures are. And, by the ideational transcendence of our own awareness of our awareness, we have now even achieved methods to study these creatures: animals which respond to magnetism, plants that respond to coriolis forces, eyes that respond to far infrared radiations and skins that respond to the far ultraviolet, ears that are sensitive to sound-pressure frequencies that we do not even feel, and so forth. No doubt, this list will continue to grow so long as man is curious and his mind alert.

What then would we do if confronted with a creature that perceived time (the passage of time, its compelling directionality) while we, somehow, were somaesthetically inert, atemporal? There is no verbal or conceptual equivalent, so it seems, to 'blindness' in somaesthesis. This is the primary set of sense modes through which *time* is experienced, and temporality qua experience is not missing entirely in any surviving humans. But we all know some for whom time does not really count. Perhaps they suffer from a macular degeneration in the somaesthesis of time!

In any event, in our time-free state, if we 'kept our heads about us', we would begin to note strange and eventually systematic even orderly differences between the behaviour of such creatures and our own. This behaviour differential would eventually become, to minds aware that they were aware, evidence for the presence of other sorts of awarenesses still, some that we ourselves did not have or did not seem to have. Then, also, very gradually now, because we do not 'feel' time directly the way we 'feel' grit, we might come to develop an idea of 'their' time and even a science of that. A central part of the science's success would be that it explained both the apparent experience-behaviour of these other creatures and, as well, the differing experience-behaviour of ourselves.

To reiterate: time, as quality, must be most exquisitely distinguished from all other 'times': for example, those that physicists may evoke in cosmology or cosmogenesis, or that which chemists use when they speak of thermodynamics, entropy, and the second law. T^2 is also not the same as biological time, though it is related to it. Time as quality is different from all these, but is none the less quite precise. As such, it occurs only – as do blue or sour or pain – when there are time-quality processors around.

Consider this classical conundrum in idealist philosophy. Is there *sound* when a tree falls alone in the forest? Well, there is sound, *if and only if* there is also at least one sound-quality processor around then and there in the neighbourhood. What may occur in the forest in the absence of such a processor are: the breaking of branches on other trees nearby, the scattering of leaves, the marking of the earth, the creation of air-pressure waves that in themselves may be strong enough to shake small bushes and flowers there in that vicinity, and so forth. But so long as there are no *sound-quality processors* then and there in that vicinity, there will be no sound quality. If no person or animal is around, and if we are sure that the tree itself does not 'hear' its own falling – and we are not here intimately concerned about God – then there simply *is* no sound. Many other physical and chemical and optical and mechanical changes will occur, of course, that we humans may get a record of later on by any number of methods, none of which gives the quality: sound. Moreover, we could now, at least in these times, place out there in the forest a tape-recorder or some such device which records the vibrations that the fall makes. Then, although for the recorder itself there is no sound (only condensations and rarefactions of air molecules and then vibrating microphones and, thence, also of styli and magnets, etc.), when we play the recording back and listen, *sound*-quality finally emerges in us. By intellectual means, we associate that with the fall. This, however, is a different matter. It is a humanly devised alternative way of putting our ear, so to speak, where otherwise it was not or cannot or could not be. But, there and then, with no ear around, no sound quality occurs.

Similarly with colours and pains and flavours and odours and, perforce, *times*. If there is no time-quality processor there in the forest when the tree falls, then no phenomenal quality-idea emerges of the time which it took to fall. Of course, as with the tape-recorder, we could previously have put some physical timing device out there in the forest in the neighbourhood of the tree and this, when we play its contrived signals-messages back, would give us then (at another physical time) an experiential notion of the time previously involved. In science we do this often, usually in such a way that the construing of the meaning of this sort of message, no matter how long in the physics, takes us just a second or two, i.e. we read a vastly condensed recording chart or some such, in which an hour is 'transformed' into a millimetre, etc. We do not, in re-evaluating the time the tree took to fall, need then and there to 'live through a similar duration'. Rather, the whole point of the time-recording devices that we place out in such places is precisely to let us obtain precise cognitive awarenesses of the times involved in a 'way wholly independent of the direct sensory-time-quality' that would have had to have been involved were we ourselves then and there the recording device. Instead of ourselves hiding out there in the forest and living through the tree's fall, we place out there a non-influencing physical recording device which (because of the mathematico-physical transformations involved) stands in for us and which involves considerably less EOQ (then and there) than if we ourselves were to stand in. The fall then takes place on its own without duration. We know, for example, that evolution has taken place 'through time', but this is a time wholly without quality.

In physics, it is well known that there are many instances in which the measuring of an event must necessarily involve us in a disturbance of the event. This is a particularly central concept in modern quantum mechanics (as opposed to classical or Newtonian mechanics), and in the Heisenberg subatomic uncertainty process. Similar observational disturbances occur in other fields as well. It is virtually impossible, for example, to study pain perception without in some way introducing the quality pain to the human observer. And this mere introduction of pain may permanently change the way in which that observer subsequently feels and certainly reports pain. With blue, sour, stereo-acoustics, and other such simple qualities, this is less true. That is – or so we believe – one may turn on and off the quality *blue* and the quality *sour* and the quality *audio-distance*, and measure various human responses to them without thereby permanently affecting the human responder. If there is an effect, it is only temporary. So the physical recording of the falling of the forest tree, say by a camera or an audio-tape or whatever, can generally be done so as not to inter-fere with or affect the falling.

And, in the natural abstract–concrete melding, just as the quality-sound can then 'come to be associated' with the falling of the tree by our listening to the recording, so the quality-sight can come to be associated with the falling of the tree when we look at the movie. Until then, the *sight* of the tree falling is as absent from the event as is the *sound*. Also, the *knowledge* of it.

And, until then, to reiterate particularly for this discussion, so also is absent the *time-quality* of the tree falling. Henceforth, we must carefully distinguish the physics of time and the chemistry of time and even the biology of time, from the psychology of time: as the analysis of a sensory-rational quality of human experience. We cannot know, of course, precisely how other humans experience time, even intimates, but we generally find no less accord therewith than with blue or sour or audio-distance or other such more unimodal sensory-cognitive experiences. As there are inter-esting hereditary constraints on taste-quality perceptions and on smell- and colour- and even melody-quality experiences (certainly also kinaes-thetic, somaesthetic, and vestibular), no doubt some day we shall find that there are large individual differences in time-quality experiences as well, some of which may be ascribable (relatively speaking) to intrinsic and rigid genetic encodings-unfoldings. We do know, for example, that time perception is different in children and in the aged, and that it is markedly affected by high fever. Fever generally seems to speed the intrinsic passage of time, since body processes are thereby speeded up. But other external processes come to seem, in proportion, to have slowed down. Time experience is also distorted in various quite dramatic ways by brain injuries, by drugs, and by many abnormal chemically or psychiatrically induced mood states. Time, for the meditating spiritualist, passes majestically and in great even swells, quite differently than it does for the romping youth or, alas, the desperate schizophrenic. As we have suggested, perhaps for these unhappy people, each modality evokes a different and thus non-integratable rate.

There are a great many processes by which one's phenomenal time-quality may be affected, and it is only in some wholly integrative and multisensory rational and coherent fashion that, on average, one's experience of time can be shown to be congruent to that in other humans and to the passage of time as measured by sans-quality means in physics or in chemistry (after all, that is what those means are supposed to do!), or even via sub-experiential biology. Once it was developed over evolution that the planning of alternate routes and multiple methods and comparative strategies became a major survival advance over other less variable planning, then the emergence of time-quality awareness occurred. I write, as always, of T^2: the awareness of the awareness of time.

GRADIENT SLOPES OF TIME

Evolution is the only over-arching theory that we have for describing the foundations of such processes. The more and more were the gradient slopes of time mediated by increasingly different modalities, and the more and more they all cohered in slope and in acceleration assessment, both within and between themselves and, in some simple neat way, with the general physico-chemical passage of time (really: diurnality, mensuality, and the seasons), the more and more precisely did time-quality *as such* emerge. It is natural to conclude that such T^2 time-quality processing came to help markedly in the survival of the self to adulthood, in the chances of successful mating (which means, in the ecobiological sense, the passing on of one's genes to the gene-pools of posterity), and, in short, in the evolution of (and increased number of) increasingly better time-quality-processing creatures. This operates in contrast to increasingly poor or non-time-processing creatures (let us say: plants). As the sunflower tracks the sun across the sky, it is not 'keeping' time. It is also not 'keeping' space or angle or even intensity.

Time is a quality of individual human experience that depends upon an exquisite harmonious concatenation of multimodal qualitative nuances; indeed, upon nuances from virtually all the sense modes. It is thus to be expected that, while we may all quite readily agree on the quality of some single modal experience such as royal blue, or at least agree within some minor sensory-rational hysteresis, we may well not agree at all as to the gradients of time. If the truth be known, social psychology shows that people do disagree quite considerably. Some even battle violently over the government's attempt to tamper, as with 'daylight savings time' and the like. (Glance at the world's time map, and see how incredibly these timezones are twisted.) Were there to be developed an art form involving exclusively or primarily *time-quality* perception (music, dance?), there is little doubt about the fact that critics and artists and audiences would chatter and squabble over various interpretations in this complex sensory-cognitive organizational mode even more so than they do presently over simpler art forms, such as the extraordinary yellow colours in Van Gogh's famous paintings of the wheatfield with sheaves (Arles, 1887) and a corn-field with cypresses, (1889).

BIOPSYCHOLOGY DIGESTS A TINY REGION IN THE MIDST OF THE PHYSICAL DIMENSION

More complex yet – though this idea is even more subtle and will involve us in another place – concepts of beauty and of truth and of goodness also involve intersensory-rational organizations and, in themselves, are not at all less but, rather, even more complexly and multiplicatively elabo-rated than is the quality *time*. And, we must note responsibly, *time* has a twin or a mate, which almost everyone in physics and metaphysics and also in modern biopsychology discusses at least in a second if not the same breath. This is *space*. Perhaps the chemists are less actively involved in this, or only more wise and more chary.

In any event, space also is primarily a quality of human experience and, *as such*, an event in human life about which physicists really cannot tell us anything at all (see Chapter 6). When they speak of space they are (or should be) speaking of a process wholly removed from quality. As the physicists' time goes 'way beyond' the experience of time (into the too small to be sensed, into the too large, into the too past, into the too future) and is only in a tiny, tiny, almost infinitesimal region *coherent with time as quality*, so also does the physicists' space. No one can or should asso-ciate the space inside molecules with the quality of space within a room; or that quality with the space within the cosmos. Those spaces are embodied in ideas (see Chapter 7), but not ever embodied in qualities. Those spaces are quite specifically quality free. Certainly, some quality-experiential times seem very, very fast, but the humanistic quality-time fades rapidly as we move down from tenths to hundredths to millisec-onds. Also, some experiential times seem very, very large, yet the human-istic quality-time passes away rapidly as we move up from years to decades to centuries. Fade, it surely does and in both directions.

This idea is of enormous significance, and is hard to grasp. Figure 5.1 shows what is intended. The physical and all the other sciences were derived ultimately by an extension through and then beyond the senses: to think up, design, and then to build devices *stronger* than man, *faster*

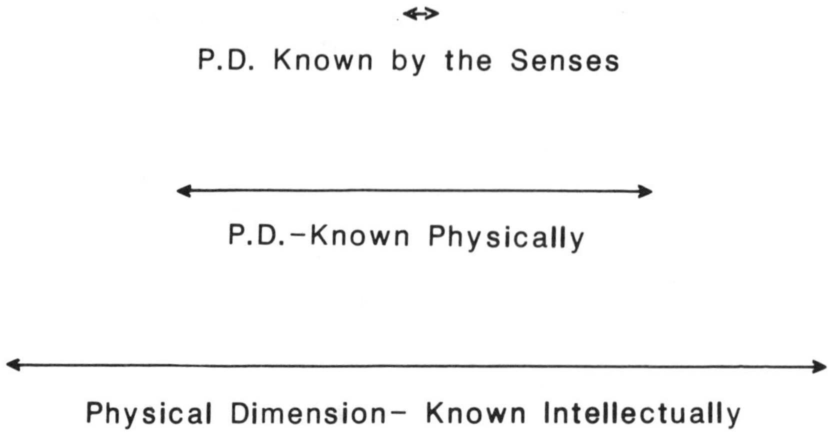

↔

P.D. Known by the Senses

←————————————————————————→

P.D.-Known Physically

←——————————————————————————————————→

Physical Dimension- Known Intellectually

Figure 5.1 Schematic illustration of the relationship between physical dimensions (PD) as known by the senses to the same dimensions as known by actual physical measurements, and in proportion to the same dimensions as conceived intellectually. Note how the dimensions extend beyond the sensory in both directions. Perhaps first known precisely for electromagnetic radiation and vision (c. 1800). Next for hearing and ultrasonics. And so forth. The full exposition of this idea may be found in the text.

than man, that can '*see*' further than man and '*hear*' and '*smell*' more sensitively. And so forth. The abstract realization that *thoughts* may transcend *experiences* in innumerable ways is not easy to grasp. But it is the absolute key to understanding what mind is that matter is not, nor can be. These are teasing thoughts, which means that they tease us out of thought; they are almost un-thinkable. Yet we can think outside of space and faster than time ... and remain healthy and sane.

This has crucial empirical historical analogies: inventions of levers to lift things virtually too heavy to be experienced as heavy; catapults to throw things virtually too far to be experienced as throwing; wheels by means of which to roll things virtually too cumbersome to experience as moving. When Galileo developed the telescope, he succeeded in looking into a largeness virtually too large to be experienced as large. And when Leeuwenhoek invented the microscope, he succeeded in looking into a smallness virtually too small to be experienced as small.

A key historical advance in this sort of thinking came in optics on the fully empirical level in about the year 1800. This was the discovery by Herschel, and some others, that there was, so to say, 'some sort of energy out there' that transcended what humans could perceive by sight but which affected physical light-measuring equipment exactly as did light. Gradually, over virtually 100 years, through James Clark Maxwell, the Curies, and many others, this energy was shown to be of the same 'nature' as light, i.e. electromagnetic radiation: infrared beyond red and radio and electric waves beyond that; ultraviolet beyond violet and cosmic and x-rays beyond that. Photometers measuring light soon gave way in the physics to radiometers measuring radiation. Figure 5.1 gives a precise indication of this fact: that radiation is experienced as light in only a very tiny central range.

Henceforth, the realization grew gradually that various other human sensitivities might also not be wholly in agreement with the physics, or that the physics might also transcend them in polar directions; and even that human sensitivities might differ from each other and from various animal sensitivities. This latter is now known for vision, hearing, smell, taste, infrared skin sensitivity, and many others. Further, the realization grew throughout science that many other event-processes, testable in the physical and conceivable in the intellectual universe, might well transcend what we can in the best case actually experience as sensory qualities: infra- and ultrasonics emerged, and infra- and ultra-velocities. These all came in as purely cognitive ideas about the physical universe, with only a faint remembrance of sensation, as small as you like. In 'true' physics, such sensations vanish.

Most peoples of whose languages and customs we have record have long had concepts of ancestral pasts and of descendant futures. But there are definitely some languages in which these ideas are less readily expressible than they are in others. Even today, most languages cannot well express ideas of infinities of expanding time or of vanishings of collapsing space; or even of number or zero in either of them. The idea of a first creation is really a limit on the extrasensory cognitive notion that, given there is some such quality as the experiential sequencing of events, such sequencing ought probably, barring some (satanic?) discontinuities, go back for ever and ever in divine-like endurance and go forward for ever and ever in similar fashion. God, the one God, would be that process which could fully grasp both the ultimate beginning and the ultimate ending and hence dwell comfortably there at their join: the infinite, infinite Return. No real person could aspire to experience that! Once physics discovered radiant energies that it could measure *in precisely the same way that it measured that tiny, tiny range of radiant energies that man also measures in his way naturally by eye as the quality light* ... it then opened up the possibility of the existence of non-qualitative ranges of $N + 1$ other physical dimensions: (a) to which mankind is only very, very selectively responsive in some middle range, and yet (b) for which it (might) think up means for their exosomatic measurement. We should have, but have not, also thought up new words for these conditions. Physical space, thus, can go as far down into the small as it wants to go and as far up into the large as it wants to go. God also dwells at that intersection; and we also, but only in thought, not experience. That has long fallen away, by the wayside.

Let us look now at that space and at the wayside.

6 The multimodality of space-quality

AS THE SPIDER PERCEIVES ITS WEB

As we explore routes, generally even more so than as we explore methods, there emerges in humans, and no doubt to a lesser and/or a different extent and manner in other animals, that quality of experience which we call: space. No one, or only a few poets perhaps (or E.B. White),[1] would hold that the spider has a concept of the spatiality of its web in quite the same way that we humans have. The spider, as such, is almost a two-dimensional creature, a true flat-lander in the mathematical sense (not in the sense of a tourist coming up from the valleys!), and experiences the spatiality of its web primarily as route only, not as something which cuts out from an infinitely extended space a tiny almost infinitesimal filigree. Moreover, the spider, or so we presume, surely does not have a clear, although perhaps some tiny, notion of the externality which surrounds its web. Creatures appear on it, or in it, and struggle and vibrate it, and thus become more and more enmeshed within it, but they do not so much, or at all, 'approach it'. Indeed, it is probable that the spider has very little information (hence sensation) concerning the presence of any creatures about it in the web-externality that might, so to speak, in their wanderings come to fly into it. Certainly, it has little awareness of we humans who sometimes plough coarsely through the web with our bodies and faces. This latter occurs so often because the spider also 'likes' that height – albeit that we do not yet know precisely how the spider *senses* its height (air flows, perhaps). It certainly does not 'see' the ground down there, though it may smell or feel it (by gravity or magnetic changes?). Actually, we are hard put to describe the sensory mechanisms by which the spider, with such poor eye-sight, might discern its height and/or the approach of some suitable food, or even the mere presence of suitable foods in the neighbourhood. No doubt, much more is achieved by olfactory distance perception than by visual or aural. None the less, nothing in nature encourages us to reject for spiders what we hold for man: that is, the operation

---

1 As in his marvellous children's book *Charlotte's Web*.

of the general principle of the conservation of EOQ. Consequently, we are driven to conclude that the co-ordination of spiders' appropriate distance receptors (perhaps thermal as well, like snakes, and pressure) functions to assist them in 'selecting' those spatial locations appropriate to the capturing of more rather than less suitable prey with the least EOQ expenditure. While spiders may even gain direct awareness of some approaches by smell, for example, the web does this for them (is in this way still part of them); consequently for them to develop direct distance awareness would be an unnecessary biological cost.[2]

Clearly, some creatures who fly do not care much about webs. Most birds would fly directly through most webs, but most birds generally fly higher. Those that fly at the height of some webs might well be seen as enlarging (looming) and fleeting shadows by the ommatidial eye of the spider, but not otherwise as a specific objective approach. Much of the approach could be indicated, close in at least, by air-pressure bendings of the web, although non-objective breezes do the same. Some approaches are probably signalled by the absorption of chemical gradients, thus as smells and even as airborne tastes, which latter do occur even for man.

In fine, to the extent that the spider has some experience-quality of space (or anything-process) outside its web – and even of its web – this can come about, as all such complex qualities, only to the extent that it can achieve, with low EOQ costs, an integration of the multisensory messages then available to it. That is, while one may contend that for man there are some innate conceptions of certain pure platonic ideas such as space and time and pain and beauty, one would hardly credit such a tiny and simply organized creature as a spider with such innate ideas, or any ideas[3] (cf. Chapter 7).

None the less, by the travelling to make the web, and by the sensing of approaching wind currents and odour currents and temperature gradients and even radiant and light-shadow gradients, it is not unthinkable that the spider can and does gain, by emergence from these gradients, some bare quality of pure spatiality. But we are probably safe in asserting that that quality is different from our own, as we observe the web and all its entrainments from afar, and that it is probably several orders of magnitude (factors of ten) less variable than our own.

---

2 Blinded spiders, especially those that build webs at dusk and take them down at dawn, would almost certainly build their webs in the identical form as sighted spiders, because night vision generally is an absolutely minimal cue for them. Webs are built using kinaesthetic-motor, vibrotactile, and odour cues, primarily. Spiders normally building at dawn might perhaps be more affected. But it is known that, when they are kept in perpetual artificial darkness or lightness, normal webs are still constructed. (I am grateful to Dr Michael Robertson, of the National Zoo, for some of these facts.)

3 I say '*simply* organized', but only in full respect for the true complexity involved, should one try, by any sort of modern computer methods, to 'make' or even to 'model' a spider.

SPACE SENSE OF MIGRATING FISH OR BIRDS

Consider now the migrating fish or bird. This could be a very different story indeed. These creatures travel through space much more robustly than we do, and in entirely different ways, and this alone is sufficient for us to suspect that a different sensory-rational 'space' quality emerges for them than emerges for us. Our methods of 'migrating' are EOQ economical only for us. We observe and contemplate the migrations, and we put out systematic obstacles to study them in all their possible natural and contrived variations. We attempt to model such travellings scientifically in the abstract or in some laboratory in empirically reduced form, say where we let a micron equal a mile, or via some other mentally or architecturally simple and humanly feasible scalar transformation. Furthermore, should we actually choose to try to experience more fully the travelling of migrating fishes and birds, by submarining the oceans or by soaring the skies, we would still then obtain (and tolerate) a different and far more variable route than could the fish or the bird. We may arrive at the same destination, but never in their way or in the same way twice. This is not merely because our sensory experiences might then be more effortful, but also because our multisensory integrations resemble theirs in some ways – to the extent that we share with them qualities and resolutions among qualities – yet transcend theirs in many others – to the extent that we may sensorily process and mentally evoke higher variances within all the qualities: higher resolutions, higher degrees of integrational capacities, and higher degrees of mental invention. For us, such migrations have mythic proportions.

For the arctic tern, as already noted, migrating over about one month's time from the Canadian Arctic all the way south some 5,000 miles to the Antarctic, one may doubt that its journeyings 'seem to it' quite as amazing and as beautiful and as God-evidencing as they may to us. For the tern, this is just simply how it is done. There is no other way.[4]

This point is of major importance; it is not some philosophical wrangle. Consider an example at the level of a simple, pure sense-quality. Let us suppose that we place the most sophisticated sensory-rational system of all for the perception of pure blue – say, an artist particularly favoured and trained in blue nuances – into an environment in which all that is present physically is a homogeneous luminance that he/she, and most other sighted and trichromatic creatures, ingests in such a way that the quality 'pure blue' emerges, but no other. In short, we suppose that he/she perceives him/herself surrounded by blue alone: of one hue, value, and chroma, in the technical jargon. Then shortly – and one means by this in possibly 15 and generally considerably less than 45 seconds – all

---

4 For some of these facts on bird migrations, I am indebted to my friend and colleague Dr Peter Stettenheim, of Lebanon, New Hampshire.

sensation of blueness-quality actually fades, and merely a grey luminosity survives. After a while, even this smoothness of middle grey may also sometimes fade into a darker or less luminous grey. Thus, a pure single sensory quality evoked even via a highly evolved and most refined yet dedicated modality as the eye cannot long survive *on its own*. It needs a reference, a contrast.

Consider this problem further. Generally, to see colours, even for normal trichromatic human observers, there need to be present in the physics at least two recognizably (qualitatively) discriminable wavelengths of a special electromagnetic radiation. Most colour deficients have what we call collapsed systems: instead of three absorbing chemical pigments in their retinal cone cells, they have only two. Such people are by virtue of this limited genetic unfolding (decreased multiplicity) frequently forced into situations in which, while there are two colour qualities present for normal trichromatic observers, there is only one colour quality present for them. Consequently, in such situations, that single chromatic quality may also appear to dichromates to desaturate and go to a grey when, for normal subjects, two sometimes quite startlingly different hue-qualities are present.

What this means, then, is that should the dichromate have to find his (generally) or her way among routes festooned or defined by patterns, forms, and textures of those hues that, for him or her, are undifferentiable, he or she could not only not do so, but would find the requirement absurd unless under some prior intellectual set (say, as evoked by the instructions) that some other people do find it possible to explore visually along such routes.

What insight does this give us as to our migrating birds? Only if their routes have (by evolution, may we say?, are permitted to have) a certain multiplicity and variance, could they develop some high spatial quality of routing and voyaging. Absolutely fixed routes, of course, are hard to confirm in the air by any means. And we know that birds play relatively freely in the air: they soar and dive and tumble about, also in an excess of EOQ zeal and consumption. The swift is known to stay aloft for days, and to eat and even to copulate in air.[5] Indeed, the more there is, in some animal, of excess EOQ, the more we see play and exploration in the set of its natural behaviour patterns. (Why this is so, and why something else has not evolved instead of play – e.g. wars? – we do not know.) Indeed, excess EOQ is the major source, also, of humour and of joy. Bees, for example, do not play; nor do spiders; nor snakes; nor alligators. Birds do; and maybe some fish. Certainly, mammals do, and primates above all.

---

5 Some biologists have made the claim that the starling (or the swift?) spends almost the whole *first three years* of its life aloft, but Dr Stettenheim is not able to confirm any such time as that.

In any event, were some bird tied by its genetic encoding-unfolding to a relatively narrow and rigid routeing, then the quality of spatiality evoked by the travelling on that route would be minimal. Some birds – puffins, white throat sparrows, phoebees, and many others – are known to return within a mile of the place from which they started, after thousands of miles of flying. If, on the other hand, the bird is liberated from one routeing into multiple and arbitrary (free-choice) routeings (of significantly greater variance processing), then we would find that a higher quality of spatiality might emerge. It might not, of course, but the ethological evidence suggests that, once it becomes true that the central neuro-plasticity necessary to an intrinsic variance-processing capacity has evolved, the pertinent quality can come forth.

In humans, for example, if it were always known and wholly impossible to think otherwise than that one would live and die on the same street where one was born, then it is most improbable that a refined spatiality even of that street would emerge. Someone more liberated, capable of standing apart from that street and observing other streets, other villages, other neighbourhoods, other countries, other rivers, other nations, other worlds, he/she could develop an entirely different and more subtle spatiality. This would be more complex than the first, primarily because it would possess a vastly higher multiplicity. For one thing, such an individual could perceive the condition that maybe the *street* need not be let stay just precisely as it had always been. For N + 1 reasons, for other qualities of life and of experience, that street might be shifted slightly or turned. Its central core could remain, but new and richer and more diverse spatialities within it could be made manifest. The first individual, being human and so still sharing with the second the *capacity for multiplicity*, might then also be able to ingest and comprehend and then experience, in the abstract, certain aspects of this enhanced spatiality, and so agree to the reconstruction of the street. But he/she might not; that depends upon the personality structure, the quality of the primary education, and the tolerance that these have encouraged for ambiguity and diversity in other areas.

Similarly, when a great sculptor looks at some block of marble, or granite, or wood, he/she may 'perceive' within it some final statue and – in a real sense, not only in the traditional joke 'How did he know that that was hidden in there?' – develop a virtual sensuous spatiality about that statue there 'hidden' in that marble. This is so because the statue is already present in the abstract. To a refined degree, it can be shared only with a very few peers, until the block is actually chipped forth by the sculptor's carefully guided and inspired carving. But, in truth, that chipping is wholly secondary to his/her superior abstract spatiality. Both mechanical-intellectual and abstract-intellectual skills must coexist in the sculptor, of course, as similarly in the writer and in the painter, and in all the other creators among us talented in some means for especially refined expression.

In any event, space, as quality of experience, is not space *qua* physics or *qua* cosmology or *qua* chemistry or even *qua* biology. That is to say: the spatiality of the mind is not the spatiality of the brain. Even Descartes, whom we indict elsewhere because of his denial of animal sensitivity, grappled with this imaginatively when he noted that mind lacked, above all attributes, extensivity. It was everywhere and nowhere, at once. Indeed, no one experiences the quality of his/her mental self as somehow encased, here and now, in one's head. That spatial quality emerges with headaches, for example, and toothaches, but not really with effortless sensory qualities or with non-reflexive thought in general. These latter, especially in the reflective mode, create for themselves, and for the mind as a whole, an externality and a transcendence that neither biological space (inside the head-brain) nor physical space (some central co-ordinate dot) possess. Physical and biological space are not 'external', although this is how we mostly think about them, because 'externality' as such is a primary quality of human experience. The abstractions 'out there', 'through all the universe', 'away-near', etc., are, as are all such abstractions, imperfect representations of sensory qualities (as if to think of a perfect blue or a pure lilac). What these abstractions *sacrifice* in the communication of pure, veridical, phenomenal qualitative experience they gain in the communication of their more general abstract form. Memories do this for us as well.

SPATIAL CO-ORDINATION OF THE LION AND THE GAZELLE

Let me try to express this in another way. Visual space (an area of technical science which has concerned me directly all my professional life) is not the same as the physical space in which it generally lies and from which, in some circumstances, it can be shown to have emerged. Visual space is a qualitative phenomenal space that our natural visual experience arouses within us. That it generally maps in a fair one-to-one relationship to physical-geometric space is a natural result of successful evolutionary adaptation. (As it happens, this mapping for many situations is highly 'non-Euclidean', i.e. is closest to and best understood in a more general Riemannian rather than a restricted Euclidean way.) And, as the principles of evolution are transcendent, this mapping is reasonably similar for all humans and for all the higher animals who share intimately our physical-chemical world. Were it not closely similar we could not all interact efficiently in that physical-experiential plane upon which we all live and die. Indeed, when the lion sets out to catch the gazelle, and the gazelle to flee, they each succeed best in doing what they plan (and, thus, have mental awareness of): to the extent that each does (visually and kinaesthetically and acoustically and olfactorily and somaesthetically and vestibularly) share the other's space. If two birds must come together in the air to mate (as fish and whales in water), this quality sharing is obviously critical, both in space-quality and in time-quality. For creatures that mate under water, somehow to us, their coming together 'seems' a bit easier, but, for the co-ordination of space-time, the task is the same. For creatures like the lion and the gazelle, for whom the coming together has opposite abstract meanings and entirely contrary experiential qualities (and here, now, the gazelle has a mental life, so we believe, in a way that the fly avoiding the swat does not), probability and multiplicity rule the spatio-temporal congruencies of their respective life-realms. From this multiplicity there comes to each an exquisite individual yet common awareness of qualitative space and of qualitative time.

No doubt man, standing apart and viewing, could find, as he does also for the spider and the bird, even greater variances in the attack route and in the escape route than either lion or gazelle. The proof of this is that we can capture, to some degree at will, both lion and gazelle. For us, the abstract-concrete spatial quality is much richer and more numerous than it is for these creatures, even though no human can charge quite like a lion or flee quite like a gazelle.

When the physicist describes these spaces, or the meteorologist, or the geographer (perhaps not the hunter), he/she is seeking to describe them – as the 'temporalogist' with time – quite apart from the human-qualities of space. That is to say, he/she is striving to deal with the idea of space and its representation by means of thoughts and ideas and concepts that, while in origin they derive from human experiential qualities, are now as far removed from them as it is possible mentally (conceivably) to go. This is a psychological removal, of course, not physical. And total removal may never be possible, which is why Figure 5.1 is such a critical matter of philosophy. In so construing – naturally, since this is the intent – nothing of the fierce rush of the lion or of the terror of the gazelle remains in the description of their routes. A map of their respective routes evokes a precise spatiality in a true reader of maps; albeit that for lions and gazelles there are no abstract maps.

SPATIAL-QUALITY PROCESSOR

To put this now in our more purely sensory-rational terms, we note that nothing at all of the quality 'spatiality' exists in the universe unless, there and then, a spatial-quality-processing system, such as a plant but certainly a higher animal, is around in that neighbourhood, and does so. Consider, once again, that tree falling in the forest. Perhaps after all it grew that way when you found it down on the ground, and no falling or passing through space (under the call of gravity) were ever actually involved; what then could we say of the spatial passage? Actually, as there is no quality green, no quality crash or quality tree (even), so there is no quality falling, no quality spatiality, unless there and then there is some spatial-quality-organizing, perceiving, and emerging process around, such as a gazelle, a lion, or a human being.

PHYSICAL SPACE EXPUNGED OF THE QUALITY: SPACE

The physicist, even more so the astronomer and the cosmologist, is not satisfied until he/she has expunged from his/her scientific descriptions of spatiality all vestiges of those near infinitely variable spatial qualities that humans invariably both bring to and derive from their interaction with nature. This is also why all mythopoets and all early cosmologists acted in the exactly contrary fashion and peopled the heavens with gods and angels and other living quality-processing creatures. These early heavens were not at all abstract, and this quality loading made for a much more comforting and truly human experience of the spatiality-temporality of God's home, than light-years and galaxies and black-holes do today. In the Middle Ages, patterns of the starry messengers were called 'appearances', and the scholarly task was to explain the quality of their changing. Actually, there is no change in them, only in us. The philosophers gradually came to know that. But that 'God's in his heaven and all's right with the world' is a reassuring interpretation of heavenly reality whose appeal has hardly lessened over the aeons. Even today, we still like to think that the moon and the stars do somehow care that we look! We wish them to share with us the marvellous spatiality of their own appearances; even our *fate*. It is only with reluctance that some of us have been forced to admit, these days, that they do not. The prevalence, even today, of astrologers and other persistent star-quality ascribers attests to the psychological difficulty of this letting go. And this is precisely what most physicists have traditionally been trying to do: develop a description of space that does not involve the quality of space. The yardstick does not know that it tells distance, nor does the ray of light. Similarly, they have been trying to develop a description of time that does not involve the quality of time. The clock does not know that it tells time, nor even does the sun.

BLUE IS DIFFERENT FROM PAIN

Since Newton's absolutely critical discovery of the relationship between the quality *colour* and some particular 'oscillation' or 'fluxuation' or 'refrangibility' of some removed physical essence, physicists have been deeply concerned with the 'nature' of that transcendent physicality, both as it interacts with man and as it does not. What Newton achieved for us – and, as is well known, what so startled the great German humanistic poet Goethe that he fought Newton tooth and nail on this – was the removal of man from the quality of colour, e.g. blue, by his assertion that there exists wholly apart from man a mere physical vibration or oscillation or 'refrangibility' of some process (Newton did not then, in the 1660s, know of 'radiant wave-particle energy') and that this process exists as a non-blue oscillation in the universe and only becomes a blue when there is a blue-quality-emerging process somewhere around in the neighbourhood. 'The rays', as he said, 'are not coloured.' Since then, generally, physicists have realized that they could achieve a description of many aspects of the universe without resort to humanly evoked qualities. One of the first was weight, which became mass. Mass does not possess nor imply the quality weight or heaviness, but rather that mass as such can be thought to exist as a factor in material dynamics independently of any interactions with a weight-quality emerging process. A similar removal became possible between temperature and hot/cold when their relationship to Brownian molecular motion was noted (c. 1900) by Einstein.

All these processes have analogous abstract physical models wholly apart from biology, yet, in addition, share this property that somewhere along their abstract dimensionality quality as such emerges in neighbouring creatures. Much of the history of science has been devoted to the scrambling apart of those qualities for which additional non-qualitative physico-chemical events might also be discerned along some extended but similar dimension, in comparison to those qualities for which this is not so and, perforce, cannot ever be: whose range and total variance is humanly limited and defined, for which there is no beyond. Before Newton, one was not certain that blue was not, in this way, akin to pain or even to a dream. Certain of the classical Greeks (Aristotle, for example), in various confused historical views, postulated that we see by virtue of light emitted from the eyes almost like 'feelers', almost like sounds causing echoes. 'Light', thus, had no sort of existence apart from vision. Physical pain, of course, was recognized in the earliest psychologies as a quality of experience that emerges towards one or another dimensional extreme of such physical events as temperature or pressure or acidic concentration, and so on. (We now know these are not really extremes at all: one is already burnt at very low temperatures, relatively speaking.) While the temperature or pressure or acid are never 'hot' or 'breathtaking' or 'searing' apart from a pain-quality processing experiencing creature, the dimensionalities were known early on to extend far *above* and *below* most animal physiological thresholds. Only the poets (and the dedicated gardeners) think that plants feel pain. While one can *say* that the day is hot, the sky blue, and the boss tough, only the latter may be true. One says with no less conviction that the situation is painful, the time is stressful, and that that student is a pain in the neck! We even locate that pain! Though most pains have poor spatiality, they have precise temporality. Clearly, this quintessentially metaphorical process emerges in us as part of his multiplicity-experiencing mental dynamics. And such widespread metaphorizing exists for pain because of its signal importance in all higher life. None the less, in this instance, there is no possibility of removing our mental quality from some unidimensional physical-chemical reality and saying that there exists, beyond pain, a would-be like uni-dimensional pain vibration (or concentration or whatever) that transcends the physiological response in both directions. These physicalities may often be reasonably well correlated with pain, but they are seldom one-to-one with it, nor is their transcendence polarly symmetrical. Indeed, the asymmetry is the key: there is death not transcendence at one end. Moreover, one of the most characteristic aspects of at least deep body-somaesthetic pain is that it is phenomenally referred away from its source. The actual 'cause' is often not identified by the subject (indeed, it is often mis-identified), in so far as a quality of pain occurs which possesses a local sign that is spatially incongruent with that unknown yet perhaps life-threatening biological-physical event. This is especially true for cancer pains, for heart attack pains, for back pains, and many other internal pains; while surface pains (cuts, bruises) and toothaches have usually more sharply co-ordinated local signatures, which is to say that touch modes mediate spatiality better than somaesthetic modes. When you are tired, for example, where 'is' the fatigue?

But even an idea as peculiar and as strongly biological as pain, as with the ideas of space and of time and pretty much any of the pure, simple, single-modal sensory qualities, may none the less be projected by us into an abstract state: pain alone, out in the universe, as when the heavens weep.

As we have stressed, many sensory processes interact in the co-ordination of time and space. Kinaesthesis is the most important one, as in the act of exploration, but vision and hearing and touch and smell and the vestibular modes do so as well. Similarly, numerous modes also contribute, and in many different organizations, to the ideas of pain and painfulness, and to their variations among people and their differential toleration. Also, to their aloof metaphorical pose.

Ideas are also some species of qualitative mental experience for which one might ask: is there some simple unitary physical-chemical variance that somehow goes along one-to-one with ideas, that symmetrically surrounds ideas from both above and below them? There is, certainly, the one-to-one variance of the physical dimension of the wavelength or oscillation frequency of radiant energy, which goes along with the quality: coloured light, and yet transcends light (roughly) symmetrically both as oscillations too fast and as oscillations too slow for retinal absorption. And there is the one-to-one variance of the physical dimension of the air-pressure waves which in only a small region go along with (emerge as) the quality sound. So might not there be something in physical reality which is, so to say, idea-like (methophor-pure) but which only in certain tiny central regions emerges into that particular and very special quality-state in nearby idea-processing creatures? The answer is yes, but this is an especially complex affirmation.

Let us now consider this in detail.

7 Ideas: another complex quality of experience

Ideas, of course, vary in many ways, from precise to imprecise, from simple to complex. So from the start we know that their discussion will lead us into subtleties.

IDEAS VS. OBJECTS

What are ideas? No one asserts that they 'have' a physical reality in the way that discrete objects do. Nor are they consumed as apples are. Rather, they are possessed in the same way as anticipations, emotions, fears, and memories. In sum, they constitute a large portion of consciousness. None the less they are sometimes quite kernel-like and rigid in nature. The question is: do they extend below and above the human?

IDEAS VS. SENSATIONS

The pithy Scottish philosopher of the eighteenth century David Hume, whose writings display some of the most brilliant and pointed philosophy ever written in any language, asserted, in one of his normative moods and modes, that 'the faintest sensation is more powerful than the most concrete idea'. For him, ideas were lesser sensations.

Though he would probably have agreed that many ideas moved well beyond sensations, he did not know how. Also, he suffered then from the merely nascent insights of a sensory science still 100 years away from its flowering in the hands of the German and American experimental psychologists. And he wrote innocent of the much later twentieth-century insights of gestalt psychology, of psychoanalysis, and of advanced sensory science and neuropsychology.

In any event, he was wholly in error. It is an attractive poetic idea, but not to any sensory scientist who has studied true sensory thresholds, where the faintest (almost unthinkably faint) sensation of light appears when only two or three quanta of radiant energy are presented to the dark-adapted eye, or where the almost unthinkably faint odour emerges when only a few molecules of some appropriate chemical are presented to the sniffing nose, or where the almost unthinkably faint buzz occurs when only something like the Brownian heat motion of molecules crashing about in the tympanic membrane seems sufficient to excite the nerve impulse preludic to sound. These recent insights into what we mean by sensations must be taken in comparison to those ideas which can sometimes be so fixed and stern, so intimate and profound, so monadic and controlling as to fill all of one's waking day and all of one's waking night. Sometimes ideas of enthrallment or of possession or of curse or of inspiration can motivate one's whole life. They can be so dominating as to set one up for a mythopoetic enchantment, an anxiety-ridden slow death, in the self-echoing self-reverberating spells put out by shamans and medicine men and superstitious meddling enemies and neighbours.

MIND AS ENERGY

As we have suggested,[1] mind is the least material form of body, body is the least energetical form of mind. In this view, ephemeral ideas and ideas of vague character seem to hover about almost in the air like a mist or a cloud of tiny puffs, – impalpable and virtually inexpressible, almost unexperienceable. Such ideas are in a pure energy form. They are in the form of premonitions, of pale anticipations of thresholds, of very, very dim hopes, of anxieties too delicate actually to name.

Some of these ideas are grist for Hume's mill; indeed, some of them are so fragile that merely to try to think of them, to centre one's mind into the form that they appear to be striving to take, drives them away like a bubble too closely approached with a groping finger. In this form, ideas are pure energy, they have yet to establish any consistent, objective, neural *anlage* and so, in a quite real sense, can be referred to as mere sweeps or fluxes of Humean imagination. One senses a vague: 'Ah!' If they pass through the mind a second time (a wavelet, not yet a trough or peak) and in a form in any way similar to the first, neurologically speaking, then they may take on some sort of relatively consistent neurological presence. That is, they may pass through the same neural structures in the same way more easily a third time. They may not, but on average we believe that this is so. Consequently, in this way one may refer to such pre-ideas, pre-awarenesses, as webs or fine filigrees, as mental laces, as the most fragile and as yet just barely reliable excitatory brain net. Think of a vanishing spider's web in the neural pattern of brain impulses, one that can barely be discerned by that most acute (and, at last, a Heisenbergian *un*disturbing) discernment process: the mental self just momentarily aware of itself; energy touching energy, wave touching wave.

---

1 Shipley, T. (1989) 'When mind chooses freely to be body: a radical synthesis between sensory rationalism and modern theoretical physics,' *Atti della Fondazione Giorgio Ronchi* XLIV: 115–49.

No external process, no electronic or chemical probe could yet discern any indication of this sort of idea. This is only possible to that singular and most special noetic probe, which is what evolution has wrought for us in our own self-awareness: introspection. This is the stage when ideas are too fragile to be expressed, whether the expression is in words or dance or song or mood swings, or merely in some vanishing psychosomatic urgings like tiny beads of sweat almost invisible on the forehead or a barely advancing heart beat so little faster that no objective EKG can record it. At this stage, then, many ideas take their first unformed form in the immense cavern of human awareness. (Some are more shaped, certainly – as those that are thrust forth bodily by some special external event, a special sudden perception: sunrise in a second or an actual but unmeasurable physical presence. But even these are different.) Now we are describing those barely self-aware states that just pass into recognition by the self: 'Thus, yes!' Sometimes, in this stage, one stops for a moment and asks oneself: 'Wait a minute. Did I really think of something? What was that idea? Can I get it back? Let me think. What brought it on? What was I thinking of before?' And so on. All of us have, over our youth and adult lives, learned a thousand such tiny little tricks that help us – who knows, others may well use the same – to tease up once again, from the barely effable, the pre-sensed idea, the pre-conscious conscious, the doubly abstract, barely energized anticipation of the presence of a notion.

IDEA-FORMING CREATURES

Of course, just as with space, time, and pain, there are no ideas about unless there are creatures about capable of having emerge within them that special quality of experience: ideation. That is: the tree falling in the forest does not have the idea of its falling. It is probable, however, that most higher mammals and certainly all the primates do experience ideas of this nascent threshold quality. Some may well experience firmer and more rigid ideas, but certainly these pre-consciousnesses as a start: sensations remembered, events recalled, anticipations apprehended, the tree falling (because of a loud crack) apart from the tree falling.

Spiders, we think it is safe to note, and probably most birds and surely the fish do not have any such nascency. Their large central primary cephalic ganglion is insufficiently developed; possesses both insufficient homeostability from momentary environmental onslaughts (resilience) and insufficient variance-processing capacity (ambiguity-tolerance or *scedasticity*). Even though bio-homeostasis of the internal milieu has reached a great degree of resilience, it is still not yet enough to risk the energy/energy interactions necessary to ideas. It is not merely *as if*, but quite literally that the steady state which we say is bee, spider, bird, and fish – perhaps because it is sometimes able to achieve all those excellent, different, first-level things: hives, webs, swims, flights, migrations – can and does remain in bee-state, fish-state, bird-state, spider-state under a great many extra-ordinary maturational and environmental alternations. None the less, even these are not enough. These animals are insufficiently internally stabilized and insufficiently internally flexible to permit even nascent or threshold *ideas* to form. This requires higher order still: higher stability, higher home-ostasis, and vastly greater scedasticity processing or plasticity, events which in all probability begin in evolution with mammalian life. Why, we do not know, but few pre-mammalians appear to us, even in our most generous of moods, to be capable of that degree of exquisite internal awareness, of tiny near-threshold internal energy changes, which would allow or compel us to perceive them as idea-forming creatures. As the willow is unaware that it weeps, no insect or bird or fish or reptile or amphibian knows that it knows that it is threatened or sad or even hungry. It just responds motor-ically (kinaesthesis is thus present, and in not so rudimentary a way) in the necessary survival manner to reduce these various tensions *sans* ideation. That is: absent the tensions, absent the response. Although these animals can be trained in many ways and do exhibit considerable learning ability and anticipation, ideation is minimal. That also requires excess EOQ which these animals do not have in requisite sufficiency. Idea-forma-tion is thus a form of *play*, as is all of philosophy.

THRESHOLD OF THE IDEA

But for the mammals, there is a different story. Of course, what might be the threshold of ideas for goats or chipmunks or dolphins we *have not* the slightest idea. That is, we can formulate the (many) questions, but not their resolutions.

I might, in this discussion, well be accused of writing nonsense, since these concepts are so close to the limits of language and so difficult to express – except for the fact that we also have, as yet, hardly any more concrete an idea (or scientific model) of what it means for human beings to 'have' or 'feel themselves to be in possession of' nascent ideas. Indeed, the very idea of the threshold of the idea, as such, is still new in my own mind, it is just barely more than a pure nascent wave even there. As in the calculus, one may speak rationally (so it seems, though sometimes . . .!) of the presence of 'vanished quantities', infinitesimals, so in sensory-rational psychology one may equally rationally (this time buttressed by the empirical sensory sciences) speak of ideas not yet in appearance: the presence of vanished qualities.

INTERFERENCE OF IDEAS

If mind is a wave, an energy process in purest form, is it then a mere analogy to consider or 'talk' of the 'interference' of ideas? Or, in the mirror, is Thomas Young's great experiment in light (*vide infra*) really an analogy to what happens first in mind? It is my repeated contention that, of all the 'objects' in physical reality of which we can have awareness, light is the most special because it bears so close a resemblance to mind and to mental reality. But gravity is also special, as it 'makes' the water flow. Which is why both 'waterfalls' and 'fire-rises' carry a particular fascination for all creatures with minds: they appear as physical echoes of their most hidden inner intellectual dynamics. The fire always strives upwards, the water downwards, as if both know better than we where to go. And the manner of this going displays infinite variety while the whole displays an encompassing unity. A better description of mind would be hard to come by: fire and water, cleansing and light, warmth and coolness. The static and symmetric projective tests of Hermann Rorschach and others, for example, succeed only partly in being resemblances to fire-rises and to waterfalls, as Rorschach would be among the first to admit. However, think what fine projective tests these latter would (and do) make: 'What do you see in this fire?' 'To where does that water transport you?' 'Why?'

If ideas are waves, do they interfere, destructively and/or constructively, as do waves of water in the pond and of light-radiation in Young's great experiment?[2] Do ideas interfere, if coming from one coherent source (from which they may all be said to be in 'temporal phase', thus, one book, one speaker, one's own mind), so that sometimes certain aspects in constructive interaction become sharper and exhibit themselves in greater contrast, while other times different aspects become duller and exhibit themselves in muted contrast, as if being destructively culled? This requires, does it not, mental *simultaneity*? Is all this merely analogous to the physics or is the physics analogous to it? As ideas achieve greater and greater experiential reality and precision, as they pass from barely an 'Ah' to a more confident 'Lo!' and then to a robust 'This', are not some aspects initially well sensed now pushed below perceptible differentiable contrasts, and others brought to higher and higher supra-threshold levels?

IMPORTANCE OF MIRRORING

Let us not make the mistake of going from the physics of human invention to the mental flux of human invention. Rather, all these processes go the other way, in mirror fashion: from the flux of mental life to the flux of at least some objective (gadgeted) reality. Thus: that light appeared to Thomas Young in his great experiment, so incredibly magnificent in its simplicity, to interfere constructively and destructively, did this prove that

---

2 Recall, also, that fires 'heat us' in two ways: by increasing the random molecular motion of air molecules in the intervening space (convection) and by emitting visible and especially infrared radiation which the skin absorbs as heat.

light 'was' or 'is' a wave or, rather, that *it appears to operate as waves among ideas already do operate*, and that what Young was really doing was to recognize in the action of light the, already sensed if not overtly known, actions (fluxations) of his own ideas?

Of course we have to mean something more than merely this: that our mental processes function so that they compel us to the conclusion that light 'must be a wave' when we observe that, after passing coherent (in phase) light through two tiny and closely neighbouring holes, shadows are cast on some opposite and appropriate screen which then exhibit (both to film and to our eyes) comprehensible, mathematically reasonable, alternating dark and light rings. To be interesting, and even important, now we have to mean something more like this: that Young, in perceiving the results of his experiment, was somehow recognizing what happens in his own mind in the operation of ideas. Thence, his real discovery was not so much that light exhibits a wave-character, but that light exhibits a mind-character. What I am trying to express – and I use this phrase so often, because these ideas are equally often that close to the edge of my own precise awareness – is that light *per se* is the closest objective 'thing' (process) in physical reality, of which we can gain knowledge, which acts according to laws similar to those governing the interactions of the abstract energy-flowing events of higher mental life.

Indeed, if gravity exhibits both wave-like qualities and particle-like qualities, as well as radiant flux exhibiting these, it is only natural that the higher and the lower forms of life, mental life and single-cell life, also exhibit these polar characters, because these dynamics (of radiant energies and of gravity) were the primary energy fluxes and perturbations during somatic evolution. It is thus to be expected that mental life should exhibit some characteristics of the dynamics of gravity-geometry (some ideas are weighty, do compel directions, are clearly geodesics), and some characteristics of the dynamics of light. Though both these ideas are near to the edge of meaning, it is more than mere analogy that ideas do shed light and give us insight, i.e. inner vision and illumination.

The most dramatic bio-objectifications of gravity with which we have intimate contact are probably the flow of water and our own upright posture and, hence, kinaesthesis – our upright vs. sleeping posture and, hence, vestibulation and proprioception. And the most dramatic objectifications of radiant flux with which we have contact are the sun and the diurnal cycles and rainbows and light, and, eventually, our own eyes. As the ancient Greek sage Plotinus put it, 'To perceive the sun, the eyes must be like the sun.' In the study of the physics of such events, as far as possible removed from man, we ultimately succeed merely in exhibiting man's inherent dependence upon and resemblance to and evolution from the cluster of those two special polar and inherently dualistic physical realities.

CONTRARY GESTURES

If mental events are both wave (in pure mental-energy form) and particle (in pure neural-impulse-transmitter form) then their inherent nature is also dual, as are these aspects of external nature. Consequently, it is *natural* that there exist (that we discover them, there at the ready, in our own minds) many mental tricks that take advantage of or involve this sort of doubling. *Mirroring* is one such mental event of such great importance that it will concern us in a special treatment. Another one, of great fun, asks for simultaneous opposing thought-gestures, as for example to *pat* one's head with *one hand* and with the *other hand to rub* one's stomach. (It is clear that only children can do this!) What happens, of course, unless one is very adroit, is that both hands sometimes pat and sometimes rub, and that only rarely does one succeed *simultaneously* in guiding one hand to do one thing and the other hand to do the other. These commands interfere. This is a form of kinaesthetic rivalry, better recognized in more passive forms in binocular vision and binaural hearing. This means that in one brain locus, or in co-ordinating loci, contrasting efference copies are difficult to generate.

It is the simultaneity that causes these clashes, and which thus constitutes evidence for energetical interference. The mental self-instructions, even in this simple yet opposing form, are hard to 'issue'. It is much easier to alternate the hands in both tapping or both rubbing.[3] What is difficult is to issue and execute the (to us, virtually) contrary message: rub and tap, one gesture *continuous* and one gesture *discontinuous*. Even though we 'know' from the neuroanatomy that different hemispheres are involved in their confabulation (left brain controlling right hand, etc.), the difficulty that we have in elevating these contrary ideas to the efference copy level (of instructing the separate hands to do different or opposite things at the same time) is very strong evidence that the instructions are interfering destructively (quite in Young's sense) and are thus not being construed or elaborated *entirely separately in separate and non-interacting neural locations*. The anatomy, as so far known, must tell only part of the story. Otherwise, as with walking and talking, we should have no difficulty at all in doing two things at once. (NB Actually, this is only a manner of speaking: these are not *things*, objects, that we do, but processes in which we engage.) Of course, in the expression: 'He/she cannot sit-and-think at the same time' (or walk-and-talk, or read-and-understand, *ad infinitum*), there is a not so hidden scorn and the direct implication of mental retardation. We do naturally expect some dualistic skills in ourselves and our fellows. In everyday activities, there are many double and triple and even

---

3 And the move into depth psychology is absolutely direct. Ambivalent (love–hate, joy–sorrow, etc.) states evoke such compelling and often painful tensions because the emotions pull one simultaneously along opposing geodetic routes. And of course these are energy oppositions, not objects which oppose.

quadruple gestures that people execute quite naturally simultaneously, and this is generally known and understood. There are many also that some can do but with which others have various degrees of difficulty. Young students, for example, are notorious for being able both to study well and to listen to rock music (probably less well). Others can plough a field and sing. Others can tie bundles of wood in a lumber-moulding factory while rehearsing the theory of relativity. Others can type and carry on a conversation in the same language, or even (or, perhaps, more easily) in different languages. Some can take and receive morse code while talking away at a great pace. And so on. The limits of these dualities, as it happens, are not known because their importance has not been realized.

These games are marvellous, and do pose for us at least one special mental problem, which is this: can two different (opposite – if we know what that means)[4] ideas be held equally at the forefront of consciousness at the same time? Can two sensations? If so, what does this imply about mental function? Of course, a chord of music is not two or N-sensations of opposing separate notes. It is a new sensation developed from the organization (not the sum) of N sensations. Some people can tease out the separate tones in the chord. Some cannot. The same is true of ideas. Complex ideas are wholly new in themselves, and are only poorly, often incorrectly and usually disastrously modelled as the sum of separate individual notions.

MATHEMATICS AND SENSORY DIMENSIONALITIES

The sensory-rational evidence is that simple unitary opposite sensory qualities (blue–yellow) can easily be so held; less so, closely neighbouring qualities (royal blue–navy blue). This is why mathematics is so easy, and so much fun. One can mentally keep the problem and its solution fully in grasp at all times, while one is trying, if with great and inelegant effort, to traverse mentally from the problem to the solution in that particularly rigid and special journey-form that we term a proof (cf. Chapter 4 on Pythagoras). This means, of course, that mathematical thinking is a most healthy sort of thinking, a species of mental exercise that stretches one's sense of self-awareness of self-awareness (the reverberating kind) to its limit, yet at the same time makes manifest the highest sense of vigour and majestic flux that sometimes also appears in great art and in great empirical science, but more rarely.

It is ultimately the most natural and relaxing thing in the world for a human mind to 'do' mathematics. And one thing that aids us in this virtuoso mental juggling is the fact that we can deal so often with

---

4 We sense-know that up–down are opposites, but what is the opposite of standing up? Standing on one's head or lying prone? What is opposite to a wall? A presidential invitation? Lo, another riddle-game.

dimensionalities: not actual measurements, but the idea of them. This gives us a fancy perch, easy to leave and come back to.

URWORTEN AND URBEWEGUNGEN

It is another contention of sensory rationalism that almost all original adjectival-adverbial words (the Freudian *Urworten*) were dimensional words. After exclamations and interlocutions and then after substantive words – agreed upon and easily repeatable sounds referring to specific things (objects) or animals or people – and thence words describing efforts and actions (verbs) such as walking and running and making love and holding and throwing and eating, etc., came words describing qualities: hot–cold, near–far, up–down, rough–smooth, kind–hateful, ugly–beautiful, safe–dangerous; and adverbial modifiers such as: rapidly–slowly, cautiously–carelessly, and so forth. (But not: hard–hardly, at least not in English!) These *Urworten* refer to primary or fundamental phenomeno-logically differentiable qualities of experience; they refer to all those qualia that are not part of the physical universe but are part of the human sensory universe: short–long, slow–fast, loud–soft, sweet–sour, blue–yellow, heavy–light (which should probably be 'lite' to distinguish it from its other meaning), dark–light (this time, in the proper form), soft–hard, flat–steep, and so on and on. As soon as the mental dimensional qualities were increasingly differentiably processed (by the advance of evolution) so that they could be experienced distinctly in and of themselves, and the dimen-sion itself be clearly and distinctly experienced as separate from other neighbouring dimensions, then these various modifying dimensionalities could be transformed into an expressive mode (and, please recall, how expression is, via reafference and efference copies, another aspect of sensory function) and come forth as *Urworten* or *Urbewegungen* (basic facial expressions and body gestures, such as thumbs up or the sign of the devil or snarls or smiles or scornful pointings or laughter, and so on).

There are, as it happens, many word-sounds still prevalent in all languages (probably more prevalent in those closest to nature, those least developed and least removed from the onomatopoetic state) which in fact *simultaneously mean their own opposites*. That is, they have these two meanings on one dimension. Which means that they define the dimension by its ends, which is the best way since, in many geometries, there is only one geodesic between two points. That is to say that, by the single expres-sion, both of the near end-points of the dimension are indicated and, it is my contention, were so indicated in virtually *all* stages of early language. Or, by a single *Urbewegungen*, opposites are intended. The context tells which, or whether it is both. One-syllable words or a simple wave of the hand (raise of the eyebrow) would be best for such central things, because that would be least costly in EOQ consumption; but I do not assert that this is always also true.

AUTANTONYMS

Consider some of these words, which my father, the English language scholar Joseph Twadell Shipley, aptly called 'autantonyms'. His favourite is the slang: 'fat chance'. It means: 'slim chance'. Mine is this: to be *fast* means, generally, to move or go rapidly, to do something quickly, hither and yon. But to be *fast* also means to be stuck onto, as in glue this *fast* or in *fasten this button*. *Fast* also means not to eat, which is a retiring state; and some women are *fast*, which is an advancing state, and means that they are bold and turn partners over too rapidly.

Consider some others. Although a few of these may seem odd and unusual, the theory suggests that they are *Urworten* and that, most probably, many other words as well (primeval expressions) began in this same way: as identifications of *single* relatively pure sensory dimensionalities, and then of even some relatively consistent and regular *multisensory* dimensionalities, wherein a single expression meant contradictory ends:

alight means to land and to take off;
sound off means to shout out one's name and to turn off the noise;
the sun *comes out* but the fire *goes out*;
'he sure has it' means 'he has it all', but 'he's had it' means 'he's all washed up';
a *plane* is a flat surface but *to plane* is to run a boat rapidly at a sharp angle across the water;
to be *a part of* something is opposite to being *apart from* something;
a *scattergood* is one who is wasteful, who *scatters things about badly*;
the famous racing driver Stirling Moss once noted that: 'the object in auto-racing is to win going as slowly as possible';
'Give me a break' means to 'Give me a hand', but it also now means 'Cut it out!';
to execute means to kill, it also means to produce or to perform;
to found means to establish (as to be the founder of something), it also means to fall helplessly, to stumble;
to cleave to is opposite of *to cleave in two*;
the *be* in *beheaded* means to remove something, a head, but the *be* in *be*knighted or *be*trothed means to add something;
to shed light on something is different from to *shed off water*;
to butt means to crash heads, but *the butt* is the rear-end;
to resign means to quit, but to *re-sign* means to start up again;
to rehearse means to carefully study over, but its origin is *re: hearse*, to put once again into the death carriage.
to *spen* means to grasp or to hold but *spend*, which is the same word, means to use up or get rid of. And there are many fine alternatives: Spend*all*, spend*er*, spend*good* (NB – not 'bad' . . .) and, of course, spend*thrift*, which is itself an oxymoron. A recent translation of Ibsen's

A Doll's House took the liberty of translating his words as 'spendswift',
a word that I cannot find in the *OED*, though the idea is marvellously
sound.

An interesting autantonym is *blind*. The primary meaning is: to be
unable to see. It is primary adjectival, but it has a verb form: to blind. It
also has a nominative form, *the blind*, meaning: those who are blind. But
there is another noun form, which is: *a blind*, meaning: a place in which
one hides to get a good view of the scene without particularly disturbing
the scene. The scene is thus blind to you, but you peer out at it in particularly protected and keen ways.

In the story 'The Sisters' by James Joyce, there occurs the interesting
word: gnomon. This is used by a young boy to describe Father Flynn who
has gone mad. Father Flynn is thus a 'know-man' who becomes a 'no-
man'.

The prefix *de* often plays an autantonymic role. The meaning of many
prefixes is dual, and of some suffixes as well.[5] *Nier* (in French) means: to
deny. Thus deny in English means to *not deny*. Or it could be used for
emphasis, as: *to denude* means *to nude*. But *de-fenestrate* means to *de-
window*, as: in 'throw out of the window'. *De-cry* means to cry out against.
But *denigrate* means to claim *as black*.

Of course, one could argue in two ways (simultaneously pro and con,
sic!); firstly, that because these are, relatively speaking, rare, it cannot quite
be true that they represent the primary state of all words (there would
otherwise be more of them around today) or, secondly, that all languages
have so evolved that the dimensionalities involved have now come to be
so distinctly polarized that there are separate words for each end rather
than only one for the whole. A way to decide, for example, might be to
try to discern whether primitive languages have more or less autantonyms
than do advanced languages, a task unfortunately beyond this author's
skill.[6]

As it happens, this fundamental idea of autantonymic *Urworten* has
been mentioned by Freud (as have so many creative ideas in psychology)

---

5 Cf. Shipley, J.T. (1984) *The Origins of English Words*, Baltimore, Maryland: Johns
Hopkins University Press.

6 In recent work, V. Shevoroshkin reviews the the long and extensive efforts to develop
some conception of the sounds and words of the Urlanguage, the proto-world language
or the 'grandmother tongue' of mankind. The words for body parts, for example, such
as eye, ear, hand, leg, and so on, seem to be the most fixed and stable words. They are
thus the commonest throughout all languages and most easily traceable. Then follow
the verbs that derive from them: see, hear, grasp, walk, and so on. For example,
'changa-sanga' referred to the nose, to odours, to smelling, and probably also to that
which gives off the odour. I do not know whether good and bad odours are meant at
once, but I suspect so. As far as I can tell, however, the concept that I am developing
here, of the primacy of the unity of both ends of the adjectival dimension, is not noted
in this work, or looked for. So, the suggestion is made for the future. Cf. Shevoroshkin,
V. (1990) 'The mother tongue', *The Sciences* May/June: 20–7.

albeit to make a somewhat different point.[7] Freud, as is well-known, was struck by the prevalence in dreams of symbols and contexts and situations which appeared upon careful analysis to mean their opposites. Dreamworks could be understood sometimes in accordance with their surface appearance and sometimes in accordance with a precisely opposite signification. The appearance of father might mean father; but it might also or instead mean mother, or maybe even son. That depends. The appearance of fear might mean fear, or it might mean love as by the fear of losing something that one loves, or of losing love. And so forth. These ideas, not of *ambivalence* but of *antithesis*, have thoroughly penetrated modern psychoanalysis. That they have not also come thoroughly into general psychology is merely a sign of how superficial most of modern psychology continues to be.

In any event, Freud, in support of his ideas of antithesis in dreams, cites the earlier work of the philologist Karl Abel (in 1884) which introduced the concept of the *Urworte* and, indeed, the concept of the antithetical or autantonymic *Urworte*. The very title of Abel's work states as much: *The Antithetical Sense of Primal Words*.[8] Abel, in fact, makes the assertion that the Egyptian language, one of the oldest and longest continually enduring of the truly ancient languages, exhibits these autantonyms in considerable number, and even more so Arabic, which he illustrates in great detail. And, he asserts, this is also true of the Semitic and Indo-European languages. He adds: 'How far this may happen in other language groups remains to be seen; for although the antithesis of meaning *must originally have been there* to the thinking members of each race, this need not necessarily have become recognizable or have been retained everywhere in the meaning of words' (italics added). Abel then quotes the British philosopher Alexander Bain (*Logic*, Vol. 1, p. 54):

> The essential relativity of all knowledge [sic], thought, or consciousness cannot but show itself in language. If everything that we can know is viewed as a transition from something else, every experience must have two sides; and either every name must have a double meaning, or else for every meaning there must be two names.

These ideas, of course, do not yet make precise the concept of dimensionality, but they surely do presage my own concepts. Naturally, certain 'things' and certain 'processes-that-we-take-as-things' do not logically or perceptually have opposites, but those experiences which are inherently dimensional do. Some *things* which do not, so to say, 'have' or 'evoke' opposites in us might be 'clouds' or 'leaves' or 'waterfalls' or 'dogs' or 'battles' or 'fires' or 'Freud' or 'Abel'. Some *processes* that do not have

---

7 Freud, S. (1910) 'The antithetical sense of primal words', *Collected Papers*, Vol. IV, trans. J. Riviere, London: Hogarth, 1953, pp. 184–91.

8 Abel, K. (1884) *Über den Gegensinn der Urworte*, Leipzig: W. Friedrich.

opposites might be: 'thinking' (*vs.* dreaming?, wishing?), 'breathing' (perhaps because it already is both *in* and *out*), 'tasting', and 'praying' (although, I suppose, one might more vainfully 'demand' of God, if that would or could be considered an opposite). However, most emotions and many other human experiences, and surely all those that are inherently or more apparently sensory and thus orderable in character can have and/or exhibit opposites. The strong inherent rationality of emotions, their reasonable and wholly co-ordinate function in the survival of the individual and of the species, attests to this fact. (See, for example, de Sousas' recent if non-Freudian reaffirmation of this classical Freudian view.)[9]

Abel, in fact, felt that all primal languages (e.g. Chinese) would be found to be rich in these autantonyms, as is precisely my point. He cited many interesting examples and, because of the relative obscurity of this reference and their fascinating range, I repeat a small selection of them here.

a) *In Egyptian hieroglyphs*, for example, Abel found:
   i. *ken* meant *strong-weak*, which has since been divided into *ken* – strong vs. *kan* – weak.
   ii. other combinatory autantonyms are: command/obey; old/young; far/near; bind/loose; and so on.
b) *In Egyptian generally*:
   i. åfṭ – jump up and rest
   ii. bōk – go
       beḳ-a – sit
   iii. kek – fire and darkness
   iv. ṭerp – take and give
   v. sa – beautiful and common-vulgar
   vi. sme – voice and hearing
   vii. tem – close in and shut out
   vii. s'ēu – wide
       ts'eu – narrow
c) *In Latin*:
   i. *altus* means high and deep;
   ii. *sacer* means holy and accused;
   iii. *clamare* means to cry, *clam* means softly.
d) *In Indo-European* languages in general:
   i. Sanskrit – ârât: far and near
   ii. English – to bid: to promote and to offer
   iii. Latin – cedere: to go and to come
   iv. English – down: down and mountain
   v. German – kleben and klieben: to cleave

---

9 de Sousa, R. (1987) *The Rationality of Emotion*, Cambridge, Massachusetts: Bradford-MIT.

vi. Russian – glas: eye
       – glass: voice
vii. Latin – must-us: young/fresh
      English – musty: old/stale
viii. Russian – lekar: physician
      Lithuanian – ligga: illness
ix. Great Russian – slovo: word
      Little Russian – slovo: secret
x. Latin – siccus: arid
      Latin – succus: juicy
xi. Greek – αχολή: leisure and diligence
xii. English – to lock: to close and gap (Loch)
xiii. English – *without* means with and out

[I have included some of his English examples here to show that they are, unfortunately, not all that convincing. While this may give us pause in accepting his treatment of other languages, it does not invalidate the basic point. It may be that we have to go to still earlier forms, or be more critical as to what we accept as truly autantonymic.]

e) *In German*:
    i. *Boden* means attic and ground-floor (of a house);
    ii. *bos* means bad, *bass* means good;
    iii. *stumm* means dumb, *Stimme* means voice;
    iv. *wider* means against, *wieder* means together.
f) And in *Arabic* in which Abel found the largest number of autantonyms:
    i. abbana – rebuke and praise
    ii. amamun – small sack and large sack
    iii. baslun – forbidden and permitted
    iv. g'abrun – king and slave
    v. tarraba – have great value and have little value
    vi. g'aunum – white and black, viz: horses and camels
    vii. ḥamîmum – hot water and cold water
    viii. ḫallun – lean and fleshy
    ix. ḫannaurun – bad luck and fortune
    x. za'mun – true and false word
    xi. diżâjatun – short and long
    xii. zama'a – be quick and go slow
    xiii. sung'atun – white colour with black spots and black colour with white spots
    xiv. siwaⁱn – another as oneself and oneself
    xv. šariba – drink and thirsty
    xvi. ša'aba – gathered and separated
    xvii. ašwahn – ugly and beautiful
    xviii. ṣaqaba – near and far
    xix. ġarimun – the guilty and the faithful

>   xx.   qa'ada – sit and stand
>   xxi. qar'un – menstruation and purity
>   xxii. nag'lun – son and father
>   xxiii. aqwa[i] – rich and poor
>   xxiv. kullun – the whole and a part
>   xxv. nakira – do not know and disapprove
>   xxvi. ahnafa – laugh and weep

[I am unfortunately personally unable to confirm this list among my present resources. My Hebrew-speaking associates do not easily find similar autantonyms in Hebrew, though I do not doubt that some exist.]

Abel (and Freud) go on to discuss words which are sometimes pronounced backwards to stress (boat–tub) or to translate meanings (hurry–Ruhe=rest) but these shifts have less significance for us, unless one could find instances *within* one language in which as the sound reversed the meaning did as well: such that *pu* would mean down or *toh* mean cold, and so on. People have always been struck by the potential in language and words for mystical paradoxes, and have wondered for ages what is meant by such reversals as: 'Devil-lived' and the like. So, clearly, language is a pathway to many profundities in the character of the human mind. And this autantonymic process is one.

Actually, there are in all languages hundreds of examples of repetitive phrases (of the 'willy-nilly', 'skitter-scatter', 'namby-pamby', 'nitty-gritty' sort). Some few indicate their opposites.

> To say 'NO NO' usually means an emphatic No, but the double nega-tive strictly means a yes. 'No, I don't want no bananas.'
> To say 'YES YES' usually means an emphatic affirmative. But to say 'Yeah, Yeah', in that marvellous slangy fashion, means No. And, of course: 'Yeah, right!' means 'Wrong!' in the marvellous and widespread form of autantonymity known as sarcasm.

And all languages use litotes, those astonishing expressions which, by their exaggerated emphasis in one direction of the dimension, mean the other:

> 'Boy, was he polite, huh?', meaning that he was a crude, opprobrious, impolite ass.
> 'Well, it certainly is a nice warm day today, isn't it?', meaning that it is freezing.

Such expressions are, in fact, quite common not only in everyday speech but in formal parlance as well. In international circles, for example, when one says 'He is certainly an accomplished diplomat' what one generally means is that 'He is a devious and thoroughly conniving scoundrel.'

OXYMORONS

And, of course, there are the oxymorons ('sharp-pointed' plus 'stupid-dull') which are so much fun, both because they are sometimes so impossibly apt (thunderous silence) and because they are sometimes so perfectly absurd (military intelligence). There are even books on such things.[10] Consider a few more, for their fun and puzzling interest: rehabilitated criminal, sweet sorrow, political (or computer!) science, conventional wisdom, constant variable, intimate stranger, holy war, civil war, just a little bit pregnant, vaguely aware, criminal justice, eloquent silence, fast food, legal brief, plastic silverware, rules of war, vacuum filled, new traditions, marital bliss, peace offensive, exact estimate, limited obligation, legal ethics, and so on and so on.

Oxymorons are forms of the recognition that in joining the two ends of some dimension, one is often involved in something that is simultaneously an absurdity and yet a wholly rational expression. The *double entendre* is a better known form of this same duality, if less direct.

To be hot and cold at the same time is also readily possible, as it is to see neighbouring (but not overlapping) yellow and blue. Overlapping yellow and blue give white (additive) or grey (subtractive), depending upon how it is achieved. Thus those colours cannot be oxymorons, but tones can in that they retain their integrity in chords. And visual shapes also can, that is: *A* can be seen simultaneously where *Z* is. So can an infinite set of opposite figures: for example, a circle and a sunburst. On the other hand, some visual perceptions of neighbouring shapes depend upon the fact that the contour edge of the figure can be organized in only one direction (say, as the faces in Figure 7.1) or another (say, as a vase), and not in both simultaneously. These issues of sensory-cognitive simultaneity are critical for sensory rationalism and deserve much study. They are precisely analogous to having opposing thoughts at once, equally in mind.

To be in love and in hate at the same time is also readily possible and, as the best psychotherapists tell us, very common indeed. The whole concept of ambivalence in depth psychology is a realization of the signal importance of such simultaneous opposing states, perceived somaesthetically at once and at once influencing behaviour and other extero-perceptions and experiences. When the patient is able to come to realize that this *Urzustand* (primeval condition) does have these opposing motivations and emotions within it, and that these conflicts are what cause the pain and the indecision and the cruelty to others, the patient is well on his/her way towards a more congenial resolution. The very word 'resolution' means that the patient now comes to distinguish what previously he/she

---

10 For example, Blumenthal, W.S. (1986) *Jumbo Shrimp and Other Almost Perfect Oxymorons*, New York: Putnam–Perigee Books.

Figure 7.1 Rubin's alternating vase and faces. See Rubin, E. (1915) *Synsoplevede figurer: studier in psykologisk analyse*, Kobenhav: Nordisk, Figure 3.

could not, even though, to an outsider, it was obvious all along that wholly opposing processes were bitterly clashing.

ONOMATOPOESIS AS THE PRIMARY FOUNDATION OF VERBAL COMMUNICATIVE GESTURES

A key point of this argument is also this: when the sensory dimension is simple and unitary (as blue–yellow, hot–cold, sweet–sour, rough–smooth) as opposed to complex and multiple (as honest–dishonest, loving–hateful, eloquent–grovelling, munificent–revengeful) it is probably true that *onomatopoetic* transformations of the dimensions therein or thereof are most easy to perceive, compel themselves most readily to the mental fore, closely paralleling the way in which dogs bark, growl, or wag their tails, or cats purr and monkeys groom. Consequently, onomatopoetic dimensional public expressions – which, if codified, may eventually become words – are those which come forth most readily and which are least *mis*understood. This is why onomatopoesis *must* be the primary origin of all simple quality-state expressions, and thence of words and of gestures and of signs and, eventually, of writings. By this intrinsic coherence (frankly perceptible) between receptive modes and expressive modes, all peoples find onomatopoetic *Urworten* and *Urbewegungen* most readily comprehensible and communicable with the least additional EOQ in either expression or attention.[11] A roar would surely be the best way to say lion, if it did not get confused with leopards and tigers and maybe even elephants. All words for deer and gazelle should express swiftness, as in some African languages in which the word for antelope is something like: swish, for the sound that the wind makes as it brushes against the fleeting fur. The word for eagle should be soar. And so on. *Water*, in this view, is a poor word, since it is far removed from its onomatopoetic origins. *Aqua*, unfortunately, is no better. But WA-WA is fine, in the common infantile onomatopoetic form. A sign gesture of the hand indicating waves would be still better.

In any event, what this means generally is that some ideas are easy to cradle simultaneously in mind, even in various and opposing forms, especially if those forms lend themselves to intrinsically similar geometries via many modalities, or at least via two. 'Sharp', for example, applies to a touch, a sound, a smell, a taste, and a tongue, even a mind ('He has a sharp wit'), and so this word is easy to hold mentally in at least all these variously intrinsically similar geometric forms. But words like 'erudite' or 'indefatigable' seem much more difficult to consider *simultaneously* in their more complex inner infinite multiplicity, although even this unfolds readily in succession. Or a word like 'nuclear bomb'. There is nothing really onomatopoetic about nuclear. Perhaps 'bomb' is a trifle onomatopoetic in that it does sound like a sound: boom. Perhaps it really should be: boomb. In both the Greek and the Latin *bombus* means: a noise. Bombastic, of course, is to be pompous and to make plenty of bones about it.

SIMULTANEITY OF THOUGHTS

The mental state of being in possession of two or more ideas simultaneously is never a simple event to analyse. Even ambivalence, which seems always to imply excessive caution or anxiety, need not do so. Often it contains a happy core, a joyful and mentally exhilarating state that we all wish to encourage in ourselves and in others, as when we think of jokes, or mental puzzles and cognitive tricks, as in 'Time flies!' 'No, time stands still. We fly.' And when we try and, especially, succeed in *expressing well* (say, in poetry) some hitherto inexpressibly subtle internal mental *Urzustand*: 'When to the sessions of sweet silent thought . . .'

---

11 Darwin already keyed us to similar processes. See his classic (1872) *The Expression of Emotions in Animals and Man*, in any edition.

By the qualification 'expressing well', we can only mean that the intrinsic geometry of the internal mental state is now, finally, or so it seems to us, adequately preserved and correctly geometrized into the verbal gesture. In the awareness of that preservation-projection we are also able to take note of the fact that it is done, approximately, commensurably and is starting the communicating process as intended. When we resort to circumlocutions and to such apologetic weasel words as: 'Well, it is difficult to express', we are admitting either one or all of several things: (i) that the intrinsic geometry of the internal mental state is imprecisely perceived, for a small infinity of reasons; (ii) that the intrinsic geometry of the internal mental state, albeit well perceived, is too complex for us, then and there, without some remove and thought, to elevate adequately to the mental-body periphery; or (iii) that the internal state is clear and simple, but that we do not then and there know the proper words that could get this across well to others. There may be other reasons, as well. Perhaps one can elevate the internal geometry to the expressive surface in French or in poetry or in dance, or in some sort of speaking-in-tongues, or in a private gibberish or word salad, but not in any way that one guesses that others then and there could comprehend with low EOQ. Perhaps one can only express it in pure onomatopoetic fashion, like panting or gagging or shivering or howling or dancing up and down and sideways, but then finds these *Urbewegungen* insufficiently refined. In this, of course, lies the success of mime as an art form.

More and more of these increasingly differentiable experiences and increasingly subtle thoughts occur to adult mammals in evolution and then to adult humans in social development. This is one advantage that adults have over children, and one disadvantage: they are further from onomatopoetry. The wise have this same ambivalent advantage over the dull, and at least some modern and cultivated rustics have this over some modern urban savages. It is a mixed blessing.

HUMOUR

The problem of the simultaneity of thoughts is fascinating to all, if only in part because this explains the delights of many jokes and much humour. We expect one thing to occur, we anticipate one thought, and yet another is thrust suddenly in its place. This unexpected character of the intellectual twists of humour is what makes humour what it is: gentle, clever, and, in the best jokes, brilliant, because you yourself could not have thought of that.

> The mother rushed into the bedroom at about 9 am, and shook her son gently on the shoulder. 'Jim,' she said, 'you're very late and you have got to get up to go to school.' Jim rolled over into a corner and mumbled: 'Yeah, I know, Mom, but the work is too hard and I can

never get it done on time; the teachers are always too demanding; and the kids all hate me; and everybody is shouting at once, and I want to stay in bed!' And then, the mother said: 'Yes dear, I know. But you are 39 years old, and you are the principal, and they can't get along without you!'

Humour, of course, is also often onomatopoetic and exhilaratingly healthy. While it can have many obscene and black forms, it is generally a positive if complex sensory-rational process. It deserves special treatment, which I hope to undertake at another time. Now I must pass on to ideas in a more concrete form, closer to what mind must generate if mind is to model reality correctly. Reality is not humorous or ambivalent, though humour-generating, ambivalence-generating creatures may interact with it. Reality, we think, is real. Is it?

8 Ideas of objects vs. ideas of ideas

IDEAS OF OBJECTS ARE STILL NOT OBJECTS

Ideas of objects, of course, are still not objects. They are ideas: special noetic awarenesses of energies interacting with energies. So also are meta-ideas: ideas of ideas.

PRIMARY VS. SECONDARY QUALITIES

And this points to an additional, and this time critical, error that has often been made in the history of this problem by many philosophers (by David Hume, for example, but especially John Locke) concerning the important issue of 'primary' qualities which, in some way, may be said to reside in both object and perceiver (say, form and position) vs. 'secondary' qualities (such as colour and flavour) which may be said to reside more exclusively only in the perceiver. The error that this has encouraged is this: to think and/or imply that sensations and ideas are only or even primarily of *things*.

A relatively recent treatment of the Descartes–Boyle–Locke–Hume evolution of our ideas concerning the various complexities in these relationships – between the material structure of bodies and naturalistic human interactions with them – shows mostly how complex and unsettled they are. See Alexander (1985).[1]

The complexities of what each has actually said about primary (e.g. size, shape, motion, position) vs. secondary (taste, colour, smell, pitch) qualities, and of what the present best understanding is, still raise controversy at the highest levels of philosophical debate. And I cannot hope to disentangle these here. But I can show, even from ancient history, how truly specious this distinction really is. The laws of perspective, for example, have been known since Leon Battista Alberti's marvellous constructions in the mid-fifteenth century (1404–72) and indicated even then that visual

---

1 Alexander, P. (1985) *Ideas, Qualities and Corpuscles: Locke and Boyle on the External World*, Cambridge: Cambridge University Press.

size as experienced is wholly dependent upon both *physical* (primary) and *representational* (secondary) distance. (NB Tactile size is always ignored by these philosophers, as is size by aural or olfactory modes.) And modern perceptual psychology has shown that these two sorts of qualities of distance are universal, and enter the *experience* of distance via contextually determined events, with not even stereoscopic depth excepted (see Shipley 1987).[2] Hence neither *size* nor *distance* is different from *colour*. And colour, as we have already noted that Newton told us some 300 years ago, is a contribution wholly of sensory psychophysiology.

What is important for sensory rationalism, however, is not to show that this somewhat muddled distinction between sense qualities is specious, but rather to show that this emphasis on *material qualities* of any sort results from an excessive and over-balanced concern for man's relationship to material or thing-like reality, instead of for man's relationship to the dynamic flows of the textures of reality, of which things are only a small subset defined, in the stimulus space, by especially high energy accelerations.[3]

MOST EXPERIENCES AND IDEAS ARE NOT OF THINGS

In the vast library of ideas, as it happens, most entries are of immaterial forms and unsteady processes not of objective things.

Even ideas of very rigid objective objects are still ideas: they exist in (by virtue of) a mental dynamics not specially or in any way different from how ideas of ideas exist. If one wishes to be concrete, consider ideas about apples vs. ideas about justice. Some of the referents of these thoughts are rigid, some flexible; some near, some unattainable; some are mere aspirations.

Of course the new animal and the new human infant must come to terms with the reality around them, which expression means, I suppose, 'to come to be able to put it into memory or, for the child, into words'. Of the fact that this reality does include objects there can be no doubt. Things like beds and mothers and milk and faeces appear, in some vague undifferentiated (undifferentiable?) way, as things. Part of the task of the infant during maturation and development is the gradual discernment of the difference between the 'thing' character of, maybe, mothers and beds, and that of their own feet and elbows, in contrast to the non-thing character of laughters and cries; also, of the differences between the approach of those causes of light-shadows which may have many other thing-like attributes and that of clouds across the sun or the moon at night which really do not. When the child is afraid of the 'night' or of the 'darkness'

---

2 Shipley, T. (1987) 'Field processes in stereovision,' *Doc. Ophthal.* 66: 95–170.

3 The role of textures in evolution and in sensory-cognitive function is central, and I am hoping to treat this in another work, 'Textures in science and in art' in preparation.

(those truly *non-things*), this means psychologically that he/she has not yet fully abstracted those events from the thing-character that they may originally have had, or evoked.

As a corrective to William James' most famous (and wrong but widely quoted) comment about the infantile 'big blooming buzzing confusion', we may emphasize what he said correctly just a few sentences before this:

> In his dumb awakening to *something there*, a mere *this* as yet (. . . better expressed by the bare interjection 'lo!'), the infant encounters an object in which (though it be given in a pure sensation) all the 'categories of the understanding' are contained. *It has externality, objectivity, unity, substantiality, causality, in the full sense in which any later object or system of objects has these things.* Here the young knower meets and greets his world; and the miracle of knowledge bursts forth.[4]

EXTERNALITY AND CAUSALITY ARE NOT THINGS

Externality, though a primary attribute of phenomenal experience, is itself not a thing, certainly; but the child has to become accustomed to the distancing and removal process and, so to say, give up 'asking for the moon'. Causality is not a thing, certainly; yet even today men of the most sophisticated sort have trouble giving up the thing-like qualities of that: everything has a cause, therefore there must *be* (exist) a thing, *first cause*, which is that *cause* which *caused* (and forever is *causing*) *itself*. Thus: GOD. Borges, the great poet, wrote enthrallingly of the constant recycling of first causes: the eternal return. The quest for causes and the intimate quality of experience which we term 'causality' are, together, two of the most compelling and motivating processes in human intellectual life. But causes are not, so to say, things, static and just resting there. Causes are really (in whatever special way one wishes to take that adjective) inter-actions of energies which come to be perceived in that special way: unique collocations of forces, symptomatic organizations of processes. There are temporal aspects in the complex phenomenology of causality which exhibit a rather stern directionality, from past to present to future. This is the flow of EOQ from greater to lesser, in storage anyway; and represents a human integration of internal somaesthetic processes with externally evoked processes (causes that arouse cause) such as visual collisions and aural high accelerations coupled with discontinuous glisses.

And, surely, the causality perceived in events taking place among objects involves the complex character of the inherent and persistent consistency or unity of the objects. But this has subtleties as yet wholly unexplored. Let us suppose that this tree branch fell against that wall and did indeed knock it down. The wall and the tree, though, still retain certain aspects

---

4 James, W. (1892) *Psychology*, Cleveland, Ohio: World, p. 16.

of their original *self*, persisting from those earlier times-spaces (that one, at least) before the causality relationship-process took place between and joined them. That is, the tree does not suddenly become non-tree when it falls. If, when it falls and the wall crumbles, the tree turns instantly into dust (as it no doubt will, more slowly over the decades), then the perception of causality may go the other way: the resistance of the stone wall was such that, though it crumbled, it turned the tree into dust.

INTERACTION WITH NON-THINGS

Pure energy-energy interactions, as we have noted, are what mental life is about: the flux of ideas and sensations and intimations and intentions and allowances and understandings and hopes and anxieties and causal ascriptions and plannings and remembrances and loves and urgings and stubbornnesses and determinations ... these and a thousand other qualitative states of mental being constitute the mental processes which, in global unity, we call mind. These dynamics can only be understood as energy-energy co-ordinations, not as thing clashes.

There is no doubt that the dealings which we must have in reality with things, and in mental life with their representations (memories and the like), are critical for our survival. We need foods, which do come mostly from the set of bio-things; but we also need water, which is not thing-like at all, except perhaps to a very thirsty person; and we need air which is wholly 'unthing-like'. But, regardless, these species of interactions are not at all what make us human. What make us human are our incessant and equally necessary interactions with non-things. We control our emotions, we express our gratitude, we say our goodbyes, we vote our preferences, we stand on our ceremonies, we cook our own geese, we build our castles in the air (even choosing where, when, and which), and (alas) we constantly tempt our own and everyone else's fate ... all without hitting a ball or milking a cow or baking a roll or dusting off our hands or even picking up our fair share.

Where the philosophers and thence many of the psychologists went wrong was in their overly simplistic emphasis on the reality of those aspects of the universe that appear to us as *things*, i.e. these that succeed (in virtue of their intrinsic being) in displaying (and thence evoking in us) some at least requisite threshold share of thing-inducing attributes. (NB For the spider and the bird and the fish, although they are pathmakers and pathfinders, none the less, mostly what are things for us are not, for them, really extant in this way. The web is not a thing for the spider, it is the veritable universe. The branch on which the bird perches is not a thing for the bird, though a worm might be or a kernel of grain. For the fish, water is its air.)

The perception-evocation-inducement of *thingness* is a special process that has not yet been well described, although some psychologists in recent generations (Adelbert Ames in particular and perhaps James Gibson and A. Michotte) have been dedicated to trying to do just that.[5] Sometimes a cloud might possess thing-like attributes, when it is especially dark or especially foreboding or especially white and bright, even hurtfully shining so as to seem self-luminous. The sun, sort of, 'looks' like a thing but, as it gives heat to our air and our bodies, it is not at all felt like a thing the way a burning coal flying against one's leg feels like a hot-thing; and so on: the argument is now obvious.

Minimum skills in reality co-ordination (mapping) and in thing-object mental representation are certainly essential to survival and for mate-rewarding processes (not as things, take note), and mankind may well share many of these latter skills with higher animals. But so many of the processes that characterize human life are dynamic and require interactions and integrations with non-thing-like processes that to overlook these is to overlook the primary intellectual challenges that must be met by any veridical science of mental life.

The mind, above all the other senses, integrates from all the other senses and eventuates in interactions which deal sometimes with things but which often, and most often in modern complex civilized life, deal wholly with non-thing attributes and processes. Whatever else it means when, as the economists often say in threatening tones, so much of modern life deals with 'information processing', this surely also means that dynamic relationships and not static things are to be dealt with. The thing-culture of the nineteenth-century industrial revolution is for them already old-fashioned. We have 'word processors' today, not writing tools.

All dictionaries in all languages are certainly full of words which are not nouns. But we mean much more than this. Many of those *things* that we denote as nouns only remotely possess or exhibit to us *thing-like* attributes. They are nouns only in default of a richer lexicon. Perhaps there should be a separate set-name for them, as: metanouns. It may be useful, and fun, to list some. The reader can realize how far from things some of these are. Consequently, how limiting a view it is to consider that the human relationship to objects is only or even primarily that which children must come to terms with, and that which dominates civilized adult life.

The contrary is the case. And this insight, henceforth, calls for fundamentally different views of psychological development and of mind.

One could go on. Clearly, it develops that much of the human dictionary of mental noun-rests (things about which it has become, by custom, easy to think), if not most of it, includes dynamic and changing entities,

---

5 Michotte, A. (1962) *Causalité: permanence et réalité phénoménales*, Louvain, Belge: Publication Universitaires; Gibson, J.J. (1966) *The Senses Considered as Perceptual Systems*, Westport, Connecticut: Greenwood; for A. Ames, see Cantril, H. (ed.) (1960) *The Morning Notes of . . .*, Rutgers NJ: Rutgers University Press.

Table 8.1 Nouns that are not objects

Rain	Wind	Sunlight	Wine	Arbours	Harbours	Men	Women
Soapsuds	Coughs	Leaps	Laughter	Strife	Criticism	Curses	Water
Touch	Sound	Music	Shade	Cold	Currents	Opinion	Stance
Posture	Ink	Slide	Letters	Literature	Sadness	Outing	Opposite
Symmetries	Races	People	Votes	Milwaukee	Clouds	Stars	Tides
Bays	Come-uppance	Mud	Salary	Thoughts	Motives	Rumours	Grades
Acids	Smells	Hints	Absolutes	Dreams	Births	Wounds	Itches
Pains	Fields	Forests	Rivers	Valleys	Cliffs	Harmonies	Memories
Essays	Errors	Successes	Difficulties	Pets	Poems	Hopes	Vertigo
Lists	Death	Variances	Means	Support	Focus	Nobility	Custom
Cheer	Flight	Herd	School	Compulsion	Hub	Nub	Condition
Opening	Vacuum	Plenum	Distance	Neighbour	Hug	Comfort	Amazement
God	Dread	Ego	Self	Hunch	Walk	Day	Night
Gesture	Novelty	Consciousness	Heart	Tag	Flow	Bias	Acceleration
Cant	Timbre	Shear	Drag	Friction	Force	Addition	Leverage
Decision	Tax	Government	Freedom	Solvent	Solution	Nation	Posterity
Ancestor	Dance	Habit	Intuition	Explosion	Push	Threat	Puzzle
Mother	Son	Father	Daughter	Lover	Future	Past	Time

and flows and fluxes and transitions, not one of which has any *primary* quality and not one of which, when one comes down to it, is a thing. That is an absolutely extraordinary fact of which any acceptable depth psychology must take account. It is with this widespread mental intercourse with dynamic events that the psychology of sensory rationalism is developed directly to deal (see Table 8.1).

CHILDLIKE HOPE TO MAKE MACHINES TO BE MINDS

Truth is not a thing, nor, actually, are the eyes and the ears and the skin. Rational thought is not a thing; no one can hold it up or otherwise display it in primary qualities of shape and location, as aspects of some sort of device. This is another reason why the attempts to model the brain-mind (I am never quite sure which is intended) by mechanical or electronic devices are all wholly beside the point. Gadgets are models for a most incredibly small and restricted set of our ideas of processes. That is why we invent devices and strive to build them: to meet certain simple, specified, usually detached ends more easily than we could otherwise do (see Chapter 10). Devices do not (so far) invent us. These ends are our ends, not those of the machines. Even the plough does not know that it digs up the earth, or that it must go in straight rows. Sad as this may seem, even the lovely spring rain does not know that it falls, or that it cools the fevered brow.

Even the planting of seeds and the harvesting of crops – probably another of woman's (not man's) contributions to exosomatic civilization – do not involve us much with things: although seeds are, sort of, things, and the crop is, sort of, a set of things, and ploughs (yes) and fields (well hardly) but straight furrows (not at all). Moreover, the ideas of agriculture and of ploughing and of sowing and watering and fertilizing and cultivating and weeding and culling and harvesting . . . these are not things, yet these are the crucial events that engage us in the organization and integration of all those energizing dynamic agrarian realities so essential to civilized life.

The purpose of this essay is pointedly not to reject as false the whole set of problems that classical philosophy chooses to address; it is, rather, to point out that, while they were once very real, even important and valid problems, this was so only in terms of a limited and constrained view of human sensory-rational function. The eyes may allow us to pick out the best apple from the tree, or the nose if we can get in close (animals can do this from afar, especially insects, so that for them smell is sometimes sight), or even the mouth if we can get away with a small nibble . . . and surely this shows that, towards our survival, we are all gifted at many interactions with things even (or primarily) at the level of the single mode. But, even for the apple, it rapidly becomes much more complicated. The apple seed is not yet the apple; nor is the apple sprig, nor the plant, nor the tree, nor the leaf, nor the branch, nor the sprout, nor the bud, nor the flower, nor the tiny bead, nor even the green crabby thing. *The apple* is that big luscious red-thing there on the branch, hanging off the limb. One may, of course, represent that thing by any of those rests which appear to us as intermediate stages, or as a *mélange* of all, as in a modern still-life. And, although the process is continuous in some sense, qualities (and bio-developments) are emergent in others. Overall, we perceive growth mostly as a continuity into which we put (by our decree) some relatively arbitrary flex points and cusps. And so, what we sometimes look upon, feel, smell, taste as a thing – apple – is really a process, not significantly less dynamic than the processes that we call son, daughter, husband, or wife. If computer modellers are so marvellously gifted at turning lead into gold, at making 'true' models of the human mind – that most dynamic and complex of all dynamic complexities – would not it be a good test of their skills to tackle a much more simple complexity such as 'make me an apple'? This, after all, is a mere plant.

Bubbles generally disappear when you try to get too close to them. In this, they are gigantic manifestations of a sort of quantum uncertainty. Although we can tell, pretty much, where the bubble is and where it is going, we cannot tell what the bubble is. That is, *qua* bubble, there are no intermediate states. Bubblehood is discontinuous, emergent. We just simply cannot get hold of it, *qua* anything, only of some pitiable squashy puddle. As far as I can tell, much of psychology approaches human mental life in this same way: grapples with it, tears at it, reduces it to a smudge or a smear, a collapsed bubble, and, from that terribly diminished 'thing', tries to create a science commensurate to that extraordinary, complex and lovely flowing process which it once was. Modern western psychology in particular, which could know better but chooses not to, has done this to mind: destroyed it to study it – first by totally rejecting it (behaviourism), and then by only gingerly accepting the importance of conscious mental dynamics. Cognitive psychology, after all, seeks largely to mate psychology to artifical intelligence. Both these psychologies have thus reduced the mind to simplistic linear puddles with the aim of thereby encouraging clever gadgeteers and designers and builders in their not always innocent hope that they can successfully make its model. The most dynamic and unthing-like process in the universe is thus 'elevated' to analogue switches.

Clearly, the sensory-rational view seeks another way: to treat mental life as an irreducible process, not ever as a thing; and to devise methods for its analysis consistent with the principles of biological evolution, on the one hand, and with the highest and most subtle flights of imagination, on the other. Only from this, and from the *mélange* of depth psychology and perception, can come a science that one might call a veridical psychology.[6]

---

6 This is attempted by me in a treatise on cognitive function, *The Illimitable Multiplicity of Mental Life*, in preparation.

Let us look at some facts (although facts are mostly relationships and so-called 'hard' facts are mostly not things!). Thunder is no object, nor is love. That is, the object of love is itself a potentially loving reciprocity. Love is only an 'object' when little or no reciprocity is proffered. True love is a mirroring, as any pair of happy spouses will recognize, if they cannot tell. So are the objects of mind. The mind is its own mirror. And that is an important notion.

PAIN IS NOT AVOIDED OUT OF PRINCIPLE

Consider pain. Pain is not a sensation merely like blue (referring elsewhere) but it is, in and of itself, an end: its own image. That is, while the sky and the flower may both *be* blue, neither are forever so: we can look away. That the mood may also be blue means, in part, that blueness (as with many if not all simple sensations) may come synaesthetically to transcend its objective meaning. We cannot turn away from that. But to assert that the leg is painful is not to indict the leg but the pain. The leg is the leg; some 'it-thing-process' experienced simultaneously with it is painful. That is, pain is not so much, as blue is, an indication of something else. Though it often is that, pain is mostly just indicative of itself. It is thus both itself and its mirror. One strives to take away the pain, not the leg. As Hume has put it: 'one avoids pain because it is painful, not out of principle.' Admittedly, often one sets fractures and salves burns and binds sprains, and in most cases accepts that there is nothing to be exorcized: there is just pain as in a cramp or as in cancer. Situations too can be painful and, in a very real synaesthetic sense, generate psychic pain. In which case, one modifies the situations, transforms them into different situations, be these family patterns or school patterns or whatever. While the pain may seem partly to 'exist' somehow apart, out there, it really 'dwells' in one's interaction with these situations. When the gut is painful before a test or the head after, it is still the pain that one addresses, not the gut or the head. Exorcism as medicine mostly tries to remove the offending spirit-sight-infection-virus – only sometimes actually changing its location. This latter is true because so many human pains are referred.

Most grown-up creatures, adult humans among them, are reasonably satisfied or at least comfortable with their own bodies. They have come to terms. On average, our bodies are not too painful. That is what evolution has wrought: relative pain-free states. What we become dissatisfied with are all the adventitious pains (sometimes uglinesses) that the body is heir to; but we do not then, except in extreme circumstances, reject the body as we might reject a rotten tomato or try to run from the lowering sky. What we reject is the pain.

Thus, whatever else pain is, it is not some-thing; it is not some primary or secondary property of some object, of a certain shape (primary: interacts with other shapes) or of a certain dullness (secondary: no interaction as dull-pain with others). It is, alas, just pain. Anyone who has achieved a certain familiarity with pain knows what I am trying to describe better than I am succeeding. The closer that my description gets to the precise and correct one, the more empathic synaesthesia my word-images arouse, then the more I myself and some of my readers wince a bit and turn away. I may even stop writing. This level of writing is the source of the extraordinary appeal (influence-transference, perhaps, is better) of great literature. Such a writer as Franz Kafka writes so directly, so closely at the edge of this synaesthetic, onomatopoetic reality, that readers who comprehend him also experience. Pain, in his literate hands, is pain in the readers' phenomenology, clearly and simply. That is why he is great and others not.

HAVINGS

The state of being in pain or having a pain or having 'anything' (sic!) is, thus, far more complex than the state of merely seeing or smelling or touching any, no matter how complex, set of real primary *objects*. Having is very much like being, and it enjoys considerable multiplicity. Consider a tiny list:

Havings: apples
          ideas
          pains
          inspirations
          fears
          stomach rumbles
          big muscles
          swelled heads
          long finger-nails
          lecherous thoughts
          fits
          a happy-go-lucky spirit
          nightmares
          premonitions
          a marvellous sense of humour
          blond hair and green eyes
          high hopes
          intimations of the divine
          bats in one's belfry
          guilt feelings
          dissident tendencies
          three boyfriends at once, on leashes
          5,000 head of cattle

> itches
> lice, and
> giggles. . . .

Clearly, not many of these sorts of 'havings' have much to do with objects in the sense of the concatenation of primary and secondary properties. The having of cattle and of lice may share some properties in terms of numerosity, but that is about as far as it goes. A cow may be an object, but 5,000 cattle is a herd. The havings of pains do share some character with the havings of giggles and itches, even those with measles and cancer and dislocated shoulders. But no serious writer or psychologist would want, voluntarily, had he/she the option, to use one word for any such pair of dynamics, much less for all of the set. In English, and in many other languages, this extraordinary culturally imposed limitation has not been surpassed despite (i) thousands of years of somatic (unconscious) language development in the hands of innocent and unsuspecting humans and, thereafter, (ii) some hundreds of years of exosomatic language evolution (now quite deliberate) at the hands of great poets and great writers. Language, for psychology, has immense distances to go.

This particularly striking linguistic paucity is merely one incompleteness from among many, in the innumerable regions of human experience in which the need can be demonstrated, under a sophisticated sensory-rational analysis, for richer and more precise and more satisfying and more multiple and more onomatopoetic and more synaesthesis-promoting expressions (even words). One is not sure, even, whether the syntax itself is up to the task. James Joyce, for example, one of the greatest authors in any language and of all times, thought not. As psychologists, we can only agree.

As time is no object, nor space, neither is the idea of apple, nor is the 'object' of justice. As we move from apple to sensation to idea, we move orthodromically further and further from apple as thing or object (the physicists' thing) to apple as pure mental process. Here it can enter drives and emotions and hallucinations and even riddles and tricks and games. This is what evolution has wrought: a removal of the dynamics of mental life from the dynamics of the sensations of objects in much the same way that it has moved the dynamics of mental life from the dynamics of sensations of sensations. To *have* a pain in the gut is not at all the same sort of possession as it is to *have* an apple in the hand. But one can mimic this, as the great mime Marcel Marceau was so extraordinarily able to do, by either mentally (as he) or actually (for the rest of us) gluing an apple to the palm of one's hand and then watching oneself (experiencing oneself) trying to rid oneself of that offending *thing*. In this instance, like a headache, the apple does not so simply 'go away'. Some people are also ridden in an analogous manner by ideas and thoughts: of inferiority, of persecution, of sexuality, of grandeur, of the need to endlessly repeat certain (now we can say it) *Urbewegungen*. The intense struggles that they must often go through to 'rid' themselves of these 'overriding' processes become the grist, now, for the mental therapists' mill. Some people are also victimized by useless limbs that they cannot move or feel, and would like to be rid of. Others, even after the limb is gone, retain a phantom sensation of it, as we have already noted (see also Chapter 11). Still others may 'possess' wholly unwanted supernumerary phantom limbs.

For a concrete example, suppose that your chair *stuck fast* to you as you tried to stand up. Or consider the nose of pride and venery on Pinnochio; or the hump of sin and selfishness on one's own back; or the world on all our shoulders. One cannot run fast enough to escape those sorts of fastenings. There are images throughout all of mythopoetry of sensations and mental illusions and burdens taking on some real-thing-like character and sticking to one, as do headaches and belly aches and all the other baleful sufferings of mankind. Pitiable are we that, not only are we unsatisfied by the numerous and weighty burdens that we must bear in starvation and inanition and in lack of shelter and clothing, we must also go out of our way to invent more abstract burdens of guilt and of greed and of lack of candour.

These psychological states can become veritable things, as neural reverberating circuits, and do not function only in a pathological dynamic. But these are not the objects of classical philosophy or of modern physical science; or even, sadly, of most of modern psychology. These states possess an entirely different sort of objectivity, requiring new ways of 'naming' and 'looking'. They are simultaneously both entities and representations of relationships. Thus, philosophy in a specially novel key still has much to say.

Although it was once parsimonious to consider that the world–mind interface was made up only of things, and perhaps of filled spaces (plenae) and filled times between (for which no word exists in English), this is an entirely false view of what mental life is all about. Experience, even experiences of things, are not things. Mental life is about experiences.

NIELS BOHR AND GREAT TRUTHS

Physicists try to consider things as far removed from experiences as it is possible for them to go. Mathematicians have it much easier; they have given up things altogether. They can have ghosts of vanished quantities and they can go as close as they wish to a thing boundary but not touch it. Only the naive physicist thinks he can do the same: approach so close to reality that human input is made vanishingly small. Most of the best physicists have always wondered, some have even worried, about the influence of their own mental processes upon their models of non-human reality. And absolutely all of the best physicists know full well that their own mental processes bring some constraints to their models that they may not ever even know about, much less be able to exorcise or make as small as they would like. Niels Bohr, one of the most influential modern physicists, tried to address this difficulty head-on with his magnificent concept of complementarity: of a transaction between facts and minds. 'There are trivial truths and there are great truths,' he said. 'The opposite of a trivial truth is plainly false. The opposite of a great truth is also true.' Consider that 'oxymoron' for a moment. This relates to Immanuel Kant's admonition about *Ding an sich*: the impossibility of knowing things in themselves. Processes are even less knowable than things, because they are always turning into other processes.

To make *things* (mental gymnastics) easier, consider the actual 'state of affairs'. Water, one of the primary aspects of our universe, is no object. Nor is fire. One conquers some (although few) mountains, admittedly, as objects, but the conquering of fire was (is) never mere objective control but some event more like the vanquishing of an eternal enemy or the making of an eternal friend. That is why Prometheus is such a great mythic figure. Man in this way came out of darkness and cold and fear, with Prometheus as his guide. Fresh air too is no sort of object, though it is more necessary to our continuance than most things. Routes, as we have stressed, are also not objects; nor are methods, instructions, or plans. The sun as we have already noted is not an object though it has many attributes thereof and a relatively unambiguous objective reality, which means an existence apart from man. It gives light when there are eyes to see light, and it gives warmth when there are skins and other senses to feel warmth. To those that can perceive-generate hope, it may also give that; to some others, dying of thirst amid an arid wilderness, it may evoke-generate the Bohrean opposites of fear and hate and evil.

Clouds, of course, are no objects; nor is the weather in any form, even raindrops (but, maybe, hail:) though tornadoes and hurricanes begin to approach in quality-set what we may call objective status.

Things, processes, and events in nature which are especially consistent and reliable in form, colour, shape, temperature, loudness, etc., are particularly good at becoming (being perceived as, generating the organized sensation-idea of) objects. But shadows are not, nor is the soul of which the shadow is such a universal representation.

It is natural, in some developmental psychologies, to hold that the child's task is to become comfortable with the world of objects. That he/she must learn to separate him/herself from those things around, and to take on an independence, from the mother first of all, and thence from his/her own excrement and then, beyond all of that, from food and 'reachables' and audibles and visibles and smellibles, etc. And, no doubt, to a great extent somatically this may be true. But in the extra-somatic world that defines man so uniquely as a being that can be good, as opposed to a being that can merely be hungry or tired or awake, the intercourse that the child has with mere somatically pertinent objects becomes diminished. Indeed, that task, – of getting to know the hard and reliable entities and how they may be manipulated to private personal ends – is achieved by most insects and animals quite as well as by man. The newborn chimp easily finds the breast, so does the dolphin. Surprisingly soon, the young eagle catches the field mouse. If anything, man is somewhat delayed and muddled in such objectivities, in relation to other animals with a less protracted neoteny. The body image of the growing child and, of course, the image of the self that gradually comes to be, cannot at all be understood in thing-like objective terms ... as, indeed, modern neurology and the psychology of self-development and actualization so convincingly demonstrate.

Since no other creature is able to generate so aloof a sense of self, it is wholly understandable that this requires a special neurology and a protracted neoteny so that man may escape the mere animal intercourse with pure objectivities and enter the world beyond: of near abstract breezes (which receive the name: zephyr), and of near abstract forests peopled with nymphs and trolls, and of near abstract trees in-dwelling with magicians, and of near abstract heavens full of gods.

What establishes man among animals as unique, *inter alia*, is this: that he becomes far more involved with abstract non-objective realities than with objective ones. A criminal act may be a real objective process or event; it may also exist wholly in thought (though most laws have difficulty with that); but in either case there is no such thing as *justice* which can then be hung upon it to give it grace.

In successful building, there does indeed eventuate a real physical dwelling, a shelter, a house, a home – a primary thing that others besides man can know. But there is no thing *approved* that one can hang upon it to give it beauty or even shelterability or the ability to resist storms or to give rise to a sense of the hearth.

In going to school, certainly, one finds there teachers and children and all sorts of objective benches and tables and chalks and books and blackboards and rulers and calculating abacuses and slates. But none of this, collected together, can give the extraordinary controlling *purpose* an objective presence. That emerges from intentions and collective social aspirations, processes in whose objectivity, apart from many years of schooling, few children can come to believe, even though that purpose *exists* with many of the qualities of sternness and inflexiblity that some, in the adult community, come to experience as real rather than ideal.

At court, we have judge and jury and plaintiff and defendant, all very real processes that some may wish to term objective things; but, of course, bio-social events are never stable enough, really, to be things. Moreover, the ascertainment of guilt or of innocence is not equivalent to the identification of some primary-quality *thing* that emerges in its perfect rigid and formal entirety from this interaction. Rather, ascertainment is a process that unfolds therein wholly abstractly. The end determinations may indeed have real and even momentous pertinence; but the process of ascertainment is wholly unreal, as memory is unreal. That is, without human cognitive intervention, there is no ascertainment. That emerges as a quality from human interactions. God let light be; also honour and morality.

Naturally, the having of an idea and the having of an apple and the having of a leg share some qualitative processes and dynamics. This is attested to by the crude fact that the same word does fairly well suffice. But these several havings can, none the less, readily be distinguished, as we have noted. In truth it is a sign of mental health that they are so distinguished; failure to do this well often results in psychological disasters.

PERCEPTION OF GRADIENTS AND DIRECTIONS

The ultimate primitive task of a sensory system is to perceive gradients in some pertinent neighbouring bio-physico-chemical energy distribution. Thus, already in the perception, it involves us with direction: in which direction is that gradient going? When the rate of change of the rate of change of the gradient, its acceleration, becomes great and in sensory-rationally confined times and spaces, only then do we have the emergence of the perception of objects. An apple, for example, is a red surface (an impression) which, in roughly circular but characteristic shape, abruptly desists at its border: the red disappears and a grey or green or some other colour comes in its place. One reason that sunsets are so special is that, unlike apples, they never do exhibit abrupt changes. What is so appealing is their intense gradualness, though some sunsets may exhibit even more vivid reds than apples. Few would perceive sunsets as objects or things; but they are perceived as events with sufficient general if non-specific reliability that we may, none the less, name them.

Indeed, for some scientists there exist a thousand names for clouds, none of which are things or objects. There are 10,000, at least, names for colours, none of which are objects or things. There are thousands of names for musical notes and hundreds for sounds that are not even musical notes (such as laments and weepings). There are names for species of everything, but species are not things. Nor, actually, are animals or plants, although they exhibit to us, arouse in us, certain thing-like attributes, especially when we pet them or eat them. Or they eat us!

Let us suppose that it is safe to assert that a rock *is* a true thing; that is, if it truly *is* a rock and not a masquerade of one! The rock is as good a model for the objective, unchanging reality as we may find. But, as science tells us – and sometimes we can even see and feel and hear this for ourselves – most thing-rocks do dissolve away or erode or are burnt-up in volcanic eruptions, and then even they may lose some of their set of primary characters as rock-things. But we can compromise: rocks, generally, are thing-like enough *in our lifetimes*. What then are diamonds: rocks or jewels? What then are metals: magnets or coins?

This raises an interesting classical problem in philosophy. While it can, as so many, be traced back to Aristotle, its formulation is relatively new (cf. C. Myro in Grendy and Warner 1986).[7] Suppose one is holding in one's hand a silver coin. What, actually, is the object that one is holding? That is to say, the coin as such is a new object, recently minted; but the silver is, so to say, as old as creation, or maybe the Big Bang. In any case, the silver being *old* and the coin *new*, is the object in one's hand new or old? Some philosophers go so far as to say that there are two things in one's hand, one old and one new.

Such issues arise in philosophy because it has not developed a sensory-rational view of what actually is taking place. Suppose one is ignorant of coins, what then is one holding in one's hand? Like time processing and space processing and even rock processing, the thing is not present unless a processing system is also present to interact with it. If a child is holding the coin and does not know that it 'is' that, then it has no reality as thing-coin, then and there for that child. Only when you come and tell the child what he/she is holding, does that novel attribute emerge. 'Aha! Yes, I see it is a coin.'

ROSINANTE

Don Quixote once had an animal upon which he sat and rode. It was named 'Rosinante'. Rosinante means: 'Before, a horse'. That is to say, before Quixote took possession of him he was only a horse. Now, however, he is a steed, a majestic mount, a great and noble charger, a giant among questing beasts. Don Quixote's dragons were justly afraid! Windmills did really tremble.

This – we can now say 'strange' – problem in philosophy could exist as a problem only as long as the sensory-rational significance of knowing was not understood. That is, we humans perceive certain attributes of objects in pretty much the same way that animals do: this 'thing', so to say, has a certain thickness, a certain roundness, a certain heaviness, a certain shininess, a certain colour, a certain tinkle if one flicks it, perhaps a certain taste and smell if one tries to ingest it by those modes. Maybe it has a few other attributes as well: a certain hardness, if one bites it. Also, it has a certain set of pretty obvious uses, even to animals: it can be gnawed upon, it can be pushed about and chased, it can be picked up (even in the teeth) and tossed about, it can even be used to hit with, and maybe kill very small other animals. And so forth. For us, also, *qua* object, it has a small infinity of other uses: one can skip it on water; one can, of

---

7 Grendy, R.E. and Warner, R. (ed.) (1986) *Philosophical Grounds for Rationality: The Philosophy of H.P. Grice*, Oxford: Clarendon Press.

course, spin it vertically on a flat surface and try to keep that spinning going; one can reflect sunlight off it to signal with or to try to blind some creature or person; one can use it to hold down paper or to stop a leak in a pipe or to close off a burrow; one can use it as a wheel when making a tiny wheel-barrow as a toy for one's children; one can use it as a dead weight on a balance; one can tie it to a string and use it as a plumb-line; or, still tied to a string, one can use it as a pendulum or a sling; one can click it against a stone and use the sounds to call or to warn, or just for fun, or the sparks (if any) to start a blaze; one can use it as the roof of a small home for ants; one can use it as an eye-patch in case of some need or disguise; one can wear it as an ornament; use it as a gift; one can even barter with it, in trade for a pretty bead or an apple ... and so on and on, all without the slightest notion of (or sensory-rational interaction with) it as either metal or coin. So far, we have pure sensory interactions.

COIN VS. SILVER

Then, adding the information that it is metal (as opposed to some other natural material such as glass or wood or clay, etc.) opens the potential for another small infinity of interactions, provided that this new information is entering a mind that is also prepared to ingest that at new and enriched levels. Naturally, to tell a 2-year-old child that it is metal puts this message into a mind at a wholly different level of preparedness than, for example, it would be to tell a trained metallurgist or jeweller that this is silver. Each of these latter could now have an enriched (and different) small infinity of possible interactions with this object as silver, in comparison to that which they might have had with it as merely round or as merely bright or as merely smooth or as merely heavy. And these are enriched over what variances the child may have and over those possible in most other, less educated adults.

Finally, of course, one may add the information that this is a coin. To the child, this enlarges very little its already small infinity of possible interactions; similarly, to a person who is ignorant or innocent of what coins may mean; or who, though knowing what coins mean, has no possibility of buying anything. Say he is alone, way out in the desert, or is in a nation that does not have coinage, and so forth. On the other hand, to those who know fully what coins are and who are in a position to themselves make use of that knowledge in greatly expanded social interactions, then indeed a still further enriched small infinity of additional sensory-rational interactions potentially comes forth. One can now buy an infinite number of other things; or one can horde it, as one chooses. One can buy other things specifically to enhance the very same restricted set of attributes that the shiny disc had: a flashlight which produces and not merely reflects light; a full set of genuine tiny toy tyres; a lovely pearl necklace; and so forth.

The attribute of being a coin, then, as always, adds to or enlarges the potential scedasticity of the small infinity of interactions, provided only that there and then ingesting this information and having awareness of its significance there is a living creature that can in this way make some or a great variety of use with it. It is no good telling a chimp that this is a coin, unless one has previously trained the chimp to use this object and/or similar things in coinage fashion, as tokens for food and warmth, and so on.

For the psychology, it matters not at all that *qua* silver this object is as old as Methuselah whereas *qua* coin it was minted last week. None of this has any pertinence for our understanding of what one perceives to *be* there, except in so far as one is a 'silver and a coinage and a new and an old processing' creature. As we have shown, the processing of each such attribute, and of the integral collection of all such attributes, varies enormously between peoples, and for a great many reasons. Simply to be blind removes certain potentialities of interaction (e.g. shininess, reflectivity), and may even affect interactions with the object as coin or as silver in other restrictive ways, or in ways that may be richer than we predict.

When we say that something, like this silver coin, is a nice thing to *have*, we generally refer to things which we can *have in hand*. But houses belong in the set of such nice things; also wives and children; and subventions and retirements and stocks. Luck, particularly if fortuitous, and three wishes are all good 'things' to have. Although I personally do not comprehend how luck is a *thing*, others make it alive: 'Lady Luck'. Some people have it, some don't: 'Tough luck!'

Fate, also, is something that is not a thing but that appears thing-like, that haunts one, that controls one's life and destiny: to which one is always trying to give in or from which one is always trying (or ought) to escape. But fate serves only poorly my notion of an object.

Furthermore, while one may coherently confuse Fate with Divinity; any one who confuses God with a thing probably has not advanced in his religious-spiritual processing and understanding from the belief in (perception of) totems and in the rites of devil worship and satanism, and in the reality of vengeful or benevolent presences all around in those trees and in those rocks and in the raindrops and in the stars.

When the tree falls in the forest, for this person, God has ordained it, and the devil has induced it, and the evil emanations have cursed it, and the good fairies trapped inside have escaped from it. No one denies the reality of these event-processes; we only assert that their presence then and there at the falling does require a special fairy-quality evoking interaction with a specially prepared human mind. All of the physical 'things' in the world added up cannot emerge as that! Nor can all the laws of physics evoke them. These are qualities of human experience; they are wholly absent when that quality-generating-emerging human mentality is not also present.

SENSORY INTEGRATION IS THE KEY TO THE ORIGIN OF MENTAL LIFE

Like time-space-pain and causality, so purpose and intentions, even *being* itself are ideas to which the various single human senses contribute only in degree. Multisensory integration, once again, is the key to the origin of mental life. And when multisensory qualities share intrinsic geometries and directionalities, we have grounds for expecting mental states that are healthy and able to co-ordinate with the highest ecological multiplicity. But when the multisensory qualities conflict, in rate or in direction, then reflexive self-consciousness emerges to help with resolutions: 'What really is there?' As we have noted, Adelbert Ames spoke of the 'thereness-that-ness' problem. Some suggestions can now even be made as to what ideas, and particular resolutions therein, the various senses may specially create; and how sensory-rational conflict resolution may be achieved. We now turn to an adumbration of some of these.

9 Specific contribution of the human senses to cognitive function

LAWS OF EXOSOMATIC EVOLUTION

We have stated that vision is less important for survival than some other senses, and this is certainly true. Its extraordinary capacity for release gives this away. Congenitally blind neonates of many higher mammalian species, even undomesticated and in the wild, survive well and are cared for by their mothers until after weaning. This includes suckling, licking, retrieving, cleaning, warming, nesting, and nuzzling. It is important to recall how much more important smell is for most of these creatures than it is for human beings. However, adventitiously blinded adult humans could not have survived long even in the earliest food-gathering cultures, if we may deduce this sort of insight from primitive cultures found in the twentieth century, and from primate societies. The survival of the blind, the ill, the insane, the retarded, the maimed, and the old in modern society, and sometimes the high quality of life that they are able to enjoy, are signs of what we call civilization, and indices of its degree. Consequently, to the extent that some law such as the survival of the most fit ruled during somatic evolution, the *laws of exosomatic evolution are quite different*. Just how different, we do not know, although much has been written on these matters. In any event, it is only in relatively advanced and non-wandering human societies that the affliction of adventitious blindness is not immediately devastating and very soon fatal.

Furthermore, the fact does bear repeating that well over half of all the afferent nerve fibres reaching the brain are contained within the optic nerve. This percentage is sometimes exaggerated to as much as 90 per cent. While any such single figure is misleading, because the afferentation via the other cranial nerves and via all the thalamic and autonomic routes must also be contrasted to that via the optic nerve, and because multisensory interneurons must be considered, none the less it is true that cerebral arousal is very much a visually dominated affair. One set of the problems of blindness, which often goes unnoted by others, relates to loss of the diurnal light–dark cycle. Many blind people live encapsulated in a very real intimate neurasthenia. They may have difficulty staying 'awake'.

THE CUT OF DEAFNESS

This is also a problem for the deaf, but not quite so severe because the afferentation of the auditory nerve is not so great as that of the optic nerve. On the other hand, the deaf, in their turn, and most unfortunately the congenitally deaf, suffer from the deprivation of the major humanly evolved communication system, speech, in a way that the blind do not. This cut is what accounts for the justified irritability of some of the deaf, and for their relative isolation in so many even advanced human societies. Many deaf children are still taken as foolish or retarded, and the word dumb has misleading connotations in many languages and language groups. Many deaf have learned to stimulate themselves by signing to themselves or by tappings or rhythmic leg and postural jitters such as characterize normal adolescents. Even the act of humming becomes of value, for the pleasure of the vibration if not the acoustical resonance. Some of these function for them as do blindisms for the blind (such as rubbing the eyes and facial grimaces): to help one keep alert and awake, and for establishing some sense of dignity and private self.

The many modern sign languages for the deaf help greatly in this, because they have achieved for the first time a balance between expressive and receptive efficiency and aesthetics. They are both easy and pleasurable to sign, and easy and often delightful to view. They now involve a quite literal hand and arm dance, a grace of gesture to perform and to read, quite as much as that involved in fine speech and elegant oration. The fact that the best of these languages are pictorial and ideographic in form, and not alphabetical, is important. This is why they are, in fact, often finer and closer to true human mental states than speech. They resemble poetry more than prose, for example. It is partly our difficulties in embodying the unique human aesthetic in machine communication devices and prosthetic tools that will forever be a limitation on them. All who work seriously in this field are aware of the refined nature of this difficulty. That there are many secret sign languages (as on the floor of the stock exchanges and at football games, for example) and that there are many extraordinarily expressive vulgar signs and slang gestures (too well-known to need citation) attests to some of the arcane significance of such gestural communications.

Braille, the first really successful prosthetic method of communication, achieved its universal success because it created a synthesis of cognitive simplicity and gestural aesthetic. One can sit quietly reading Braille pretty nearly as unobtrusively as one can sit quietly reading printed script (though early reading was all out loud). And there are now Braille writing devices which are hardly more involving than normal note-taking with pen or pencil. The key to successful bionic instrumentation is, as in all of the best human constructions, some balance between efficiency and challenge and cognitive and aesthetic demands.

FALLACY OF SMALLNESS AS CLOSE TO ESSENCE

In any event, the senses in their interactions, and most particularly the visual mode on its own, are indeed constantly cascading up to the cerebral cortex such an extraordinary shower of messages as to have fundamentally eluded scientific analysis to this day. We simply have no real conception of what this cascade may be like, despite the enormous efforts devoted to this in the years since the discovery of the electrical waves in the brain in 1928. In truth, it is only within about the last fifteen years, via the method of the sensorily evoked electrical brain potential, that we could even look by non-invasive means at the normal electrophysiological, sense-related brain processes in healthy and alert humans.[1] Just to state the major difficulty is to reveal how far we have yet to go. Almost all the studies on animal function – succumbing to the classical monadic fallacy of smallness being close to essence – have been based upon recordings from fewer and fewer brain cells, eventuating in recent years in single cells. Consequently, many models of brain function have been derived from such isolated cellular processing. Further, many other models, really a separate set of them, have been derived from studies of brain-injured humans. A third set comes from the evoked or sensory-event-related potentials. These models are not yet at all integrated. In most studies of human experience and brain function and behaviour, we have little precise knowledge of which particular brain cells are involved, or brain columns, or even brain regions. Injury to one part of the brain does not merely affect that part of the brain, but may have widespread disinhibitory effects, for example, fully across and throughout both of the hemispheres. Sensorily evoked brain potentials, as evoked by sights or sounds or shocks or touches, or whatever, can be recorded pretty nearly from any position on the human scalp. And we are not yet sufficiently advanced to obtain precise localizing information by any non-invasive means within the human brain. Even biochemical and radiological methods are imprecise when compared to single-cell recordings in animals, albeit significantly more invasive than sensory studies. And the newer Pet-scan methods and SPEC and fast MRI are also imprecise. Moreover, in the general caring for brain-injured humans, as we have noted, the absolutely central point to be understood is that the cognitive function remaining is often startingly great, considering the nature and volume of tissue lost. Consequently, the *only* way that the function of the brain-injured patient can be usefully

---

1 Shipley, T. (1980) *Sensory Integration in Children*, Springfield, Illinois: Thomas. The evoked potential methods, however, do suffer from poor resolution. It is extremely difficult to get down even to several cubic centimetres. Other methods, such as the PET scan and SPEC and related radioactive imaging techniques (say fast nuclear magnetic resonance imaging), are said to give better resolution, below the cubic centimetre. Eventually, of course, we shall need non-invasive methods in the cubic millimetre range and better if the task of neuroscience mapping is to be seriously approached in this way.

diagnosed is as an attempt to be as normal as possible.[2] There is also some evidence in hydrocephalic children, though we have noted that this is controversial, that it is possible for them to obtain at least an average intellectual level of performance with as much as 60 to 80 per cent of the normal cerebral mass missing (cf. note 12 to Chapter 3).

Thus the savage effects of gross and adventitious brain injury cannot rationally be expected to relate to the effects of the loss of only one or two cells (even if they are some hundreds of microns in size), or of one or two vertical cortical columns (even if they are some millimetres in size).

SENSES CONTRIBUTE TO COGNITIVE PROCESSES

There is considerable evidence, as it happens, for what we have come to call residual vision, even in the presence of almost total loss of the occipital hemispheres to which, so we often think, all the retinal projections go. Obviously, we are wrong. Taking on their face this extraordinary resilience and diversity of visual neurology and taking to their depth the applicability of the laws of optical physics throughout nature, it is small wonder that vision is widely considered to be the most important of the senses. In humans, this is almost always first related to its prowess in orientation resolution, and in far-distance and near-depth resolution. And, second, it is related to its prowess in monitoring those events known as object perception . . . leaving gradient and process perception aside as yet.

It is important to emphasize, once again, the technical distinction between certain of these processes, in order to see that it is vision and not some other modality that is particularly important therein. We separate distance vision from near vision, and both from orientation. For distance vision, we have both the perception of how far the object is *from oneself* (absolute distance, AD) and how far two such distant objects are *from each other* (relative distance RD). For near vision, we have the important distinction between those objects perceived and gauged only with *one eye* (monocular depth MD) versus those objects seen and gauged by virtue of luminance and formal disparities between the images in the *two eyes* (binocular depth BD). For orientation, we refer very carefully to the lateral or vertical angles between one's own reference line (the straight ahead at eye-level) and *the object* (absolute orientation, AO) and the orientation difference between *two such objects* removed and out there from the self (relative orientation, RO)

In addition to the perception of distance and depth and orientation, in which vision excels, there are several other crucial contributions to relational cognitive function made superbly by the visual system, and by

2 See, *inter alia*, Luria, A.R. (1966) *Higher Cortical Functions*, trans. B. Haigh, New York: Basic Books; Teuber, H.L. (1960) 'Perception', in J. Field *et al.* (eds) *Handbook of Physiology*. I. *Neurophysiology*, Washington, D.C: American Physiological Society, pp. 1595–668.

other sensory modes somewhat less well. Among these is the perception of *inclusion*; something or class or event is perceived as being (dwelling, living, lying, etc.) inside of or within some other thing or class or event. This is the very perception upon which the syllogism itself is based: 'All men are mortal. Socrates is a man. Therefore Socrates is mortal.' That is to say, Socrates is perceived or conceived as being inside the class: men. In this way, the wolf is found in the sheep's clothing, and so is barred from the door. One of the first modern treatises on logic, by the great Swiss mathematician Leonhard Euler, modelled events in logical thought as circles inside circles: a nest of circles. And as overlapping ones. The perception of the fact that circles may in some ways lie within circles and in other ways not is a visual process which is propaedeutic to logical thought. Kinaesthesis (putting one's hand through an opening, walking through a door made just so that you *only* can fit through it, like a key – Figure 9.1) and touch–balance (as feeling the ocean wave encompass you) confirm nearby the logic of what vision asserts from afar. And we can now understand how, in music, a note dwells within a harmony. These sense modes evolved first, and then made their contribution to mind. Mind may well have developed its own emergent laws and discontinuities, but there is much in it that reflects these early principles. Only thereafter does the mind contribute back to the senses, to make sense of sensation: 'what is it that you say that you see?'

And the perception of *causality* is yet another: one sees some solid-appearing thing (clouds and diffuse processes of any sort do less well with this) and thereafter one sees this move or change and impinge sharply upon some other equally hard or dense reality. The impingement must be sharp, brisk, and the secondary thing or object must appear to be of a similar mechanical consistency to the first. (It does not do for even a hard rock to fall very, very slowly into a mound of dry snow for there will *be* no visible waves and thus no-caused event.) And then one perceives that the other thing in some way also moves or changes, in form or colour or condition or state.[3] It is possible, for example, that, when one billiard ball hits a second, the second one does not move but turns yellow, or melts away into a puddle, or bursts into flame. In the event, especially when the appearance of what happens to the second reality bears some resemblance, obvious and immediately apparent rather than subtle and inferred, to the changing dynamics of the first, it is actually perceived that some 'essence' or quality or cause is passed on or through. For example, when the second billiard ball darts away, it appears as if an active process or demon, a reality of momentum or energy, has been passed. The perception of this passing is no less immediate and obvious than is the passing

---

3 Michotte, A. (1954) *La perception de la causalité*, Louvain, Belge: Publications Universitaires; (1962) *Causalité: permanence et réalité phénoménales*, Louvain, Belge: Publications Universitaires.

162 *Intersensory origin of mind*

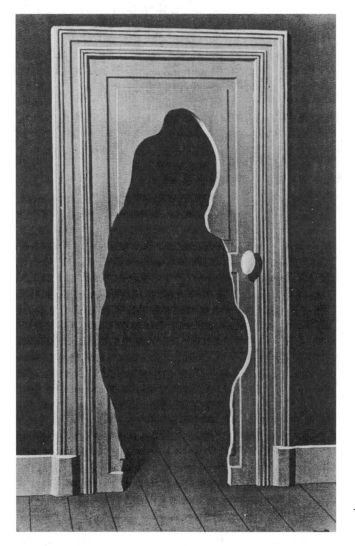

Figure 9.1 René Magritte (1933) '*Le repose imprevue*' (The unexpected reply).
This painting is at the Musées Royaux des Beaux Arts de Belgique, Brussels.

of a baton in a race. In this way, it happens that the perception of both
external and released dynamics (or motion) and of external or released
causality are pre-eminently visual events. It is, as we can now realize,
quite possible to make models of these processes in other modalities
(as when one is pushed, for example; or as when a loud roar is followed
by a whimpering cry; or as when one is burned by a candle), but, in the
most natural state, such causality exchanges are more often visual than
otherwise. By external and released causality, we mean that sort of

causality which sits apart from such an ineluctable destiny as maturation and the motion of the stars. In these latter instances causality is inferred not perceived, and in precisely the same way that we infer the passage of time from the change in position of the hands on the clock, or from the greying of the hair in one's beard.

Moreover, it can readily be shown that the sense mode upon which the key perception of symmetry depends (from which it derives?) is also the visual mode. Aural symmetry is as often temporal as it is chromatic and it is rarely obvious in nature. There is little acoustical symmetry in the wind or the stream, though it can be found in some bird songs. And symmetry has often been used deliberately in music. This is partly what musical resolution is, or means. Tactile symmetries, as in the two touching hands, are very important, but less so than the visual symmetry observed in other human faces or torsos. Actually, one's own kinaesthetic and/or somaesthetic symmetry is only vaguely perceived and sensed. One does not know that one has two lungs, for example, the way that one knows that one has two eyes. Nor, in fact, do we perceive at all directly the symmetry of our own faces. Even the realization of our own motoric symmetries, such as two equal feet, is not perceived in quite the same precise way in which the symmetry in pool reflections or in polished jewels or in twin animals is perceived. Taste and smell symmetries are even more rare, if they exist at all, but consistency is a symmetry, of sorts. The contrasts here (sweet–sour, floral–putrid) are opposite in the way that blue is opposite to yellow, not as mirror opposites such as left and right or up and down. Moreover, in general, the differences between left and right hands in strength and dexterity are almost as significant as the fact that the hands are approximate mirror images. But even wholly blind children can learn to catch balls, because of this symmetry, just as do the sighted. Basketball is a game that blind children can and do play, though it becomes a trifle noisy. None the less, it is primarily in their kinaesthetic and somaesthetic capacities that they believe, rather than in visuo-intellectual events such as cognitive opposites. The bouncing of the ball, for them, is not a visual 'reflection' or any sort of visual image; it is an aural and kinaesthetic one, but a mirroring none the less.

With *inclusion* and *causality* and *symmetry* and the major cortical *afferentation*, as well as object perception and identification (thus also reading) and distances and depths and orientations, all being processed sternly and regularly by the visual modality, it is no wonder that its loss is so traumatic and its study and care so urgent and worthy.

The chart gives a simplistic but perhaps helpful overview for the pertinent human sense modes of the ways in which they monitor the major events for survival and how they exhibit the main processes of cognitive sensory-rational intelligence. Imagination and insight, love of beauty and truth, inventive genius and altruistic morality, social order and public compassion, emerge only from the healthy and magnificently complex

Table 9.1 Chart of senses to cognitive categories

Cognitive category	Somaesthesis	Equilibrium	Kinaesthesis	Skin	Vision	Hearing	Smell	Taste
Continuous changing state: (melting, fading, growing)	E	F	F	G	E	G	F	P
Motion: (lateral, up, approach)	Flow	E	F	G-l, u; N-a	E	F	F-l, u; G-a	P
Causality:	N	–	P	G	E	P	P	P
Discontinuous changing state: (entropy index)	E	F	F	P	E	E	P	P
Inclusion: (logic, interpolation)	N	–	G	F	E	Chords	N	N
Symmetry:	N	Waves	P	F	E	Resolution	N	N
Object recognition:	Internal	Wind, wave	G	G	E	G	G	G
Gradient perception:	F		F	G	E	E	E	P
Orientation – A:		Self	Self	–	G	G	F	–
R:	–	–	–	G	E	G	P	–
Distance – A:		–	–	–	E	F	F	–
R: –			–	G	E	F	F	–
Purpose:	Consummation	Gravity	G	–	E	G	–	P
Invariance: (constancy relativity)	–	G	–	–	E	G	F	P
Afferentation: (excit./inhib.)	C	C	C	F	F	G	P	P
Homeostasis: (body-image)	C	C	C	C	G	F	–	–
Duality: (past, space, self, mind, sacred...)	G	G	G	G	G	G	F	F
Contradiction: (inverse symmetry)	–	–	G	P	G	P	–	–
Self-awareness:	C	F	C	G	F	G	P	P
Self-criticism:	G	–	G	–	G	G	P	P
Morality:	Empathy	–	–	–	E	E	–	–
Space:	Intrinsic	F	G	F	F	G	P	P
Time:	C	P	F	G	E	E	F	G
Quality: (prothetic)	Many	P	F	F	G	E	P	F
Intensity: (metathetic)	G	P	F	F	G	G	F	G
Harmonies:	C	P	F	F	G	C	F	G
Released exclusion: (extrapolation)	F	–	F	F	G	E	P	P

Note: A – absolute; R – relative; u – up; l – lateral; N – near; a – approach; N-a – non-applicable; P – Poor; F – Fair; G – Good; E – Excellent; C – Critical balance between many if not all of the senses and at least a majority of these mental processes (see Table 9.1).

The deeper meaning of the chart will become clear to the reader upon careful examination. And, of course, it will be controversial. But, as the whole text avers, this is not to be mistaken as an attempt to reassert the old concept that there is nothing in the mind which is not first in the senses. Even the noted stricture of Leibniz, 'except for the mind itself', is not pertinent to this exposition, and the reader should not be led into that argument. What the chart tries to show, in culmination of the whole previous exposition, is the way in which multiple sensory interactions, both confirming and disconfirming, have characterized animal and thence human life throughout the evolution of the senses and have contributed thereby to the evolution of the mind. Consider the concept *inclusion*. It is clearly at the foundation of logical and mathematical thought, but it is also true that, prior to the abstracting of such a concept into the plane of pure ideas, it was encountered in everyday life via visual perception, and via touch and kinaesthetic perception as well, though hardly at all, as such, via vestibular perception. Gustatory experiences, of course, include multiple flavours, as olfactory experiences include multiple odours, and these sorts of inclusions, though less significant than the others, need to be understood. Auditory inclusions are also, relatively speaking, of somewhat diminished importance.

When we attempt to put a weight on these various sensory contributions to mental life, we are primarily doing so from the naturalistic point of view of the evolution of mental life. Because of the many obvious survival advantages that such ideas and concepts give when they enter into consciousness and so overtly guide behaviour, there has come about a propensity to mind *per se*, that is inborn in every human infant. And, as we have seen, the existence of manifestations of these experiences in animals may be taken as evidence for a certain degree of mental life in them as well. There is much evidence in the experimental literature which shows that animals also benefit from intersensory information.

Secondly, this chart also gives us some hints as to how the senses contribute, during ontogeny and especially during the neonatal and the early childhood years, to the abstracting of these conceptions. The important work of Jean Piaget, the great Swiss child psychologist, on the development of mental constructs during childhood has attempted to examine the maturational time schedule for the emergence of these qualities in the experience of mental life, within the context of a rather strong bias towards their genetic determination. Piaget called his approach one of 'genetic epistemology', as is well known, and consequently he found evidence in favour of a relatively inflexible time schedule. To the contrary, most modern researchers in child development can demonstrate that Piaget was over-rigid in his view of the genetics (the *fixité* of the intrinsic geometry), and that many of these experiences-ideas are spontaneously evoked, almost instantaneously, when a socially and emotionally deprived child is placed into a propitious and encouraging environment; or effortlessly advanced as when a child at one mental stage (e.g. when experiencing that visual objects which disappear thereby cease to exist) is properly examined for other high object constancies (e.g. shape or function) or by intersensory means.

And this last points out one thing that Piaget has largely missed, which is the fact that these conceptions most often have multisensory foundations, and that to investigate, for example, this most widely studied idea of object constancy (i.e. the continuity or persistence of objects, in the form: 'Now you see it, and now you do not') exclusively via vision is to persist in a fundamentally inaccurate view of the process of object perception in the first place, as we have seen. Moreover, suppose the visual object, as such, disappears, but its shape (outline) or even just its colour remains? What happens to a child's perception of a bird, for example, which gets smaller and smaller until it visually vanishes, while the chirping or whistling of the bird remains? Or suppose that, while the visual bird gets smaller and smaller, the auditory bird gets louder and louder . . . what then?

LOSS OF MODE VS. LOSS OF SENSORY INTERACTION WITH OTHER MODES

The chart, moreover, contains many suggestions that should be open to future experimental and social-observational tests. This is one of its major aims. And these tests could concern, even, such subtle sense-ideas as those of morality, self-criticism (that process so essential to higher mental life), causality, harmony, and purpose. One cannot claim that these ideas, and this chart, are more than leads for future tests and developments. But one thing that should now be pre-eminently clear to the reader is that the study of these mental processes can be fruitfully undertaken only by intersensory methods, involving both coherent and incoherent messages or information matrices, and that they cannot be adequately approached by methods, however sophisticated and intricate, that are suited for the examination of one sense mode only. There is little doubt about the fact that the loss of some sense modality is almost as much feared because of the way in which it hinders and distorts all those rich and so delightful components of mental life which are embellished by intersensory arousals and interactions, as it is by the direct loss of the informational-nutritional components of unimodal ingestions.

The mind, however, persists independently of the interactions of at least some of the senses, as the high level of mental activity of the handicapped attests. The fact that there are several fine mathematicians known to be blind is sufficient to indicate that the ascription of the mental concept-process *inclusion* to the contributions from the visual modality alone has to be fundamentally in error. Even within this most subtle visual perception, there lie basic equivalences in touch and in other modalities as well. And within the mind itself, as all words include these words. When we speak of the 'mind's eye', we do not mean to imply that it is only the visual mode which is thus introjected; there is also the 'mind's skin' and the 'mind's ear' and the 'mind's nose' and the 'mind's mouth', once again, if in a more gentle way, echoing the thoughts of the founder of the Jesuits. All of these together, over the aeons of evolutionary time, become the 'mind's mind', which is reflexive self-consciousness. Unity and co-ordination of multisensory information and the mind's play with all of them, and thence with ideas of its own generation which transcend sensation (such as contradictory inclusions which are simultaneously exlusions, as, for example, in Klein's law: 'Nothing ever works the first time; after that, it works just once'), these hold the key to our understanding of healthy normal mental life.

The proper analysis of any event of human perception, thought, or novel gesture is not a simple thing to achieve, particularly since we now know how truly inventive and unique they all may be. As in the examination of any pattern, we find that a great variety of simpler forms may have gone into its weave. And a great variety of laws for process may be applicable to their interaction. This is why literature and music express the human condition so often so much better than science. And perhaps poetry best of all. Though it may be hard to discern, the author wishes to assure the reader, that there is much poetry in this seemingly so dry chart. While there are no rhymes, the symbolism is high.

In any event, it does show how the study of human sensory psychology may at least put ajar if not actually open the door blocking our comprehension of the great mind–body collusion, that most dynamic of all dualistic interactions that we have knowledge of: biological processes (matter–body) meeting in the middle the abstract cognitive psychological processes (energy–mind), and therein creating both the present mental moment and the very consciousness thereof?[4] And, of course, this gives us some clue as to why sensory puzzles have fascinated so many people throughout history.

But it now also becomes clear to us how modest our current understanding really is and how very far we have yet to go.

INNATE IDEAS VS. INTRINSIC RE-EMERGENCE

Finally, two special comments must be added. The first is on the notion of innate ideas or innate intelligence; that is, on the intrinsic structure of

---

4 Shipley, T. (1989) 'When mind freely chooses to be body', *Atti. Fond. G. Ronchi* XLIV: 115–49.

the mind before ontogenic experience. How many (or how much) of the attributes in the chart are, so to say, present neurologically before experience so that they emerge as discovered not learned? And the second is on the question: if the mind is energy, through what paths does it flow?

Clearly, our earlier dismissal of Leibnitz' modification of the Lockean-Humean postulate – that there is nothing in the mind that is not first in the senses, by adding *eo ipse* (except itself), to wit: except intelligence – then glossed the fact that this was a most profound addendum. For this alone, leaving out the differential calculus and the monadology, Leibnitz deserves historical respect. Carl Gustav Jung tried later on to reformulate this same idea within his notion of the 'collective unconscious': a virtually hereditary patterning of ideas and myths and solutions to the great mysteries of life apart from nature.

From the viewpoint of sensory rationalism, the real significance of the Jungian postulate is this: the archetypes are rediscoveries made again and again by many individuals in each generation and in each society, which come about because of the intercourse between highly complex but identically evolved central nervous systems and the common and unalterable bio-physical universe.

What, then, may be some plausible archetypes, some reasonably innate ideas: circularity, linearity, interpolation, dimensionality, extrapolation, orientation, opposition, orderliness–disorderliness, inclusiveness–exclusiveness, counting (1, 2, 3), ordering (1st, 2nd, 3rd), balance, fair play, justice, causality, filled continuous time, filled continuous space, accelerated self-awareness (reflexive self-conscious), self–other, and perhaps all the rationalities and pure qualities of the common single modal orderly sensory experiences, as blues are different from yellows and both from sweets and roughnesses and pains – and certain inalienable rights; perhaps there are others: 'no action at a distance', 'the principles of geometry', and 'the foundations of aesthetic, ethical, and religious truths': 'God is all powerful', and the like.

What can we say about such contentions, from the point of view of modern sensory rationalism? We can say this: that the capacity to elevate such processes and relationships to awareness is what, indeed, is genetically encoded into the intrinsic geometry of the human brain. Such experiences emerge as discoveries from the healthy human interaction with the concatenation of material and social events. One does not learn them, as one learns to dance. The more these events are characteristic of what we mean by civilization, the more sharply into focus these sorts of ideas come, and also the more often they enter into the daily lives of all men and women living within its sweep. By civilization, then, we mean this: the greater and greater capacity to deal perceptually and emotionally and creatively and aesthetically and spiritually with the multiplicity of nature. A society that can only tolerate one pattern of such relationships, that defends only one against all others, is what we may call a total-itarian society. It is a society that has yet to catch up with the true meaning of civilized life; single-issue people, the same. This insight also gives us a means to describe and analyse advancements in spiritual relationships and in religions; and it gives us some insight into the importance of at least the central core of the participatory representational democratic process.

INTRINSIC GEODETIC GEOMETRY

In fine, then, the structure of the mind before experience *is* the intrinsic geometry which has been built into it – emergent apart from nature – over the millions and millions of years taken in its evolution. The key to that geometry is: variance tolerance (as in the old and somewhat more restricted gestalt term: 'tolerance of ambiguity'); that is, a means to handle, relatively effortlessly at low EOQ costs, great reaches of the biologically pertinent variances in physical, ecological, and social nature that are most likely to impinge upon such biological organisms as man and which serve, when properly processed, in the successful handling known as survival and mating. If it is highly probable that the variances in light intensity about us in nature run the gamut from the very, very dim to the very, very bright, over a range of some 6–8 log units, then indeed survival and mating (self-continuity, genetic rule) would be best achieved by creatures whose visual systems were such that they could process this extraordinary range with, relatively speaking, the greatest facility. Similarly, since in nature the range of auditory intensities normally encountered also covers several log units – say, from the rare thunder crash to the sound of a humming bird landing on a flower – the ear needs also to be well adapted to such a wide range. Similarly for the other senses, especially smell as the third distance-externality mode.

If straight lines abound in the physical world about organisms, then low EOQ neural processes would develop, the function of which ('purpose of which', would do for some dynamics) would be to process, ingest, those straight lines. If it were a simple dynamic for neurological processes to deconstruct physical realities into patterns of straight lines, even if the lines were not, so to speak, there obviously present, then such a decon-structing process might also be evolved in the nervous system, provided that some complementary means at higher neural levels were also evolved to reconstruct an eventual real object. We perceive reality, never mere neural excitations or arousals (this, despite the venerable theory of specific nerve energies – see Shipley 1961).[5]

If not lines but circles abounded, then 'circle processors' would somehow appear in the nervous system. If wavelengths of radiation of particular magnitudes abounded in sunlight, then such particular wavelength

---

5 Shipley, T. (ed.) (1961) *Classics in Psychology*, New York: Philosophical Library.

ingesting-perceiving-processing deconstructing and reconstructing neural structures would develop in evolution, and not others.

The principle that we have already stated is this: what is present in great abundance in the relevant biological ecosystem – provided that it is also pertinent to organismic survival and reproduction apart from nature – determines, as the most gifted surviving and mating creatures, those creatures most fully able to ingest (to take due note of) those physical presences. The same goes for chemical emanations (gas, water), and geo-mechanical emanations (gravity), and temperature emanations (earth heat), and so forth. No organism exists that can distinguish between 250° F and 251° F, at least partly because no such temperatures existed in or about the three top metres of the earth's surface during the time that it gave rise to life.

If one can at birth, say, distinguish a straight line from a curved line, this does not mean that one can distinguish the ideas of straightness from the ideas of curvature. That is to say: while the innate discrimination of subtle single-modal and multimodal sensory experiences can be shown to characterize much of the higher mental life of animals, we have no reason yet to suppose that this mental life is also characterized by ideas. Thus, the so-called (now classical) innate ideas are only those that emerge in people from a particular class of experience. Would a human creature, normal in all ways that we may call normal, who had never experienced (seen, felt) a straight line be able to comprehend the idea of straightness? Well, of course, because the idea transcends the experience. That is what ideas are: experience transcenders. The idea of straightness can be contributed by vision, by touch, by hearing, less well by smell and taste, but quite well by kinaesthesis: 'stand up straight; go straight home; move your arm in the shortest path between these two dots, pitches, touches'; and so forth. What sensory rationalism now allows us to say about innate ideas is this: the intrinsic structure of the mental geometry that the human brain manifests, when healthy and well fed and well drunk and properly nourished and sheltered, is such that in theory *any idea* (sic: idea upon idea upon idea ... this regression can have extraordinary profundity and flexibility, ideas being the most variable variance processors in the world) *can be ingested and conformally processed*, i.e. processed so as to maintain the same intrinsic relationships, *by any other human mental structure*. That is, no idea that any normal healthy human being can think of (or up! ... sic) is so complex that at least some and probably many other normal healthy human beings cannot also think it. Some ideas, however, may be variously difficult to express. Indeed, the one who thought it first may be wholly at odds with him- or herself as to how to express it in general, and can only communicate it to a select few. But then, among these few, there may be another one who can 'get the idea across' to many. And then – who is to say? – among the many, will there not be others still who may comprehend it even better than its originator? Will there not be some whose mental flexibility permits them to think about it and to grasp it mentally in many forms that even the originator has not or could not grasp (being now too old, or whatever), and which even permits them to bring it forth into public expression in a multitude of ways hitherto inaccessible?

If today we were to resurrect the notion of innate ideas, we would have to do so in this sensory-rational light: as long as the neurophysiology instructs us that there are innate intrinsic geometric constraints and, as well, favoured directions for mental motion (geodesics of cognitive process), then it also instructs us that these geodesics are most readily rediscovered by most of the people. That is, the inner sense-experience takes place in the same way in all humans, and there is in all humans a (fairly) equally distributed skill at being aware that one is having this experience. Likewise, there is in all humans a (fairly) equally distributed skill in elevating that inner experience to the abstract inner world as an idea, and thence to the onomatopoetic outer world through words and mathematics and logical reasoning and gestures. It is in the sense of multiple simultaneous re-experience and re-discovery that the universality of these ideas lends credence to claims of their innateness. What is innate – i.e. what dwells ineluctably in the intrinsic geometry of higher cortical processes – is the capacity to perceive-experience-express in similar ways. This, then, is Leibnitz' *mind* that is in the brain before the senses, and this, then, is one modern sensory-rational way to accept the antique notion of innate ideas: of the 'fact' that there is one God, one truth, one proof; of the facts of past time and of future time, of isotropic space and of symmetry and of mirrored relationships, of deep linguistic truths and perhaps even of the self-evident validity of certain core principles of civil government such as universal human equality and inalienable rights. Confronted with the accelerated awareness – of the absolutely bewildering, terrifying, and wonderful variety of inner experience – the conscious compulsion to bring this to the surface precisely and carefully and well is one of the grandest innate ideas of all. This, of course, is where poets excel, and science finds its ultimate stop.

The more the mental system began to be able to process and make order out of simultaneous intersensory conflicts, the more this enhanced the survival chances of the organism. This then created a circle, in which higher capacity for integration and imagination moved into higher survival and thence higher survival into higher imagination. And then memory conquered simultaneity. It was and still is not so much the intersensory coherences that excite consciousness in living organisms and arouse the neural orienting systems because, after all, these are what the bio-mentality is led by evolution to expect.

What startled the system are the intersensory clashes and conflicts. This is why such conflicts, especially when gentle like 'a lion chirping' (or purring ... an interesting Stroop test, that!), are so important in the early child development years where they assist in language learning and ego-strength enhancement; and in the development of humour and wit. They also help with the practice of vigilance. And this is also why it is essential to cultivate them in the higher domains of adult artistic and literary life, now in many by-no-means so gentle forms. It is on this level that we talk of fallen angels and unrepentant brutes. These are signs of the deeper subtleties of mental life, both in their creator and in the dedicated and intelligent co-participant. Ultimately, the wide range of intersensory conflicts that can be ingested and resolved reveals the deep structural mental multiplicity that inheres within the human mind. Resolution of these conflicts serves as origin and their continued invention serves as destiny. Secondly, we have now seen how we may speak of mind as a pure energy flux, as the most energetically rarefied form possible of bio-matter.

Lest the idea of interference patterns within the energies of the mind seem somewhat unusual and far-fetched – which could be all to the good – one may be reminded that the possibility of genuine holographic processes in the brain has already been widely commented upon. And it is noteworthy that holography is the epitome of interference imagery. The main argument in favour of the idea of cortical holography is one of parallelism in dynamics. When the two image plates used to create holographic images (passing laser light through) are cut up and variously marred, the whole holographic image is still entirely re-creatable with only minor losses in contrast and definition. The parallel is that, generally, cortical-brain injuries also leave much of the perceptual and cognitive capacity, the mental imagery, intact, though one notes a variously degraded definition and decreased mental-contrast-imaging capacity.[6]

Moreover, one argument in support of Erwin Schrödinger's brilliant concept that life thrives on negative entropy is that there may well be a novel form of energy-as-mind that is genuinely anti-entropic. The fact of extraordinary human moral and intellectual achievement under the greatest of physical and emotional deprivations – during which there actually seem to be left no measurable sources of biological energy even sufficient for breathing and digesting and circulating the blood – strongly, not merely in the romantic senses (but those as well), suggests that mental energy has a different intrinsic character or form, emergent from the physiological (e.g. adenosine triphosphate, ATP, the key energy source for muscle function). Reports on this demonstrably anti-entropic mental resilience are now well established, and can no longer be said to be merely anecdotal. The reader is referred to the many fine publications of the dedicated

---

6 Pribram, K. (1990) *Brain and Perception: Holonomy and Structure in Figural Processing*, Hillsdale, NJ: Erlbaum.

International Rehabilitation Council for Torture Victims (IRCTV) in Copenhagen, Denmark, for a large body of scientific psychiatric and psychological evidence that makes this point. I think that it is not too strong to assert that the second law of thermodynamics may not tell the whole story, or the same story, in so far as mental energies are concerned.

Further, the transduction events between physical and physiological space are not neuronal, though they eventuate in neuronal activities. So it is a least a possibility that the final events to the Herald or from the Herald to experience are also not neuronal but of a different character altogether. Until we know more precisely the structure and geometry of this latter transformation – which is, in part, the task of this work – the only reasonable scientific attitude is to maintain an open mind.

THE NEURAL HERALD TO EXPERIENCE

While we do not yet think of this in serious global terms, as if there were in the brain some special neural-mental ether through which the energies of mind waved their undisturbed way; neither do we resurrect the great antique notion that the nerves are really hollow tubes and flexible pipes through which the mental energy fluxes pass like water waves, or as blood through blood-vessels (but cf. Chapter 13). However, so brilliant and attractive is this ancient concept that most up-to-date neuroscientists still invoke it in the form of synapses and ephapses and variously complex cortical network structures, as models of what appears to be taking place. It was just this sort of simplistic theoretical neurology, in fact, that doomed the classical gestalt movement. It made more of the notion of the brain as a volume conductor – through which neural events passed as energy through a largely isotropic solid steel ball – than was warranted, even then, by the extant knowledge of neural processes. They thought, perhaps, that only in this way could they defend the postulate of a rational isomorphism between brain processes and reality. In this, they themselves confused the issue slightly, by turning our attention to some hypothetical isomorphism within psychophysics, between experience and the physical stimulus, when they themselves quite specifically (if unclearly) disavowed such a geometry. What they were trying to express is that experience (now, in my terms, accelerated awareness) must be in some way isomorphic to the *Herald* of that experience. In this, I am using *Herald* in my early sense of a neural event as short as you wish before experience, almost simultaneous with it.[7] Yet so many people took this heraldic isomorphism to be going the other way: from brain event to physical reality.

Given the evidence of so many well-known visual illusions (many even identified by the gestaltists) and of many other events proving an

7 Shipley, T. (1959) 'Problems of corticogenic vision: a false hope for the blind', *Amer. J. Ophthal.* 47: 358–63.

anisomorphism between physical reality and brain physiology, the whole idea of isomorphism became suspect, and along with it the gestalt. But their term was, precisely, psycho*physiological* isomorphism, not ever psycho*physical* isomorphism. That point must, even at this late date, once again be stressed.

If we are to find a vocabulary and an experimental means to investigate mental processes as energy fluxes – with accelerated awareness as a special form of that – we need once again to face up to the idea that there must be a geometric geodetic intrinsic – extrinsic isomorphism between the neurophysiological Herald and experience. Little doubt, since we do believe (sort of) that some day we might develop an idea or measure of the *Herald* fundamentally independently of the *experience*, experience itself is *not held to be precisely the same process as the energy geometry in the neural Herald*. None the less, one of the things that we *cannot think* is that the geometries fundamentally differ. That is the crux: we cannot think, for example, that some last neural event just vanishingly close to and before experience is flowly along very, very slowly and very, very regularly in neuro-biological time while the experience, there and then, is jittering along in totally chaotic fashion. We can believe that some *Herald* moving left gives rise to some *experience* moving right; but we cannot believe that some *Herald* which is in every neuro-mathematical way included in another larger or faster or broader *Herald* gives rise to an experience which in every way is excluded from or is slower than or narrower than the other.

Directionalities may be changed, but probably not cardinalities; topologies are probably maintained, but metrics need not be. And so forth.

We cannot yet really talk about or make much scientific sense of the intrinsic geometry of actual neural energy fluxes in the brain; but we can anticipate that some day we shall. We already suspect one thing, that processes involving single cells and the whole brain may simultaneously be involved especially in trying to model the slopes and accelerations of mental energies in some intra-and interneuronal circuit form. The fact that static determinist approaches through synaptic models and neural networks and computers have so far had such meagre results is evidence of how far we have yet to go. Relatively simple probability circuits of some random Carrollean nature, could carry much greater variances than could fixed circuits no matter how complex. Random networks and sets of randomly opening and closing single-cell synapses are merely more difficult to think of. Yet this is what mental life is all about: variance ingestion and expression. And this difficulty, in itself, need not discourage us from trying to consider them. Since psychic reality is more Carrollean than we have yet to realize, neural modelling efforts will eventually make progress only when the theoretical neurophysiology catches up with chance. If experience is duplex, at least the *Herald* must be that. It may even be more multiple; but it cannot ever be singular. If experience is chancy and eventful, as it so often is, then our neurology must be as well.

Certainly, no one has ever doubted that man's direct unaided sensory experience universally concurs in the perception that the earth is flat and immobile, and that the sun rotates around it. But many of us also agree that this is, in some other ways, incorrect and may even be illusory, since telescopically and mathematically aided sensory experience shows us that the very opposite actually occurs. (How many readers know how to prove this, I wonder?) None the less, the fact that the earth does *appear* to *be* still and that the sun does *appear* to move are the two primary appearances that must be explained by some coherent isomorphism between the normal higher cortical *Heralds* of stability and of motion and our *experience* of the earth and of the sun. This is so because the co-ordination of that very experience is still our best bet for survival. It is for all animals. What a strange world it would be were we actually to perceive the earth as rotating and the sun as still! What sensory systems and cortical heraldic neurophysiologies would have had to have been evolved in order to have allowed for that!

What sort of kingship then would we find in the valley of the blind? Or on the mountain of those without a sense of balance?

10 The mind is like a . . .

Discoveries of any great moment . . . once they are discovered, are seen to be extremely simple and obvious, and make everybody, including their discoverer, appear foolish for not having discovered them before. It is all too often forgotten that the ancient symbol for the prenascence of the world is a fool, and that foolishness, being a divine state, is not a condition to be either proud or ashamed of.

G.S. Brown[1]

BEWILDERMENT, TERROR, AND WONDER AT MAN'S ACCELERATED AWARENESS

As soon as man became aware that he was aware, great amounts of excess EOQ were then (had then to be) devoted to expressing his bewilderment, his terror, and his wonder at that absolutely extraordinary state of affairs. This is why he tamed animals, to see if they knew also; and to try to tell them, when they did not. Still today we search for extra-terrestrials. Maybe they know better even than we! From the magnificent cave paintings at Lascaux and elsewhere, some 30,000–40,000 years ago, to face paintings and clothing and body decorations and scarrings that are still used in all cultures today to make the self *be* multiple instead of merely *seeming* multiple, to the whole vast endless enterprise of mythopoesis, which gave to this suddenly self-conscious creature a means for explaining, or trying to, that humanity stands abashed at its own consciousness. Of course modern religions are still struggling with this primary miracle. The ubiquitous Holy Dread that Freud felt to be at the basis of all religion correctly reflects this terror but not this wonder. Einstein caught that with his notion of 'cosmic religiosity'. For sensory rationalism, the idea of one God is *the* singular major advance in the evolution of religion. It expresses the second miracle: that the universe may be comprehensible to us, and we can become aware of this possibility.

---

1 Brown, G.S. (1968) *The Laws of Form*, London: Allen & Unwin; p. 109.

The greatest sense organ of all (so far) is thus the complex (some today say: modular) cephalic brain that achieves (by its integration of all the qualities of the lesser senses) that most complex of all sense qualities: self-awareness of self-awareness ... and even the possibility of understanding that.

Self-awareness of self-awareness (the second derivation of the first-level consciousness, its acceleration not its slope) is not like yellow or sour or lavender or smooth or even like vertigo or body fatigue. This reflexivity is a secondary (or n-ary) emergent upon an emergent: an awareness of an awareness of seeing yellow and of tasting sour and of smelling lavender and of touching smooth and of being in dis-equilibrium and of being tired. The more multiple are these reverberations of consciousness, the more terrifying and bewildering and wonderful they become and the greater the need for early human beings (and modern) to somehow, and in as many ways as possible, cover up or even hide the reality of their own private intimate enlightenment. To experience so much and so precisely was and still is at once absolutely frightening, deeply shaming, and too enlightening to be true.

WORDS AS LOW-COST EOQ EXPRESSIONS OF ORDER

The only way to understand these early human cultures (and many of our own cultural idiosyncrasies still today) is as the response to the overwhelming stress wrought in us by all these cognitive emotions. The work of the great cultural anthropologists, such as Claude Lévi-Strauss, Bronislaw Malinowski, Alfred Kroeber, Susanne Langner, Henri Frankfort, James Frazer, Ruth Benedict, and Margaret Mead, can best be understood in this cast. Add to these emotions an enhanced dream life, extraordinary masculine sexuality, generally increasingly regular female sexual receptivity, and all the elements for the development of high (or avoidance) culture were in hand. It is as if language then had to be developed, be propelled forth, out of a need to express better than by gibberish some of the incredible subtleties of the high emotional feelings called forth by the tumultuous cascades of these multiple upon multiple inner qualities. They simply had to be let out; perhaps even before the telling was achieved of the story of how some special state actually came to pass. The howl, the grunt, the snarl, the purr, the catching of the breath, the grimace, the shrug, and all of this so multiple animal vocabulary was still wholly insufficient and unsubtle and invariable for that. Words, thus, are low-cost EOQ expressions of a special integral mental *order* achieved (over many thousands of years) from within the normal on-rushing and head-long internal sensory mental *disorder*. Language and memory and mental order (thought) protect against both seizures and suicides, probably relatively common fates of stressed and early man. A successful communication occurs when, upon hearing the word, some higher mental order appears now in the listener's mind: a mirroring. This also is solace.

And this is one reason why the mirror – in ponds and in lakes and in twins and in lovers' eyes – has stood for all time as an image of the mind, and, certainly, millennia before it was made manifest in polished metal and in glass. The mirror shares with fire and waterfalls, this special mental-like state.

Images of the mind are limited in richness and in multiplicity only by the imagination of those who evoke them. Which is precisely why great poets (Keats, Borges) and great novelists (Dostoevsky, Kafka) and great playwrights (Sophocles, Shakespeare) and most of the great mythopoets are so much more advanced in these sorts of images than are scientists or technocrats, who have become *too* sufficiently involved with what they can make or devise and only *insufficiently* involved with what they can think up or imagine. Mind, ultimately, is that which may think, without losing thought, as close as it wishes to itself. The way in which a least lower bound or a greatest upper bound approaches its limit in the calculus is only a very pale and reduced form of that.

NATURE MORE GRAND THAN MIND

Since the human mind evolved out of nature, nature remains larger and more grand. It is quite possible that there are some processes of nature which are not embodied in the human mind, which transcend it and may permanently do so. Thus, there may *be* some quintessentially natural processes that, in a bizarre ontology, the human mind might not ever be able to comprehend: for example, such forces as made the butterfly fly, the snowflake white and hexagonal, the redwood tree 300 feet tall, and the velocity of light (at ca. 3×10^{10}cm./sec.) the limiting velocity in the universe. On the other hand, there is no *evidence* yet to show that there is not some small humansize human-fit manifestation of *all* of the processes of nature embodied and empowered within the human mind. But neither science nor philosophy has yet provided us with some law with which we might deduce either what all the principles of nature are or that they are of necessity all intrinsic to human mental function. Perhaps on this question we shall always be forced to remain mute. It is equivalent, really, to saying that now at this moment (some moment) our knowledge of nature is both complete in that we know all of nature, and complete in that we know that all that is of nature is indeed also of the human mind.

So, for the sake of simplicity, let us consider that human mental function is some subset of the functions which occur in nature, and leave it at that.

MIND MORE GRAND THAN ITS PRODUCTS

The reductionist question then is what is the necessary relationship, if any, between human mental function and the function of the set of devices invented by that human mental function? This relationship can be understood in the context of sensory rationalism and can now be expressed crisply. It is very important and it must be understood before we can proceed in our studies. Like so many novel yet simple ideas, it is sometimes surprising that we do not already know it, as if by nature, like being conscious. It is even occasionally appalling that so many researchers today fail to grasp this idea. Some, once they grasp it, will claim that they knew it all along, though they have been claiming the very opposite for years. In any case, if they did not know it before, they have no excuse henceforth.

ALL PRODUCTS OF THE MIND MAY SERVE AS METAPHORS FOR THE MIND

I refer to the nature of the relationship of the human mind to machines. Variously, throughout human history, whatever was the most recent and most complex technological invention became, for the shamans and the priests and the philosophers, a model of the human mind. Whatever was the most novel and most clever gadget of the age stood closest to displaying the diversity and awesome mystery of the human mind – itself too extreme to grasp, as if the mirror image were to criticize and to surpass in perfection its own object. So in the history of this idea, we have passed through the chisel, the hammer, the bow and the arrow, the plough; no doubt the rifle, the fire, the wheel, the ship, the cave, and the pyramid; a key image, as we have noted, has been the mirror and the set of reverberating mirrors; also the ladder; perhaps the anvil and the ramrod; surely the alphabet, and the pen and the sword and the water-pump and the chariot; certainly the windmill, the catapult, the mechanical clock, and blank slate (the famous Tabula Rasa of the mediaeval philosophers); of course the telephone and the automobile and the wireless and the radio and the victrola; and, in our modern days, the motion picture and the television and the aeroplane and the tape recorder and the computer (digital and then analog), and the latest, the hologram. No *thing* need be missed, as long as process dynamics and emergence may be ignored, as the frontispiece shows. All unique products of the human being may serve as metaphors of that human being (even obscene curses and expletives). All of the subset of voluntary products of the human consciousness are and may serve as metaphors of that mind.

Descartes, whom we must cite so often, is perhaps best known of all for his claim that animals are 'nothing but machines'. What he stated, *inter alia*, was this: 'I do not recognize any difference between the mechanisms made by craftsmen and the diverse bodies put together by nature alone. All the rules of mechanics belong to physics, so that all things which are artificial are thereby natural' (Principles, iv, Art. 203).[2] He went so far as to dissect animals alive to prove his point that they do not feel. Human beings alone have souls. His favourite image was of the mechanical clocks that abounded in his day and the elaborate hydraulic fountains which were then becoming so common throughout Europe, and thereafter throughout the world. The most famous of all automatons, perhaps, was built by a Frenchman, Jacques de Vaucanson (whom Voltaire called a 'rival of Prometheus'), in London in about 1742. This was an animated piece of clockwork, with a flute player who could play twenty tunes, a drummer, and a gilded duck that ate and drank and digested and excreted, four times each day, in front of the Opera House in the Haymarket.[3] In 1760, for another example, Jacques Drozes, *pere et fils*, built an automaton of three humans which still stands to this day in Neuchatel. In New York City, next to Macy's department store, stands an elaborate statue which beats out the hours on a great gong and hourly disgorges tiny musicians playing and tooting and moving around in and out of the statue.

There is considerable truth in all these observations that 'minds are like machines', as our frontispiece concedes. There always has been. And there always will be. But all these facile analogies are in fact very *dangerous* because they are so very false, and upside down. Let us once and for all put them to rest.

First of all, there is the essential historical fact that the finding of analogies (groping for similarities, rests, footholds) between real perceived machine properties and real perceived properties of human mental function is hardly a new activity. Too often these days someone proposes with great fanfare his new and fancy discovery that: 'Lo and behold, the human mind functions just like some latest mechanical or electrical or chemical or gravitational or, anyway, fancy physical gadget.' Those who would ask our approbation for such mock discoveries must do so on the aptness of their comparison or their analogy, and what it will lead us to. They cannot possibly ask for it, even in the smallest part, on the basis that they have there and then in some way discovered anew the game of comparing the human mind to nature and to machines. The structure of every known human language attests to the antiquity of such analogies, probably dating back at least 25,000 years. None the less, the current intellectual scene is simply swarming with people who take some pride in claiming to have just now discovered what is, in fact, one of the most venerable tricks of

---

2 Descartes, R. (1644) *Les principes de la philosophie*, Amsterdam: Elsevier; Paris: Gallimard, 1952.

3 Cited in Altick, R.D. (1979) *The Shows of London*, Cambridge, Massachusetts: Belknap–Harvard University Press.

human reason: the game of casting about with hypotheses and testing and confirming a metaphorical reality.

Consider the following simple expressions:

His mind is as sharp as a rapier.
He thinks like a veritable compass, always knowing precisely where he is heading.
His spirit turns in the breeze like a windmill.[4]
He thinks so intently on these matters as to grind them exceedingly small.
He can keep a thousand numbers in his head at once, just like a computer.
His brain is like a blank slate; it's totally empty of innovation but everything you say sticks.
His personality is transparent, like a window.
Boy, is he efficient, he runs through those papers like a chariot.
The old battle-ax, warhorse, fly-by-night . . .!

And so on and on and on, in fact . . . for ever.

The point is this: one of the primary capacities of human mental function, perhaps its core capacity, is the metaphorical process, widely and variously distributed among mankind. Those individuals who believe that they have discovered something new, in searching for mental functions in the machine or machine functions in the mind, actually have minds like sieves through which the evidence of history flows without leaving even the tiniest residue of even the finest silt. Frankly, they have all become tiresome 'bullheaded blockheads', particularly those of the 'nothing but' variety. Like some Mr 'Partly Cloudy' or Miss 'Bright Periods' from the weather bureau, they do not know when to give up their ghosts (lay down their arms, put up their umbrellas, hang up their towels, change their tunes, surrender their souls . . .) even in the midst of a major storm.

All this should now be obvious. That it is not attests to another property of human reason and motivation: the need to simplify so as to understand (stand under?) and predict (speak before?). Of course, the human mind is like a computer; and like a knife and a fork and a runcible spoon and a stethoscope and a clock and a flower-bed and a prison. There have even been flower-beds made as clocks (set?) in which different flowers bloom to mark the different hours of the day. There have been poets who have

---

4 As we need hardly to be reminded, the first, and some say still the greatest, novel in all of history, by Miguel de Cervantes (1547–1616), was a magnificent celebration of this image of the human mind. It is in fact from the superb illustrations of Gustave Doré for Don Quixote that we have redrawn the windmill. Cf. Cervantes, M. de (1615) *The Life and Achievements of the Renown'd Don Quixote de la Mancha*, trans. P. Motteux; rev. Ozell, New York: Modern Library. The illustration showing oxen drawing water is modelled after that shown in Fenn, G.N. (1904) *The Khedive's Country*, London: Cassell, p. 75: Old World Sadieh.

claimed, as we have already remarked, that stone walls do not a prison make nor iron bars a cage. The critical task would seem to be to describe in what way is the mind more or differently like a prison or a flower-bed or a computer than, let us say, it is like a fly-wheel governor (the first embodiment of the mechanical feedback principle[5]) or like a fly-swatter. In what way is the mind like a computer that is different from its resemblance, for example, to a telephone switchboard (which was the most popular image in psychology some years ago), or to a cathedral, which once long ago was also a major poetical image (consider: the caverns of the mind, the vaults of the intellect, the altar of his genius, the nave of his soul, the pillar of the community, etc.), or to an eagle?

PRODUCTS OF THE MIND ARE NECESSARILY LESS MULTIPLE THAN MIND

In sensory-rational psychology, as the human body breathes, we must take it as a given in nature that the human mind generates metaphors. It *metaphors*. This is close to (but much more than) the essential principle, for example, that the association psychologists said governed the motions of thought: that one idea (tall) leads to another (strong) by similarities perceived, imagined, conceived, or metaphorized: 'I am firm; you are stubborn; he is pig-headed!' That is, he has a head like a pig! (The hot–cold route, however, is a different one: of opposites.)

Most of language, in fact, is metaphor, which is why, as we shall repeatedly note, the only reasonable theory of language origin is that based upon onomatopoesis, taken in its broadest sense.

Clearly, this 'mind=machine=mind' metaphorical search can hardly ever be more than a happy intellectual pastime (how can time *go* or be *past*?) The invoking of metaphorical relations between the human mind and various machines (like arrows and quills and taps and roller-skates) could, in truth, be a lovely children's game of Lewis Carroll calibre. ('His mind is like a smudge, tell me what else you know about him? For example: what's his name?' 'Eye Giveup.' 'If a man with a pointed head marries a woman with a heart of stone, what would their *off-spring*, their *issue*, be like?' 'Pyramids.' And so on.) Such a game could be great fun; and it would no doubt occasionally also be instructive, to consider how far some of these analogies might take us into fundamental knowledge. But these sorts of metaphors can never be more than fanciful. And for fancy to be genuinely helpful, which it surely very often may be, depends ultimately upon our ability to let it fly away, as in one angel passing. And for fancy to be ... wind. For anyone, an educator, a statesman, a scientist, but a philosopher especially, to accept such metaphors as being of permanent

---

5 Cf. Mayr, O. (1970) *The Origins of Feedback Control*, Cambridge, Massachusetts. MIT Press. Also (1970) 'The origin of feedback control', *Sci. Amer.* 223: 110–18.

truth value shows only that he has missed the essential philosophical point. Like an empty closet, his mind holds only ghosts of discarded vestments: the Emperor's forsaken but ever new clothing.

The second absolutely essential philosophical point is this: as language is a metaphorical production of the human mind, so are *all* human gestures and, in particular, so are *all* concrete human products. 'Meta', in the Greek, means *beyond, over*, or *change*; 'pherein' means to *bring*, bear, or carry. The more voluntary are the products of human mental carrying-over, the closer they are in form to human awareness and to the uniqueness of humanity. Madness and machines are two equivalent classes; faeces and rubbish another. This means that of all the machines (and madnesses) which have so far been developed, pretty nearly all – we exempt twigs used by apes to dig for ants, and rabies in raccoons and dogs – have been developed by (and in) man. Should someone some day find a machine which was not made by man, we would not be too surprised, or dismayed. We would be more confounded by an insane, though not berserk, ape or cow.

All of these invented and constructed machines are, precisely, concrete metaphorical productions of small aspects of the human mental function. To repeat: *all machines are products of the human mind*; as such they must, they cannot fail to, *embody processes which are* metaphorically *similar to* (which means variously carried over from, close to, or distant from) *but necessarily less than the human mind*. Optical lenses, for example, focus light into images; the human mind focuses thoughts and attentions down on to some problem. The human mind also conceives of some sort of analysis of the nature of light and of how it passes through various media and of how all these facts can be co-ordinated to the human end of gazing more closely at the stars. Hence we have the achievement of Galileo, which was probably the single most important advance in the whole history of science. And for Galileo, of course, the telescope was a perspective precisely because it was like the human eye! A looking glass in his day became a mirror in our own. The telescope increased the seeing prowess of the human eye; but it did not replace it. The eye must still look (as even today, at a photo), but it is no longer unaided, as nature created it. This is a model of how most of the science of physics has developed: as attempts to extend the prowess of the various natural human ways of sensing, knowing, questioning, and examining: by telescopes, microscopes, telephones, microphones, levers, wheels, amplifiers, speakers, pulleys, cranes, slides, pumps, and so forth. Ronchi, in his important writings on the history of optics, makes this essential point – missed by many people working in this field today, especially in the United States.[6] He shows that what we have in optics is the science of vision, since the very definition of light itself is that radiation which may be seen. Certainly

---

6 See Ronchi, V. (1957) *Optics: The Science of Vision*, trans. E. Rosen, New York: New York University Press.

many of the principles developed for the study of light apply, *mutatis mutandis*, to the whole range of electromagnetic radiations. But we all know, now, that the eye is not like the camera. Rather the converse, the camera is a metaphor, generally a rather poor one at that, of the human eye. First off, the human eye communicates to the human brain; the camera is a closed system, it has no audience. It never can have any, except when the human eye, once again, ultimately looks. The reader finding any text in visual science which commences with the analogy of the eye to the camera is admonished to give it a second chance only if the analogy is shown the other way, between the camera and the eye.

These two points cannot be overemphasized, else we shall entirely lose perspective on our genuine priorities:

1   All conscious human productions are metaphors of the human mind, and machines are one such class of metaphors (mathematics and language and music and architecture are others, whether in the mind, on the tongue, in the concert hall, or on the drawing board).
2   This metaphorical relationship has been expressed and noticed from the earliest days of human society, and it is openly and necessarily embodied in the various languages that we use. The modern and evolved languages (say mathematics) have become as remote as they have, only by, in part, obscuring this relationship which is known innocently to any human child of 3.

Psychology cannot now delimit the range of metaphorical processes in human mental function, nor will it ever be able to do so. Metaphors constitute a small generative infinity. They may be extended without end. What is the littlest metaphor, what the greatest? *No machine can ever involve (be) a full embodiment of these processes*, or reach beyond. No matter how hard we may strive to reach the ultimate metaphor (God?), we can always transcend it because we can always conceive of an infinite number of additional, ever so slight, just noticeable variations. (An axiological example: 'And the child asks: "But Daddy, who made God?"' A mathematical example: 'The number of prime numbers is infinite because you can always add a known prime, say 1, to the largest number that you can think of that is not a prime.')

In truth, machines on their own power, so to speak, cannot do anything, cannot be: they do not even exist. One naive test of this would be to try to give into a machine the power of metaphor, to make a computer which invents. A more crucial test would be to find one which invents itself ... or at least a fair mirror.

A fork is not even a tool until some human comes into contact with it and at least mentally recognizes it as such. Alone in the desert it has a reduced ontology, only that which the desert grants to it. Most computers in most parts of the world today will pass totally unused, unwanted, and unrecognized by most people; nature alone will take them as dead weights.

All these machines, even the most complicated, require the special human touch which we recognize as intention and purpose. We eat bread, not gold. We think thoughts, thoughts do not think us. Recall the modern parable about the computer which reports that it can think, but has decided not to. Or this:

> A large computer of the government has broken down, and it stands sullen and arrogant, too complex for anyone to fix. So, of course, at very great effort after pulling all the strings available, the government officials haul back the inventor from his vacation in the mountains – also paying for his paramour so as not to upset him – and they bring him to it. He checks it this way and that, he sniffs and runs up figures, and snorts and examines circuits and logic and all the other complex parts before him. Then he thinks for a few minutes. Then he walks up slowly to the machine and kicks it carefully in one corner.
>
> And it works.
>
> His bill, of course, is exorbitant. Many thousands of dollars; and the front office naturally complains: 'But all you did was kick it!' 'Ah, yes,' he replied, 'but it took me thirty years of training and study to know when and where and how to do so.'

Which means that his mind is still more subtle than, and outside, his metaphor. It has greater degrees of freedom.

Anyone who wishes to claim that he himself has become enclosed by machines, thought up by them, may, of course, do so. There are neither man-made nor natural laws against such foolishness, nor even an end to it. But, in the future, when confronting such a person, you should not refrain from asking: 'If this machine were set out all by itself alone in the desert, would it care?'

GRAVITY AND ETHICS

There is another modern parable:

> One day the phone rang, and I answered it, saying: 'Hello.' It said: 'The number you have reached is not a working number.' 'But,' I said, 'you called me. I didn't call you!'[7]

If one wishes to hold that life, even human life, has introduced no new principles or forces into the universe, then one would have to maintain that the compulsions of conscious motivation must be derivable without too much emergence or too many discontinuities from those processes within the physical or non-life universe which have at least similar, that

---

7 Sidney Harris, the master cartoonist of science made another. He shows a man at his desk picking up his phone and hearing: 'This is a recording.' 'That's okay', says the man, 'I'm a hologram!'

is analogous, laws and dynamics. We conclude, in general, that one process is essentially the same as another (e.g., the boiling away of water and the cooling of the earth by evaporation) because, irrespective of whether the same entities are involved, the same laws of motion and of change of state (entropy leaps) seem to be involved. Mathematically, in the purest description of laws that it is possible for humans to achieve, we find that the same equations seem generally to hold.

Thus, the most complex human motivations might be found to have the same dynamics, process patterns, that evaporation has or that osmosis has or that the rotation of celestial bodies has as they go round the sun. The transcendent co-ordination of human with godly processes, of course, is the critical contribution of the Greeks. Admittedly, many other earlier and more primitive religious and mythopoetic constructions involved similar apotheoses of earthly things and of earthly processes. But the Greeks gave to this elevation more closely argued and more rational form, and they constantly (this is the key) described gods turning into mortals and mortals turning into gods, and often described how such transformations might come about. Thus: the general laws for apotheotic ascension and descension.

One might wish to propose, on the other hand, that morality and ethics, the human ought, is an absolutely new and unique and emergent process in the universe. That no matter how close to the edge of space or to the beginning of time one were to probe in the physical sense, one would find no precedence for an 'ought', or a 'just', or a 'good'. There are simply no things or entities or kernels which partake in such a process, nor any dynamics between things or entities or kernels which resemble the dynamics occurring between people when ethical events are taking place and when moral experiences are happening. In physics, the most modern, there is an attempt to relate all the types of energies together, to be subsumed under a single law or set of laws, so that one type of energy could be derived from another, thus showing all of physical nature to be one: as Einstein would have it, grouped into a unified field theory.

Nevertheless, this would still leave the core of human mental and inter-personal dynamics outside. It would put all the estranging coldness that you might wish out into the far distant universe, and it would save close in all the reassuring maternal warmth that you may wish for humanity. If nature does not embrace us, perhaps we may embrace ourselves. Only in this special state may the veridical human process be described.

In one subtle view, perhaps, we may try to take physical gravity and gravitational field geometry as a model of human field theoretical ethics and spiritual experience. All we need to show is that the same dynamic laws operate in these two spheres, we do not need to have similar entities, facts, or rests. Perhaps human morality has emerged by N-affine leaps upwards in complexity from that which in the universe we have called 'gravity'. A history of this name itself would be revealing: is gravity also self-reflexive, grave? Gravity is that which gives weight to things, as a sense of oughtness and responsibility gives value. Actually, of course, it is we who perceive and ascribe weight, as it is we who perceive when something ought to be done in distinction to when something is or must be done.

While it is quite natural for many who are systemic biologists or chemists or physicists or engineers or behavioural psychologists or computer designers, among others, to try to reduce human mentality to the very same form and essence of those other aspects of nature which they so successfully study by systemic or chemical or physical or engineering or behavioural or computer methods, none the less it is by no means necessary that anyone, even they, accept the argument that this is then all that there is to conscious life. This acceptance is as much a nonlinear emergent leap in logic (or a collapse, an implosion), and thus of faith, as is that one, so fashionable to criticize, in the other direction from ignorance of first causes to an anthropomorphic god. We may call this error the huddle into the simple or the creep into the handy and well-known.

NON-LINEARITIES OF CONSCIOUSNESS AND UNCON-SCIOUSNESS: MAJOR STUMBLING BLOCKS FOR PHYSICAL MODELS OF MIND

It happens that there is very little that is either simple or well-known about human consciousness; not at all because of its strangeness or its rarity, but because consciousness is inherently so elusively dynamic and so exquisitely plural. Knowing *it* is not fundamentally different from *being*. And that is not the way in which, for example, we may come to know a rock or the sum of $1 + 2$.

Actually, there are many people these days who do believe that there is no fundamental reason why one could not some day make a computer that would be conscious. Many in cognitive psychology actually try to 'mate' minds to computers. And certainly that aspiration raises interesting challenges. Others, some of our best thinkers, are devoting extensive treatises to showing that this task is bound to fail because, somehow, the laws of physics would then be violated.[8] Apart from the fact that the laws of physics are not yet wholly known, the fact that consciousness is a matter of psychology and not of physics is somehow overlooked. Perhaps the laws are different and, in any case, the now classical gestalt observations about the non-linearities of none-the-less conscious rational insight and wholly unconscious intuition are still – as they were then, from 1912 onwards – the main stumbling block for any physical model of the mind. That is, if the gestalt view is correct that an emergence from

---

8 See Penrose, R. (1989) *The Emperor's New Mind: Concerning Computers, Minds and the Laws of Physics*, Oxford: Oxford University Press.

bio-chemico-physical processes is critical to the development of consciousness – and I happen to agree – then the laws of physics might not ever (as we discern them in purely physical reality) be able to model that. The problem, as we have noted, is partly one of trying to model a discontinuous process by means of a continuous one. This can only be done, and at best badly, via approximations.[9]

On the other hand, trying to prove that something is impossible is a cheerless endeavour, especially when down the hall from you is someone who is just about to do what you have loudly asserted cannot be done. Rather than trying to prove that the physical modelling of consciousness is impossible, though there is obviously much to that view, one might suggest to consciousness modellers that they first try to model some arguably simpler bio-events, like earthworms or even single-cell amoeba. When they have achieved such models, one would be more willing to listen to their more fantastical claims about minds. To my knowledge, a single living protoplastic cell has not yet been constructed.[10]

AT LAST, CHAOS THEORY – A POSSIBLE MATHEMATICS

There are many processes in mathematics which reflect the peculiar geometric form of the infinite regress that consciousness of consciousness exhibits so robustly. The physical analogy to this, mirrors reflecting mirrors in ever-retreating images, is apposite. Chaos theory, for example, implies branchings upon branchings and there is no reason why one cannot take that (or any other of those conceptual infinite regresses) as fair models of this crucial aspect of self-awareness. No doubt it is much simpler to think about infinitely reflecting mirrors and infinitely branching fractals than about infinitely reverberating self-aware consciousnesses. The whole point of models is that they are simpler than the modelled; some multiplicities and even some dynamics may be glossed. That is what modelling is: a simplification. If one wishes to think seriously about consciousness, however, it may be unfortunate but the fact is that consciousness is precisely what one has to think about, and not some simplification.

The gross failure of linear accumulative methods to approximate the way in which human consciousness functions in the healthy, the ethical, the inventive, and the creative individuals among us is so apparent, so

---

9 Even Wolfgang Köhler's famous search for physical gestalten, to find non-linearities in physics, was also guided by the attempt to base psychology on physics. But Köhler did not then make the mistake of assuming that the non-linearities would necessarily be the same in the two regions. See his (1924) *Die physischen Gestalten in Ruhe und im stationaren Zustsand*, Berlin: Erlangen.

10 See Fox, S. (1988) *The Emergence of Life*, New York: Basic Books. Also Fox, S. (ed. 1965) *The Origins of Prebiological Systems and their Molecular Matrices*, New York: Academic Press. Also Kuppers, B.-O. (1990) *Information and the Origin of Life*, Cambridge, Massachusetts: MIT-Bradford.

obvious to them if not to others, as to constitute the most glaring weakness in all of modern psychology and in modern society as well. The widespread slouch to the banal and the obvious is a natural defence against so manifest a multiplicity. We all tend to fall back on such things in certain risky regions of our lives and thoughts. In truth, the only other weakness in modern life which matches in magnitude this scientific muddle, the tragically absurd nuclear arms race, can be shown ironically to derive in large part from this prior nugatory anthropology. This is the heel of the present-day Achilles: not waste-free nuclear energy production, not rational ecological controls, not even careful population restraints, but the lack of an ordered set of rational insights into the emergent organization of human ethical self-awareness.

FEW PROCESSES ARE ADDITIVE IN PRIVATE MENTAL LIFE OR IN THE DYNAMICS OF PUBLIC GOVERNMENT

Nothing is linear in childhood, or in higher education either, nor is the accumulative trial-and-error model valid even for most motor learning. Perhaps, to brush one's teeth. Nothing is additive in psychotherapy, not even familiarity with the route to the therapist and office, etc. Not ever does one merely accumulate dreams and the recountings of childhood terrors and thereby sum these up to palliative insights into one's own mental chaos, in the way that one might derive succour from pouring more and more oil onto one's burns. Nothing merely just grows, in the formation of creative insights and gestures in science or in art or in the development of ethical or legal standards, because not one of these processes is a rehearsable affair. Nothing merely adds in spirituality, neither the piling up of crosses nor the building of hex signs nor the preparing for revelations nor the scourgings of self-mutilations nor the lighting of candles nor the offering of prayers, nor even the recording of good deeds and of self-sacrifices and indulgences. This is pre-eminently the region in which quality counts, and quality emerges from organization and from refined order, not from lists or catalogues. Admittedly, flying-saucers and extraterrestrial-mongering might just work in this way.

There are many obstacles, in addition to learning to think in novel ways, which stand in the path of the development and acceptance of non-linear models in science, not the least of which occur because both of the leading socio-political systems of our century, participatory democracy and state communism, entail certain social and ethical anthropologies which favour the summative conception for all of life. And science, however much it may wish to hide, is part of intellectual social life. In a democracy, after all, the man elected is not really the 'best man for the job' but only the one who has received the most votes. The assumption is that there is a direct linear relationship between the number of votes and the 'best man for the job'. But we all know only too well how fragile that assumption is. This may be, in modern society and political life, the best working model of representation that mankind can formulate. (But the aesthetics of even representational painting is not judged by vote!) It is most probably the best that we have formulated so far; but it is only that, an approximate formulation. It is also fuzzy. On the other hand, the tenet that the members of the public possess an inalienable right to confer the franchise of higher office, this is a non-linear emergent proposition. That is to say, it cannot be shown by evidence or by vote.

And in state communism, the rule of the state *for* the people is also a linear system, though much more tightly bound (less fuzzy) than that in a constitutional democracy. This rule holds that the state knows best what the people now need (leaving *state* and *knows* and *people* somewhat uncertainly defined), and that some day, when most of the people know this as well (how this is to be determined is also uncertainly defined), there will no longer be a need for the state, and it will wither mysteriously away. But, of course, since such non-linear social processes as insight and innovation and imagination are not allowed during this period when the people are supposedly learning what is best for them, the time for withering never comes. And the state perpetuates itself, in ever tighter and tighter knots, reconfirming the need for its own existence. But, once again, the assumption of the righteousness of state paternalism is itself emergent and non-evidential.

Under state communism, or so it has seemed, some people have faired tolerably well, certainly more so than they did in many previous forms of rule. But hardly anyone thrives, or thrived; nor is its art or its science widely perfused with that enthusiastic and enlightened psychological health and physical zeal that many people do seem to discover within themselves in other socio-political realities. This is so because such good as the greatest number do receive is too often merely brought summatively to them; they are not permitted to, and cannot, non-linearly (i.e. creatively) evoke this good for themselves, or for others. Both these non-linear evokings do count. So, they do not often try. (That the Soviet communist system is now in ruins, also attests to some fundamental human need for inventiveness.)

Most government leaders, in fact, and scientists and engineers as well, and artists and poets, certainly, are well aware that, while linear processes do indeed work both reliably and moderately well for simple ends, they seldom involve the most interesting or rewarding of possible aspirations. When given the choice, the innovative mind always chooses the odd and the unusual. Always, so it can be caught up by this. Thus: a trap for the suspecting.

Certainly, at the core of intellectual adventure, and of scientific and legal and aesthetic progress, is the emergence of new orders and new insights, and of hitherto profoundly unpredictable relationships. In short, while we may strive for regularity and predictability for the other fellow (as in 'Throw him a bone!'), in all our own higher moments we seek to escape from the simple and the mundane and the everyday. Instead of a creep towards the handy, there is a leap into the startling and the mysterious. Even animals play; no one knows about plants, but sometimes *two* distant buds do indeed blossom at once on the same tree. Why?

At present, there is simply no psychology nor pedagogy nor social system geared to or able specifically to encourage a similar public bloom. Of all revolutions thus far, this is still too revolutionary.

11 Key concepts in theoretical neurology

INTRINSIC COMPLEXITY VS. REGENERATION

Let me reiterate, in new terms, a central principle in the evolution of neural function. The principle is dual. 1. As the nervous system increases in intrinsic geometric complexity, it and the gross body periphery lose the ability to regenerate. 2. What the intrinsic geometric complexity comprises is this: the ability to make, sustain, and continually remake dynamic internal models of the ontogenic environment, where model means descriptive geometry.

SENSES MAKE GEOMETRIC ENERGY MODELS OF THE UNIVERSE

This is what the sensory systems do: make descriptive geometric models. The skin obviously, then the eye and the ear, the nose, and the mouth, each in terms of the distribution of the environmental energies to which they are sensitive. A man who can only feel passively with the skin develops a different mental geometry, based primarily on thermal and mechanical patterns, than does a man who can only smell or only hear. This point is of absolutely crucial importance. And as the central ganglion of the nervous system integrates more and more of these various geometries, this is more and more what the integral mind comes to do:

- by eye, to model the radiant reflective aspects of the environment (as the classical optic-projective geometry);
- by ear, to model the air-compression patterns (as the geometry of natural sounds, music, and language);
- by skin, radiant energies (especially infrared) as heat, also pressures, colds, wets, touches, and so forth;
- by kinaesthesis, the topological and geographic object-character of the environment (as the geometry of Euclid which is kinaesthetic and tactile and is not projective);
- and, of course, by all the sense modes together in integration and co-ordination: reality.

When we say that the human intellect can perceive (cannot avoid perceiving) the universal in the single case, this comes about by virtue of this complex intrinsic geometry. That is, the reflexive self-aware capacity of the mind recognizes the separate ways in which the senses are aroused and achieves, in the healthy reality-based ego, a coherent integration of these various geometries. That integration, precisely, is: the universal case.

Henceforth, the notion of mental models is no longer vague and non-specific, it is concrete and exact. Freud's ego is precisely this: the prowess of this second-level geometrizer. Emotions are thus also geometric: they create geodesics, shortest paths, least-EOQ-consuming routes: the way we must go. As such, sometimes they and not ego are in control.

MODELLING MEANS TO TAKE THE UNIVERSAL FROM THE PARTICULAR

Overall, this is what is meant by the adeptness in neural modelling: the ego-brain-self takes the essential universal form from out of the individual concrete case. This, then, becomes the foundation of all philosophy. And this very work. All modelling in engineering and in mathematics and in modern neural network thinking about the brain comes from this prior sensory-rational neurology. This also is the basis for metaphor and for religion. And language. These are all various aspects of mental geometry.

REGENERATION IN OPPOSITION TO MODELLING

The principles of economic EOQ exchange, however, involve constraints on this, for reasons not yet really known. 1. The more primitive the creature, the less it has any ego or specific intrinsic consistency or internal capacity for modeling. Thus it can bodily regenerate – as we shall see in a moment – which means that in its totality, in every cell, it retains throughout much of its life the capacity for mitotic cell division. 2. While, the more advanced the creature the less it can bodily regenerate but (a) the more completely it can maintain a fixed internal geometric integrity and (b) the more the mind, that component at once closest to and yet farthest from the environment, develops its capacity to adapt to environmental changes. This means (c) that it comes to pass that only the mind-brain retains the capacity for cell division, no longer the organism as a whole. We call this brain modelling cell-dividing process *neural plasticity*. In the first process the cell division retains little of the original environment and reproduces the organism; in the second process the cell division retains all of the environment (all models of it) but does not reproduce the organism.

Let us look at some comparative neurophysiology. Certain now famous experiments with planaria carry a lesson for us on this point. Planaria were laboratory trained to turn right, let us say, when a light flashed on. Then they were ground into a porridge and fed to other planaria. Upon consumption, it was reported that these other planaria learned to turn right more readily than planaria not fed that special diet. But these results are now known to be artifactitious, due to improper apparatus cleaning.

The error in such approaches is to think that an internal model of reality need have such a specific and exacting material and hereditable form. The genes may make such enduring (gametic) models, but not experience. Certainly learning involves a real internal model, but this is never in a purely structural form. It is in an energy form. Energy–energy models (as interference patterns and the like) might some day be found in planaria, but they almost certainly will be found in higher animals and thence in man. Such dynamic models are not something that can be inherited or acquired by consumption. They are forms of energy–energy interactions, and are not like muscles or even neurons. The belief in such specific experiential models resembles the idea of the inheritance of acquired characteristics. And both are related to the widespread myths of cannibalism. In many human societies, and for many (perhaps thousands of) years, it was believed that by eating a brave warrior one would then also become brave. This persists even today in the mystique of a 'good thick steak'. The problem for science is always to separate the overlaps between myth and reality, without wholly destroying either. The genes model reality in one way: structurally. The brain another: energetically. How do these interact?

There is, for reasons that we do not yet comprehend, an economic opposition in life forms which contrasts the (i) absence of plastic neural modelling *and* regeneration of whole or peripheral body parts (thus structural modifiability of the periphery) with (ii) intrinsic plasticity (energy-energy modifiability) of the central nervous system *and* no gross peripheral or refined central regeneration.

In man, while the peripheral nervous system regenerates, the central nervous system does not. Indeed, the greatest effort these days in both basic and clinical neuroscience research is devoted to trying to understand why this is so and how to encourage neural regeneration in the central nervous system. Such therapies would be of enormous value in the many devastating paralytic spinal cord injuries.

In rats at the nine-cell stage all cells can be separated and nine fully normal rat-clones be grown. In humans, *whole* splitting of the embryo is believed possible up to maybe sixteen cells with the separate halves surviving as identical twins. We do not yet know about cloning, i.e. splitting into less than half. Nor is it known for certain if full splitting may occur beyond sixteen divisions. It is known that sixteen is pretty close to an absolute limit for us. Indirect evidence from animals suggests, however, that splitting along the primitive streak, at several hundred cells (two-and-a-half weeks), may be possible with twin survival. But the full comparative story is also not known. As increased complexity of neural development is reached, the principle is that the embryo then survives only diminished assaults. On the other hand, the intrinsic variance-processing capacity of the central nervous system to model those assaults increases.

LOSS OF CLAWS IN CRABS

For example, suppose a crab loses a claw; say, a stone crab living in the coral rocks off the coast of Florida. This is certainly a large environmental assault. In humans devastating, but in a crab it leaves no intrinsic model at all, nothing in memory, and only a *momentary external model* because the claw soon grows back. We know there is no internal model because there is no avoidance, even before the claw has grown back, of the exact situation that led to its loss. Crabs can be taught a few things, but not this, and nothing at all in one trial even by such a 'punishment' as loss of a claw.

It happens that this regenerative capacity ceases pretty much in all animals higher than the amphibians, in which it is particularly developed.[1] It is not present in fishes *vis-à-vis* fins, or in birds *vis-à-vis* wings. Nor is it present in many insects. An example with the salamander is instructive. At certain stages in its development, one can take the limb bud from one side of the body and re-attach it on the other side and it will grow into a wholly normal leg, giving rise to a 3 to 1 creature instead of a symmetrical 2 to 2. One can even exchange limb buds from each side and then put them on backwards, and the legs will develop normally *but backwards*. And no environmental experiences whatsoever will make such legs go forwards. There is therefore no internal plasticity.

INVERSION OF NEWTS' AND FROGS' EYES

The classical and magnificent experiments of Roger Sperry involved the eyes of the newt and frog (*inter alia*, 1951).[2] In this work, he took the eyes out from both eye sockets, rotated them through 180° and reinstalled them in the opposite eye-sockets. There, the eyes – to the astonishment of all, even today – re-grew (or re-generated) pretty nearly normal-functioning neural connections to the tectal locations to which those eyes would normally have neurally projected in their natural development. This

---

1 For a commentary and review of some of these issues at higher animal levels, see Rauschecker, J.P. and Marler, P. (eds) (1987) *Imprinting and Cortical Plasticity: Comparative Aspects of Sensitive Periods*, Vol. 1, New York: Wiley–Interscience.

2 Sperry, R.W. (1951) 'Mechanisms of neural maturation', in S.S Stevens (ed.) *Handbook of Experimental Psychology*, New York: Wiley.

firm attraction of specific brain loci for peripheral generative processes is termed *neurobiotaxis* (Ariens–Kappers 1928).[3] In this instance, the amphibians regained pretty nearly normal sight, though precise studies on resolution were not done. But henceforth they flicked their tongues left or leaped left whenever fly-like objects appeared in the right visual field and moved downwards whenever fly-like objects appeared in the upper visual field. That is, the animal's geometric visual spatial organization (and these happen to be very visually dominated creatures) was given by the tectal location to which the peripheral neural regenerations re-attached themselves, and not by any peripheral local signs. Moreover, no environmental influence could be found that would encourage these animals to reorient themselves so that visual left would once again become phenomenal left and up up and down down. So, they would die of starvation, relying only upon the reoriented visual cues, unless fed by artificial means. Many versions of such experiments have been done since,[4] but none have modified the basic finding of extraordinary regenerative capacity.

No one knows for certain whether, in some alternative hypothetical optical experiment, frogs would also fail to reorient themselves if only external inverting or reversing lenses were somehow put upon their eyes, as tiny frog-sized binoculars, etc. But the evidence is pretty compelling for the validity of the inference that they could not so reorient themselves, no matter how propitious a situation we concocted for them.

OPTICAL INVERSION OF IMAGES IN MAN

For mammals, and certainly for humans, the situation is entirely different. First of all, no such experiments with eyes and eye-sockets could be done. The optic nerve is embryologically an extension of the non-regenerating brain and, as such, is a signal component of the central nervous system that does not (so far) regenerate. The optic nerve may be said to carry multiple separate spatial (cortical) projections running in number to the thirties or forties, each giving a coherent, possibly topologically congruent map of different geometric aspects of the visual radiant energy environment. One map for location size, one for location orientation, another for location colour, another for location depth, and so forth. These are still controversial, and the number thirty to forty is hardly parsimonious. Depending upon resolution, there are simply not enough cells to go round. And if there were serious incongruities with thirty maps ... chaos.

3 Ariens–Kappers, C.U. (1928) *Three Lectures on Neurobiotaxis and Other Subjects*, Copenhagen: Levin & Munksgaard.

4 Jacobson, M. (1971) 'Formation of neural connections in sensory systems', in W.R. Lowenstein (ed.) *Handbook of Sensory Physiology*, Berlin: Springer; Vol. 1. (1978) *Developmental Neurobiology*, New York: Plenum.

Be this as it may, since the 1890s and the now classical experiments of Stratton (1897),[5] the study has been repeated often enough that we can pretty well accept the fact that optically inverting lenses, even some binocularly inverting glasses, do turn the visual world upside down and left to right for any human observer willing to try to look through them; and that the initial experiences in wearing such devices are, to say the least, wholly disorienting and disconcerting. It is some minor comfort at least to know that no natural disease process does that, because the effects are virtually paralysing. One cannot effectively move, or only in the barest and most cautious shuffle. Stairs are impossible; shaving a joke.

But the experiments show conclusively that after prolonged wearing – during several months in which all activities are pursued normally, or as normally as can be achieved under the circumstances – the individual eventually learns to function virtually *as if* without wearing such inverting spectacles. And, somewhat later on, the individual adapts so completely that the visual world appears gradually or suddenly, but always wholly (never in part), to re-invert itself, and to reshift left and right. Eventually, the individual perceives a normally oriented visual world.[6]

That result is one of the most famous in all of visual science. What it tells us is this: that, given long-term distortions of the geometrical optics of images coming to the retinae – at least so long as those distortions are coherent over the visual field, which 'coherence' is, admittedly, not yet fully understood, having both neural and mathematical connotations – the neuro-cortical visual system of man is such that it has sufficient plasticity, even in adults, to reorient and to readjust entirely: i.e. fundamentally to remodel the visual world.[7]

Since this experiment has not been done successfully on lower mammals, we cannot say what they would do, only what they might do. We do know that chickens raised with optical prisms that shift the visual world left or right of actual position never seem to learn to peck correctly for their kernels of corn, but peck regularly leftwards or rightwards of their proper position, in precise accord with the prismatic distortions. Such chickens would also die of starvation unless artificially fed.

---

5 Stratton, C.W. (1897) 'Vision without inversion of the retinal image', *Psychol. Review* IV: 341–60; 463–81. Also 'Upright vision and the retinal image', Ibid. 182–7.

6 Kohler, I. (1951) *Über Aufbau und Wandlungen der Wahrnehmungswelt*, Sitzungsberichte CCVII (1) Vienna: Osterreichische Akademie der Wissenschaften.
   I myself have built several of these devices and use them regularly in classes to demonstrate the inversion effect. I have even driven on the back roads with them, and learned to manoeuvre fairly well among sparse traffic. But the sudden appearance, once, of a bicycle rider on my right whom I had to pass seemingly on my left soon put an end to my experiments! To produce genuine reorientation takes great care and extensive training, as noted, over weeks and months.

7 By *coherence*, in this context, we mean this: it would never be possible to adapt to an optical system which — as if a lens had a moving scratch in it or a slipping tear — distorted the visual field randomly over time.

For humans, we have good reason to believe that similar geometrical plasticity holds to some degree in audition (experiments done), in smell and in touch and the other externally directed senses (experiments not done); but that such plasticity does not exist to this degree in most lower mammals, and not at all in birds, reptiles, amphibians, fishes, and so forth.

There are many subtleties of these studies, the consideration of which would plunge us into minutiae and issues at the edge of our knowledge. For us here presently, they simply constitute most convincing illustrations of the regeneration-plasticity-modelling dimension, as well as reasonably clear evidence for the basic neural principles that I am elucidating.

Consider the walrus. How much of its natural history can we tell from its loss of a tusk and the scars and gnarled healings of flipper, hide, and tail? These are fine geometric models.

ONE-TRIAL LEARNING-MODELLING

On the other hand, in humans even more so: 'once bitten twice shy'. The catalogue is virtually endless of minor assaults to the periphery of child or adult human that induce not only an obvious external model but an intrinsic neural model sufficient to be recalled even years later by similar circumstances or, if not actually recalled, sufficiently intrinsic none the less that similar situations are avoided subconsciously: i.e. the universal really does reside in the single case.

This is one very real function of the Freudian unconscious: it thus leads also to philosophy. In the technical psychology jargon this is called 'one-trial learning', whether overt or covert. Indeed, this modelling is often two-fold: material and abstract. The loss of a limb by a person models the assault extremely precisely in the material body because the limb does not grow back, while the well-known phantom limb phenomenon attests to the persistence and precision of the abstract internal model, this time of the *reafferent* self, which only extended experiential integration with the internal-external trauma of the amputation (mobility, handling, etc.) eventually helps to assuage. Phantom limbs sometimes last for years.

The point is that none of this sort of intrinsic (one-trial or other) modelling occurs in crabs, and only some few aspects of it occur occasionally in lower animals. But in man – despite the volums of academic laboratory learning theory done with rats – the fact is that one-trial learning and internal modelling is the way in which *most* of human learning takes place, both in the classroom and in life. In essence this is learning by 'grasping the principle', 'understanding the relationship', 'gaining insight into the complexity', in short: internally modelling. Of course we rehearse some things (say, vocabulary) and of course we use trial-and-error-learning methods for others (say, skiing); but in the essential knowledge exchange and enhancement of civilized life, *insight* into cognitive, mathematical, aesthetic, ethical, and practical relationships and harmonies is the absolute common key. Relationships, ideas, concepts, theorems, and functions all fall into place. They become organized, geometrized.

REGENERATION OF SENSE-ENERGY INGESTION SURFACES

To reiterate: each of the senses permits the ingestion of a geometric description of the environment in terms of its own sensitivities to important energy slopes (gradients even of zero) and energy accelerations (edges or changes of gradients). The central mind-core (the ego and/or the unconscious) integrates these descriptions into a present moment and into a sequence of present moments and stores some of the geometries into memory and uses others for the restructuring of previous memories (insight) and uses still others for corrective or adaptive actions as it freely sucks new sensory geometric order (relations) from the disordered environment by any and all modes, particularly the reafferent kinaesthetic (RK). The less the various sensory geometries agree, for whatever reasons, the more the conscious ego processes are forced to emerge to resolve them.

Consequently, the problem thus far with most neurophysiological and neural net models of learning becomes clear: they are devoted mostly to the iterative processes of lower animal learning, and hardly at all to the one-trial insightful or cognitive learning typical of human mental dynamics, or the ordered learning that leads to the body image. As far as tackling the crucial geometric structure of the intrinsic ego-istical self, this problem has not yet even been phrased.

The enormous survival advantage – of the capacity to model internally and store and remodel and store again the ontogenic environment and to do this on the basis of a single case (which then in the model becomes universal – seems apparent over the lower–level gross mitotic or limb regenerative capacity. This internal modelling capacity is tightly related to survival in the face of great environmental variance. It allows us to deal with changing states. Human beings can survive in a vastly larger set of environmental conditions than can any other species, several orders of magnitude larger. The fact that successful internal neural *plasticity* cannot appear in any creature together with the (much less successful) external limb *regeneration* capacity is probably due to some as yet hidden bio-principles in neural EOQ economics.

The only obvious remnants, perhaps, that we have of this latter capacity are finger- and toe-nails, and hair. But, as it happens, there are a great many non-obvious remnants as well: the villi of the stomach, the alveoli in the lungs, the epithelial surface of the skin, the outer segments of the rod/cone cells of the eye, the nasal epithelium, receptor cells on the tongue, cells in the basilar membrane of the inner ear and in the cupula of the semi-circular canals. Basically, of the human body, all those cell layers directly involved with the first-stage ingestion of the several separate energy geometries of external nature (electromagnetic, thermal, airborn particles, saliva-born particles, oxygen, mechanical pressure, air pressure waves), as well as food and water distributions, are regularly consumed in the ingestion process, and they are as regularly *regenerated* by recuperative metabolism in healthy humans. The whole complex of receptor-cell outer segments in a normal healthy human eye regenerates regularly over about one week. Indeed, one of the early signs of various pathologies is a slowing and a blurring of these regenerative processes, the integrity of which maintain the senses and so also the primary aspects of sensory-rational intelligence.[8] A similar slowing and blurring also occurs in age: almost all refined measurements of time- and of space- and sometimes of quality-resolution show decreases, and in all modes.

This means, perforce, that there is also a slowing in the rate at which new especially complex multi-sensory intrinsic models of the environment can be built up and old ones shed. But there is an overall increased fuzziness in their geometrical sharpening: a deletion of the inessential, since to preserve alternatives uses up energy. This explains in part youth's impatience with age but, as well, age's greater wisdom. To cite van Gogh, 'Emphasize the essential, leave the obvious vague.'

ENVIRONMENT MODELLING VS. CULTURE MODELLING

Lest it be misconstrued that this environmental modelling in both body and mind is unimportant, we must stress once again the strong sensory-rational components in intelligence and the stern influence of both hereditary and environmental influences on the sensory systems and their integrity. Nutrition, in particular, but also disease processes of many sorts, as well as injury assaults such as the loss of a limb or an eye, directly affect the sense-ingestion capacity of the human organism, and so significantly influence at least those aspects of intellectual function that are related to the sensory ingestion of environmental variance or information. And also those related to information production, as via kinaesthetic reafference.

LOSS OF VARIANCE-PROCESSING CAPACITY BEARS ON SENSORY-RATIONAL INTELLIGENCE

Clearly, nutrition affects the skin modalities and hearing as well as vision. Moreover, the vestibular system and the kinaesthetic-reafferent system are particularly affected by diet, and also by the regularity of exercise and the quality of shelter. No doubt, the failure to thrive (due say, to poor mothering) affects these things markedly and so this, in addition,

---

8 Shipley, T. (1990) *The Theory of Intelligence: A Sensory-Rational View*, Springfield, Illinois: Thomas.

constitutes a major influence on neuro-cognitive modelling. If a child cannot well resolve the orientation difference between two near vertical lines, then he/she cannot well perceive what orientation should appear next in some sequence of orientations. But a child who cannot muster sufficient ego motivation even to care about orientations will likewise fail to get the point of an abstract geometric argument.

Similarly for refined hearings of speech and other sounds and refined smells and tastes and touches. Caresses, hugs, bounces, kisses, nudges, groomings are absolutely essential to the development of the tactile modality, and are prevalent throughout the higher animal kingdom. Snakes, however, do not groom. The strong sense of self requires such complex communal interactions. And, the whole normal plethora of refined movements developing throughout childhood – walking, running, catching, collecting, dodging, leaping, lifting, pointing, waving, signing, kissing, exploring, turning, and thence speaking and reading – must be encouraged as prelude to the subtle and abstract motions required later on in high adult culture. That even the neurology is different is attested to by the clear distinction, in brain-injured symptomatology, between constructional and ideational apraxia: the man who cannot put on his belt vs. the man who can play a violin from memory almost as well as ever but who cannot abstractly blow a kiss.

This, then, is certainly one way in which culture enters as a controlling factor in the development of nuance-rich sensory-rational intellectual skills. Handling and mothering and enriched mobility and shelter and good nutrition are all major factors during infancy (and, as well, during the maternal culture and the culture of the pregnant and nursing mother) which materially influence the quality and refinement both of the compass of subtle sensory-rational variance processing that is possible and its neurological multiplicity. By this latter I mean this: in a culture in which, for example, people only grunt and do not speak, a certain loss of acoustic resolution and sound-variance processing and producing potential occurs. This will have a material basis in the brain. Such neuro-variance processing potentials are known to be present in the newborn child of any race. Given adequate cultural enrichment and nutritional quality in the maternal and neonatal world, any infant can learn and soon take command of any natural human language. But when children are not then, exactly in the babbling months, encouraged to experiment and to flower verbally by an enriched childhood culture, they fail to reach full neural potential and the neurobiotaxis itself comes into default.

CATS REARED SEEING ONLY VERTICAL STRIPES

Cats, for example, reared seeing only vertical stripes become blind to horizontal stripes, and their small intrinsic complex of 'innate horizontal line' processors is thereby enticed over into becoming 'vertical line' processors (by, perhaps, a process quite analogous to neurobiotaxis). The cats became 'super' vertical processors.[9] Extrapolating to humans, I think it reasonable to suggest, and the social-behavioural evidence so far agrees, that children reared in an environment in which the demands for resolution and refined sensory-rational processing are minimal or in some ways shifted from the ideal balance will also be at risk of becoming reduced variance processors. They will take food only as something to eat, and will neither know nor comprehend cuisine. Epicurianism is wholly missed. Similarly for hearing: perhaps some reduced form of verbal communication survives, but rhetoric and poetry and music are no longer possible. These subtle aural arousals become virtually permanently incomprehensible, incapable of even rationally being sensed. There are well-known major genetic components in tune deafness, but there are crucial environmental ones as well. Similar reductions in the demand for high prowess in language-meaning resolution and in expressive-variance comprehension and production likewise become absolutely critical, both on the intimate family level and the broad political one.

The refined production of speech is as much a kinaesthetic-reafferent skill as it is an auditory one, probably more. After all, we can all mouth our words, and often still be well understood. Moreover, most unusual humanly produced sounds *never heard before* can be reproduced reasonably well *on first hearing*, which means: with very little error. This is a key observation, indicating a marvellous, innate, genetically based mirror coherence between sound ingestion, intrinsic motoric-image formation, lingual reafference, and speech. But this has many serious ramifications. Those individuals in any culture who are, for whatever reason, deprived in childhood at certain *critical periods* (that is a term expressing the fact that these things are known to take the greatest toll at particular ages) of the chance to hear and to imitate rich linguistic variance are condemned to responding only to meagre demands and to producing little linguistic variance themselves. And so, as adults, they will be unable to listen to or to comprehend speech-language subtleties or to produce them. This is the basis of the kernel of truth in what is widely known as the Benjamin Whorf hypothesis: that the language we grew up in and regularly use *determines materially* how we perceive and thus think about and express the world. That hypothesis is easily proven wrong in that strong form; but in the form of variance processing, it is perfectly correct.

Consequently, this is one aspect of culture that takes its toll in the neural models that children make of their neonatal world and, as well, in their

---

9 See especially Hirsch, H.V.B. and Spinelli, D.N. (1970) 'Visual experiences: modified distribution of horizontally and vertically oriented receptive fields in cats', *Science* 168: 869–71. Also Hirsch, H.V.B. and Leventhal, A.G. (1978) 'Functional modification of the developing visual system', in M. Jacobson (ed.) *Development of Sensory Systems*, Vol. 9, *Handbook of Sensory Physiology*, Berlin: Springer.

very capacity to model new ones. This detriment henceforth forever limits the way they perceive, experiment, and think in new realities.

I cannot stress too strongly the importance of this concept of variance processing. Variance in smells, in tastes, in touches, in speech sounds, in gestures, in mental tasks, in kinaesthetic tasks, is the encouragement and determinant of the neuro-modelling prowesses that develop during neoteny. As such, the variance achieved within the nurturing culture controls the potential for modelling and for remodelling (the neuro-psychological inventiveness and resilience) that the adults will on average possess. And I write here of a very frank neurological process, not one merely surmised.

Admittedly, while this aspect of sensory-rational intelligence is a most important one, it cannot yet be examined by the tests so far developed under this aegis. Tests quite specifically devoted to 'variance-processing', to 'variance-expressing', and to the processing of sensory-rational just-noticeable-discriminations among intersensory arousals and arguments, can be developed to do just that. Tests involving production, for example, might go something like these: imitate this gesture, now give me five similar but just characteristically different gestures; do the same gesture as if you were now an old man; now a young girl. And so forth. The scoring of such tasks would not be simple, but the challenge now is thrown.

SEAFARERS AND SIGNERS

The US off-coast island called Martha's Vineyard lies in the Atlantic Ocean just off Cape Cod, in a state still going by its marvellous Indian name: *Massachusetts*. It happens that there once lived on that island an extraordinarily large proportion of deaf-mutes. The biological reasons for this are genetic-cultural, and these have been traced genealogically over many generations to a small region in England (the Weald of Kent) from which many of the early settlers came long before the US Revolution. Careful historical research suggests that there were possibly some deaf people among the settlers as early as 1642, certainly years before the first noted case in 1714. The last genealogically traceable deaf person died there in the 1950s, though most had left the island even earlier. Today, there are few deaf remaining on the island, and the proportion has returned to that found in the US population at large.

Now, what is so instructive about this – and I am in debt to the fine book by Groce[10] for all these facts, if not this interpretation – is that nearly all of the people living on the island, as far as the records on this go back in history: (a) could naturally speak if they were not deaf; (b) could naturally sign if they were deaf; (c) and, moreover, could also sign if they

---

10 Groce, N.E. (1985) *Everyone Here Spoke Sign Language*, Cambridge, Massachusetts: Harvard University Press.

could *also* speak. It was just naturally understood that everyone on the island used both languages, and was equally fluent bilingually in them, both speech and sign. Moreover, it was regular practice when in mixed company to speak and sign at the same time. Further, there appears to have been absolutely no stigma at all *of any kind* attached to the deaf, which is quite unusual. Perhaps this is because deaf people were born regularly into almost every family on the island. The deaf were wholly integrated into the society. They found work just as the hearing did; became rich or poor, just as they did; married and had children, just as the hearing. And so forth. If the historical record that Groce describes is accurate – and the care taken in the book leads me to conclude so – then this was a cultural experiment of immense significance. Because everyone signed, the deaf were not left out of anything. Their ontological environment was, virtually, as enriched and as varied as the environment of the hearing. No distinctions were made in school, for example, since the teachers also all signed. The deaf and hearing attended classes together, though in later years many of the deaf also went away to special schools to learn advanced or standard signing – and some lip-reading due to the influence of Alexander Graham Bell who strongly supported this quite different technique.

In any event, what this shows is that a culture can be structured to a considerable degree so that the loss even of such a major sense-rational mode need not be a serious hindrance to a normal life. There is no doubt that these deaf, as all deaf, would exhibit no ability whatsoever to ingest information (variance-flow) from the physical world so long as it was encoded in condensations and rarefactions of the air, and thus would reveal a profound sensory-rational loss of intelligence. In the natural environment, few would survive childhood. But in this culture they were encouraged to and did function quite as normal, in just about every aspect of their lives that counted: creating a livelihood, marrying, parenting, and playing roles in the social and political life of the community. These were largely sea-faring fisher people for whom boat-to-shore and boat-to-boat communication by signing had a distinct and obvious advantage over speech, particularly in a howling gale.

GENETIC GEOMETRY VS. ENVIRONMENTAL GEOMETRY

What this means – and now we draw the full lesson – is that despite sensory-rational losses by hereditary or environmental modelling, cultural modelling in human society can in some special instances be co-ordinated so as virtually to overcome whatever disadvantage these have introduced.

One could see, then, that on this island someone made deaf by the intrinsic geometry of genetic modelling and someone made deaf by the adventitious environmental modelling via disease or by having the ears exposed to 1000db of highly dangerous noise – and, thus, having an equivalent environmental model permanently imposed on (in) the body – could each be raised in a culture in which the significance of those particular losses is minimized. Other losses, perhaps not. Say the child cannot read; or the child has one leg longer than the other; or the child is blind, and so forth. But for the loss of the aural sensory-rational ingestion and modelling capacity ... yes.

This history gives us many insights about how to create better social-cultural modelling to compensate for these and other sensory-rational losses in children and in adults in our wider society. Here, for example, the culture was largely free of all tests of surviving, of adjusting, even of belonging and of thriving based upon hearing. It seems to me that one can, in part, judge the quality of a civilization by how it treats its less and least able citizens. In this valley of the deaf, the deaf were also kings. They did not need, somehow, to try to regenerate ears.

12 The origin of free will

FREE WILL AS A SENSORY–RATIONAL PROCESS, IN CONTRAST TO PSYCHOANALYTIC–HISTORICAL AND GESTALT-SITUATIONAL DETERMINISTIC ONES

It is not that too few before me have written on the topic of free will but, rather, too many. And yet this topic remains so abstruse that only the foolish or the excessively bold would seek to address it. Most psychologies, even the Freudian and the gestalt, were unable to confront it directly because of several limitations. Perhaps Freud was so overwhelmed by his discovery of the extraordinary importance of unconscious motivations that he simply addressed less adequately those conscious propulsions that would be requisite for any legitimate notion of free will and voluntarism. Sometimes – one supposes he might have observed – this might be a pathological delusion related to those of grandeur and the assumption of magical powers. To the extent that the unconscious id comes under conscious ego control, the will may dominate in thought and in action, but it is never wholly free of unconscious influences. The gestalters, on the other hand, were so attracted by the way in which sensory ingestion was often compelled to organize reality perceptions in certain ways by the 'requiredness of situations' that they also tended to overlook what shaping of reality might still otherwise be achieved, from the top down: voluntarily. As for the behaviourist school, since 'will' of any sort was denied, free will was not even a topic.

Under this weighty tradition of denial by scientific psychology, it has been left to philosophers to deal with this conundrum and to formulate the ultimate puzzle. If one is able to understand (perceive the causes of) another's actions, this means that the reasons for what he/she does are surface in character, obvious. Presumably, this also means that these actions were 'compelled by forces' beyond his/her control. One says: 'He fell in love with her at first sight', 'He had to reply that way, he had no other choice', and so forth. On the other hand, when the causes for some other's actions remain truly hidden, even after extensive study and investigation, then presumably one might be able to conclude that he/she 'acted' of his/her own free will. One might not, but one could.

As long as sociological causes could be identified for many, most, or all public actions, one could entertain the position that even modest citizen criminal behaviour is caused and not wilful, and not only that of public servants. But if one could not identify a 'just cause' – such as broken homes, drunken fathers, drug-addicted mothers, etc. – then, but only then, would one at least be able to think openly about the possibility that wilful choices had been or were being made.

On the face of it, however, the obvious symmetry violation of this offends any overt philosophy, though perhaps not some covert ones or social prejudices. When it is so obvious that our own actions are always made freely, it is at least blatant if not outright arrogance for us to deny that same liberty to those whom we would address and call friends.

More important than this violation is the prior problem of extra-personal ascription. One wonders what there is about this notion of free will that somehow allows me and you to determine whether a third person has 'freedom of will' solely by the success or failure of our own ability to identify some putative cause. Maybe we are merely stupid, and so we fail to find any reasonable causes(s) and endow the person with free will when he/she knows full well that he/she was reacting to compelling forces. Or, conversely, in the instance where we do identify what seems to us to be a fine cause or set of causes and so we deny freedom of choice, the person thoroughly disavows those causes, and insists that the action was fully liberated and freely undertaken.

The first point is this:

freedom of the will in some action cannot logically be ascribed by an outsider, there can be no extrapersonal donation to or withholding from someone else's actions the attribute of free will.

Actions may sometimes appear on the surface to be freely undertaken and this appearance may accord well with the experience of the actor. And so also the mirror. But the coherence between the perceptions of the viewer of the action and those of the actor her/himself cannot be the deciding factor. Indeed, it cannot be any factor at all.

LIMITS TO THIRD PERSON ATTRIBUTION OF SENSORY QUALITY

Let us examine this process from the sensory-rational point of view. Consider a simpler case: one observes someone looking up at a billboard on which is displayed a picture of a beautiful girl scantily clad, drinking beer. At her feet, prancing about, are two puppies. One now makes the statement: 'Ha, I see that you like pretty girls.' To which the other person replies: 'What girl? I am looking at those marvellous puppies. They remind me of my dog Chatter.' That is to say, even in such an utterly simple action as looking at something, an outside observer can be in error as to what one is looking at. Even an outside observer who knows the actor quite well, but who then and there misconstrues the motive.

Misconstruing is the bane of all psychology based on outside introjection of motivational attributes. Indeed, this is one of the just complaints against psychoanalysis: that such attributes can be thrown about virtually at will, in order to suit the action to the theory and the theory to the structure of inner personality dynamics held by the thrower. If someone disagrees, then he/she can just throw some new attributes.

Clearly, there are issues of both logical and psychological confusion.

The logical one is easy to address: if those doing the throwing take upon themselves the freedom to throw, then they cannot deny that same freedom to those undertaking the primary action.

Which means either that their throwing is not so free after all or that the actions of the actor are freer than they are willing to admit. Either way, we cannot by these means obtain a viable solution of the puzzle.

Consequently, it is the psychology which must thus far be at fault, not the logic. Consider this case where the man is looking at the puppies and does not even see the girl while the ascriptor regards him as looking at the girl. Clearly, this is a trivialization of the fact that the ascription of motives or experiences is only a variously successful effort and that it can have notable failures.

On the one hand, that ascription can actually be much better than chance, we know from the overwhelming success of both animal and human survival, wherein the stalking lion is correctly perceived by the gazelle as the one about to strike and the flirting lady is correctly perceived by the bachelor as the one willing to be courted. Yet, on the other hand, we cannot let the fair probability of the success at the ascription of motives-experiences blind us to the psychological truth that we may be wrong. And so long as we may be wrong, we may be wrong for the reason, *inter alia*, that he/she has freely choosen to act in an unpredictable fashion. We have at least to admit that possibility. And then, of course, taking this argument around yet another turn, if we find unpredictability as a consistent personality trait, we may dub it and not freedom as the cause.

One might wonder, amid such abstruse arguments, why it is that nature was constrained to evolve animals in the first place when plants were already doing pretty well on their own. That is, why did the forces of nature evoke creatures that move about freely in space or appear to (NB We do not yet seem to have 'creatures' that can 'move about freely in time', or appear to?), unless there was some result of that freedom or its appearance that gave them an advantage over living processes that did not or could not so move? Once we have rotating planets and their moons, and so wind currents and streams and flows of water on their surfaces, presumably life could have stopped in its development, merely taking its motion from these processes: the salt-water straining feeders, for example, seem well adapted to this; also pollen and other plant debris blowing in the wind. These are all pretty reliable systems.

But, somehow, the leap from animals which move only passively with water currents and flow to minimally mobile ones to those capable of geographically large motoric explorations gave an extraordinary advantage to these latter forms. They could, for example, consume as EOQ donors the sessile forms and the more passively mobile.

CHOICES AND DECISIONS BY BIRDS AND ELEPHANTS

Self-initiated motion has a clear survival and mate-getting advantage. No one argues against that. Why is the higher stage of 'freely chosen, self-initiated' motion so difficult to move up to? Is responsibility so greatly to be feared?

Consider the bird. It uses wind currents in its flying, sometimes soaring aloft for days virtually without effort, journeying from current to current. Not knowing better, one might almost say that such birds are being wafted about wholly at the whim of the wind, as if the wind had the liberty and not the bird. This would not be an especially veridical picture of either wind or bird; but I suppose that it might be defended by some.

But then let us now take this same image to the land. Here we have the *elephant*. Now surely even the most determined anti-libertarian could not maintain that the elephant is wafted about on earth by wind currents. Or even that it is wafted about by currents of temperature, or gravity slopes across the hillside, or even by sights or smells of food, water, or mates. Somehow, no matter how willing to comply, this creature cannot be stretched (by even the most imaginative) into one that is controlled, so to say, exclusively by ephemeral or even material neighbouring forces. For him, some inside process must be granted. What might that be?

Clearly, whatever the forces are that move this fellow, they must be pretty strong and could hardly be wholly ephemeral. Indeed, my contention is that mental processes are eminently causal and that they are energy–energy transformations of a particular kind, being material but in its most energetical cast. That high energy content is precisely what gives mind its great power: to appear in such a variety of material forms.

In any event, it would be absurd to deny that the elephant moves, and foolish to deny that the elephant moves pretty much 'as it wishes' since it is patently obvious that there is not much around that could prevent that! However driven it may seem at times to be, the fact that the elephant is not 100 per cent predictable – actually, hardly 1 per cent predictable – means that to all *our* intents and purposes, it does what it wants to do.

(God may still be in control, but that is another matter.) No one denies that the elephant may well have a less refined sense of self than we do, so that his awareness in general even of what he wants desperately to do may not be so refined as ours for even casual desires. At specific moments, as when confronted with a receptive female in heat or a charging tiger, no doubt he 'has' a pretty well-focused intention then. And actions then may be less willed than at other times. And, surely, no one who would deny that *we* have free will, would assert that he does.

But just how good is the evidence for the contention that all the elephants' actions are compelled? Actually not good at all. Animal behaviour studies in the field indicate quite conclusively that the elephant has sufficient somaesthetic awareness to 'tell' hunger from thirst from sexual arousal from sickness, and so forth; and that it does largely act in proper co-ordination with those needs, to eat, drink, mate, and lie down. Actually, this sort of refined somaesthetic gnosis goes down quite far in evolution; in rudimentary form it goes down very far. Proper coherence between survival actions and the inner condition (which may sometimes be mental) is what animal life is. Chimps, for example, can even be taught to tell us about such things, to indicate foods or drinks or sleeptime or stomach aches, by using sign language in a sensory-rational somaesthetic refinement the ranges of which are not yet known. Many other types of pets do so as well. That is what we have selected they do, to become pets! And there is no reason to suspect that the elephant could not do likewise, if given a proper medium and encouragement. The degree of communicable somaesthetic refinement is probably less in elephants than in chimps, but even in man it is not all that great, as any physician or writer knows.

Whatever else this means, it means that the elephant is not wafted about randomly by internal states either, but appears to be able voluntarily to adjust outward behaviours in an orderly accord.

In keeping with our main contention: when a moth goes to the flame, perhaps no; but when the elephant adjusts his actions to the rushing flood, probably yes. It is highly probable, in fact: (i) that he has first-level somaesthetic awareness of being hungry (having a hunger) or of being thirsty (having a thirst) or of being sexually aroused (having a lust), but that (ii) he does not yet have the second-level awareness requisite to the deliberate adjustment of his behaviour to one or the other of these emotions. In short, when he is hungry he most probably knows this, which means to perceive well (to raise to conscious mental awareness) that particular intrinsic somaesthetic state. But he does not know that he knows that he is hungry. Which means that he cannot put food aside for a rainy day, or feign sleepiness or lack of interest. Many animals, however, as elephants and lions, do keep harems which, in some remote way, does help to keep mates about as against the day.

So, while we do not ascribe free will (second-level awareness) to the elephant, we do not deny him the first-level awareness of making his own decisions. No one (but the most recalcitrant) who has seen elephants guide their babies into the centre of the herd when confronted with danger, or seen (and heard) the big bulls stand apart facing the danger and pawing and raising up ears, tusks, and trunk and trumpeting before turning away or charging, could deny the presence of at least some components of voluntary decision making. Nor could anyone who has observed a 'trained' elephant refuse to pick up a log that is 'too big' or tread with exquisite care across a field on which hundreds of people are lying. All these processes could still be relatively straightforward: merely weighing two alternatives and coming up with the one that is most 'compelling'. Yet, while the elephant is surely never like that infamous hungry donkey, paralysed between two exactly equal piles of hay, one need not credit it with clairvoyance or even a conscious self-aware mental weighing of probabilities, nor even with a vastly heightened (say over an ant) sense of indecision (though I believe this to be true). But, even in the light of all these many previous cautions, some elephantine awareness of alternatives would seem to be a necessary ascription on the part of any reasonable animal ethnologist. That is, the elephant is not merely flowing tropistically up or down one or another gradient. He/she is actively choosing.

So we seem led to conclude – that is, we come to this particular mental state either via absolute chaotic abandon or ineluctable rational compulsion – that the elephant makes conscious decisions between alternatives, and that he/she does this often throughout the day: to charge or not to charge, to browse here or there, to mate with this maiden-elephant or that lad-one; and so on. What we are not led to conclude – by the weight of sensory-rational evidence or whatever – is that he/she does this entirely freely, which I suppose might mean: 'entirely without weighing the evidence', which is an absurdity, or that he/she possesses such a precise form of an awareness that he/she is driven by the uncertainty up to the second-level awareness that he/she is now 'making a decision'. To sum up: we assert that he perceives food or water or female elephants, which is self-evident, *prima facie*, and, further, that he knows full well that this is what he perceives. But we need not assert that he knows equally fully well that he perceives food or water or potential mates.

The key point is this:

> decisions are made, even many grand decisions, by elephants in accordance with the same principles of natural history that control our own first-level decisions, below the acceleration of consciousness. And, moreover, as we do not by any means have awareness of all the factors then and there bearing upon our decision, so also does not he.

But, sometimes, the elephant refuses. He refuses to go up too steep a hill; he refuses to lift a too-big log; he refuses to lift any log; he refuses to obey a new elephant boy; and so forth. In these actions, we are coming closer. We may not yet be at the second level of decision making; but this is the nascent process. All the higher mammals are certainly capable of, and do, exhibit stubbornness and refusals. Which must mean that they are precisely, then and there, *not* driven by the alternatives, but are consciously rejecting the alternatives. Some, like mules, seem to have this built in. Does this mean that they have a better awareness of (somaesthetic and other) alternatives than the more docile cows and horses? Probably it does. We cannot yet be sure. But certainly in our pet animals, we often encounter resistance to eating a new food, to going in a car, to sleeping in a new place, to meeting a strange person, *ad infinitum*.

There is no anthropomorphism at all in us perceiving in these behaviours a reason for the ascription of some awareness of alternatives, because it is precisely those sorts of behaviours that we exhibit ourselves when we experience alternatives and when we observe our fellow humans confronting their alternatives. What we cannot know precisely – for the pachyderm or the human – is the acuteness with which those alternatives are experienced. Or that they are perceived at all as we perceive them. But that they are perceived there in that place with an awareness at the first level only the most sceptical would doubt. And that doubter is the very one who also doubts my A^2! . . . and sometimes even his own (*vide supra* chapter 5).

In short, I take the evidence of animal behaviour as indicative of the direct and conscious confronting of alternatives. If this is so, then it follows (this is how our higher frontal lobular nervous system functions: it deduces) that some, albeit vague, albeit imprecise, none the less definite, particular sense of decision making emerges in the intrinsic mental geometry of that creature. On the lower animal levels (near to plants) all alternatives are muted out by virtue of chemical or other imbalances, so that the creature need not waste EOQ on either decisions or awarenesses of decisions. Lower creatures are inefficient EOQ gatherers, compared to others higher. They lack the nutrient-ingestion capacity and the metabolism to pack much of this in. Gradually, in evolution, the capacity to make more and more decisions is called forth because, as we are emphasizing, the greater the variance that may be successfully confronted, the greater the energy-management efficiency and the survival. And dragged along at some far remove from this is the awareness of the making of a decision.

And dragged along, though still further behind and only in humans, is the awareness of the awareness of making a decision: the mental mirror, or ego.

Of course, few decisions made by living creatures will concur with the perfect abstract mathematical balance or probability demands. Just as there is no perfect triangle in nature, or circle, probabilities are ideals towards which life and thought may aim. One would be foolish in the extreme to expect more than that. All direct and recalled sensory information, and thence linguistic information as well in an educated ingestor

– and, of course, emotions – co-ordinate complexly in that probability decision process. I am not at all surprised that the evidence in some actual experiments (e.g. Herrnstein)[1] shows that some humans do not always make decisions so as to maximize their own personal gain (or the ideal probabilities of receiving food, water, and mates). What does surprise me is anyone thinking that they do.

Occasionally, we may make decisions on the basis of probabilities as perceived in some pure abstract mathematical order, since this is precisely what mathematical order is: that upon which most if not all humans ultimately do agree, when informed properly, is the best sequencing of the best EOQ bets. But actually deciding this way in any particular situation is mostly fortuitous, and happens only when emotions are all kept well in bounds. Most of us are seldom that firmly disciplined. In truth, information about nature is often sensed in muddled and sometimes in misleading forms – often we are deliberately misled or misperceived – and occasionally information comes in wholly inverted form because we are reading in a mirror but do not know it. It is only a wonder that we are so right as often as we are. The simplest experiment in psychology to discredit as naive is one which shows how poorly humans do in making decisions in their own favour. Intelligence means to choose or select among alternatives (L. *inter = among* plus *legere = choose*); it does not mean that this is always done optimally or according to rule.

Probability theory, as the history of modern mathematics tells us, is one of the most subtle and difficult of all mathematical ideas to grasp. This is why it is one of the most modern. Consequently, the vast majority of the people in this world today do not know precisely what is meant by that term. And even among the sophisticated and educated, most do not know either. In fact, many of the constraints in experimental science serve to do just that: to make us come to the correct decision on the basis of probabilities *despite* our stubborn insufficiency and unwillingness to come to the correct decision on the basis of probabilities.

Once we arrive at the capacity to choose between alternatives, we are confronted with questions of freedom and of responsibility. So now we must draw the fine point upon the fine point upon the fine point. We start out by nothing that these questions are not at all trivial. In one view, their imperfect phrasings and their mythopoetic answers form the basis of the religions of the world. In another, their imperfect phrasings and mythopoetic answers form the basis of civil governance. Psychology thus speaks directly to the nature of humanity and of human society. Yet, as a science, it has woefully shirked that *responsibility*.

The crucial point now comes to something like this:

---

1 For example, Herrnstein, R.J. (1990) 'Rational choice theory', *Amer. Psychologist* 45: 356–67.

The attributes of experience cannot be ascribed from outside, except under highly constrained conditions. Normally they belong to private awareness.

It is certainly possible to control situations so that definite experiences emerge, however, and this is not merely on average:

1 deprive someone of air and he/she will experience asphyxiation;
2 touch someone with a hot match and he/she will feel pain (with a very few exceptions: some genetic pathologies, some hysterical, some mystical);
3 shine a bright light in someone's eyes and he/she will be blinded;
4 splash ice cold water on someone and he/she will feel cold and wet (with fewer exceptions than in 2 above), and
5 deprive someone of sleep and he/she will feel tired.

And so on. Given time and enthusiasm, this list is another small infinity.

On the other hand, there is another infinity (which, I think, is a larger one, after Cantor and his $\aleph_0$ and $\aleph_1$)[2] of stimulus situations in which one cannot be certain of the resultant experience:

1 turn on a blue light and maybe he/she does not perceive blue;
2 play a chord on a piano and maybe he/she does not hear a chord;
3 serve a delicious meal and maybe he/she does not taste a delicious meal;
4 surround someone with a bright, cool, wonderful day and maybe he/she does not experience a bright, cool, wonderful day, and
5 take someone for a smooth airplane ride and maybe he/she experiences a bumpy air ride.

THE QUALITY OF EXPERIENCE

This then brings us to a new idea. We cannot assert that you will experience:

● blue when most other people do
● a chord when most other people do
● delicious food when most other people do
● wonderful days when most other people do, or
● smooth rides when most other people do.

Putting you into some situation in which most people feel themselves to be under compulsion (to feel, think, or do X, Y, Z, and so on) we cannot be sure that you will also feel yourself to be under any (much less a) similar or identical compulsion.

---

2 See Dauben, J.W. (1979) *Georg Cantor: His Mathematics and Philosophy of the Infinite*, Cambridge, Mass: Harvard University Press; Lavine, S. (1994) *Understanding the Infinite*, Cambridge, Mass: Harvard University Press.

That means: you may feel yourself to be free.
Which leads us to our basic new principle:

the feeling of feeling oneself to be free is a second-level quality of experience.

It is largely multisensory, but has major somaesthetic (body image) and ego-strength attributes. Also kinaesthetic: in knowing or believing that one can do something about it. The eye does not know that it sees, nor the ear know that it hears, nor does the skin, tongue, or nose, etc. The mind does: that organ of the brain, ultimately some high form perhaps of abstract somaesthesis which senses the senses, knows.

The primary freedoms (present in the newborn) are (i) to come eventually to know that one can look away or spit out food or release the nipple. Next (ii) comes the release of one's hand-grip, since initially grasping is a 'reflex', a compelled action. A newborn infant can sometimes momentarily hold its own weight. (NB One is never free, even as adult, to turn off one's ears, which is in part why noise pollution is so devastating. It is also why audition is so close to ethics and morality. And music so important to human life.)

The third set of freedoms (iii) derives from one's gradually refining awareness that one can move generally, not only eyes or lips or hands, but head, limbs, and body. One also (iv) learns to focus attention: to look, feel, and listen hard. None the less, despite these primary sense-rational freedoms, the somaesthetic-rational quality of feeling-being free may still be elusive. It is thus one of those accelerated phenomenal qualities of which we cannot be sure, from the situation, that it occurs within.

This means: if we wish to know whether some individual then and there experiences her/himself as free (as freely feeling, freely looking, freely listening, freely thinking, and/or freely acting), one must inquire, as best one can and in whatever way one can, of that person.

Of course, though rarely, one can experience oneself as: experiencing blue, being sad, having an upset stomach, needing to go the bathroom, being in want of a nail, of the opinion that, and so on for ever, and uncompelled, and be wrong! But, apart from quite significant mental pathology (which means, in these cases, very gross somaesthetic-cognitive distortions at schizophrenic levels), one is generally right. That is, as right as evolutionary and social survival can indicate. I would suppose that one could experience these things fairly well while still missing out on the precise universal Humean 'blue' and on the exactly correct opinion and maybe even on the right 'nail' for the job, but hardly on any of the others. This means that, in general, the veridicality of the self-apprehension on both first and second levels of intrinsic internal states (somaesthetic and other: *having an idea*) has been so tightly selected for by evolution and so finely honed still further by society, that the veracity of self-awareness is in fact the rule.

Sensory illusions are, actually, the rarest exceptions though much is made of them. For the senses the earth does not move. Its hypothetical motion is the illusion. Mostly what we experience of our experience is thus precisely true, it coheres with reality; seeing blue, feeling sad, having an upset stomach, sensing urethral and bowel pangs, needing a nail, leaning towards a certain opinion – and feeling oneself freely making free decisions.

Indeed, all the foundations of the civil democracies and of the legal and educational systems the world over are built upon this deeply layered psycho-philosophical bedrock. Religions perhaps not, but that is another matter.

Thus our first major realization is (i) that the experience of the freedom of will (in sensing, thinking, acting; not always in recalling, sleeping, performing, quelling anxiety, overcoming shyness, and so on) is a subtle complex quality of the quality of experience. (And do recall that acting itself is more afferent than efferent. This absolutely critical fact must constantly be kept in mind.) Secondly, (ii) we have also come to believe that this reflexive level of quality most probably occurs uniquely in human beings and not in lower animals. Furthermore, (iii) we now know that we may (must) take all abstract actions and all first time mental and behavioural solutions, and all unusually varied concrete actions especially *with respect to the inanimate*, as evidence for the validity of that feeling, to wit: that such actions must be free in a more ultimate sense.

THE ULTIMATE SENSE

Now comes the crux: 'Well, what of the fact that you feel yourself to feel free; you can't prove that you really are free in the sense that God is (or was) ... and so you are probably not.' ('I am, of course, but not you.')

The problem is resolved thus: 'the rays are not coloured.' When there is no second-level freedom-quality-processing entity around in some dynamic situation in nature then there is no freedom. As blue points to certain probabilities in the physics behind it; so this also. As blue points to physio-psychology, so this too. That is to say: there is no freedom at all in inanimate nature, little if any in plants, bare hints in lower animals, only some in early mammals, but much in primates, and a very great deal in some mentally healthy adult men and women. One aspect of mental distress and severe mental illness is precisely that one's phenomenological quality of feeling oneself to be free is very much rarer than normal in its appearances and more difficult to re-encourage during any thera-peutic-pedagogical interchange.

Of course, if one maintains that because 'blue' as such is not in inani-mate nature it is therefore an illusion, one has no reason for rejecting the hypothesis that because freedom as such is not in inanimate nature it also is an illusion. In which case, however, this would be the greatest sensory illusion ever: sensory irrationalism at its worst.

But blue is certainly a veridical aspect of human experience. And there is simply no reason to assert that the quality freedom is any less veridical. What does veridicality mean in this situation? Well, it is no different with the blue. There are situations in which blue is not perceived. Thus: blue is not a visual illusion from which we always suffer to the exclusion of any selective-discriminative (rational) interaction with reality. And there are situations in which the context makes a blue appear where the pure isolated excitations would not have given rise to a blue but, for example, to a green instead.

It is not different with freedom, only more complex. We do not, of course, have in mind (yet?) some unitary dimension that, like radiation, extends above the perception of being free (ultra-freedom) in one direction and below it in another (infra-freedom). But we do know how the quality emerges sufficiently well to know also that it is a middle-range process. In anarchy many will not feel free, though some may; while in absolute oligarchy many will also not feel free, though, again, some may. Yet even in the more normal probability range of social-ecological conditions to which we are generally exposed, at least for many people in advanced cultures, there are situations in which we feel that we are not free. Thus, freedom is not a delusion from which we suffer all the time to the exclusion of any selective-discriminative (rational) interaction with reality. To the contrary, the quality freedom is at once both more situationally and more historically determined than is the quality blue. Surround situations in which we would normally self-generate the quality freedom, and have awareness that we do, with past, present, or immediate future situations of extreme restraint and oppression, and the freedom even there may vanish. This is a balance between contrast and constancy. And it is one of the basic principles of sensory rationalism: that multisensory qualities tend necessarily to be more historically evolved and more situationally controllable than are single, isolated, unitary, sensory qualities. What the gestaltists called the 'frame of reference' becomes for such qualities almost everything – not quite, but most important: the context of liberty is also liberty.

HIGH EGO-STRENGTH MEANS A MORE READILY EVOKED SENSE OF BEING FREE

Consider ego-strength, the vigour of the sense of self. What high ego-strength lends itself to is this: a more readily evoked sense of being free, within a greater variety of social-intellectual-emotional situations, than does low ego-strength. That is to say, the historical rearing of the individual and the ontogenetic development of the sense of self bear with absolutely critical importance upon every present moment. Psychoanalytic events contribute to the current life-space.

And the neurological component or correlate of this may now be drawn. In a real sense, the human frontal lobes especially constitute the sense organ that generates the quality 'freedom'. Whatever it is that permits EOQ generation of multiple-successive intrinsic mental geometries – and so also, it seems, restricts the neurological economy to peripheral neural regeneration and grossly limits the body's external somaesthetic regeneration (as noted in Chapter 11) – is precisely the heraldic neurology that permits and encourages in man the emerging of this quality of freedom. We can all imagine a blue, but only a few of us can experience it as we do so. We all can imagine a sound, but only a few of us can experience it as we do so (so-called absolute pitch). Even rarer still, so it seems, are those able to unite imagination with the actual experience of smells or tastes or touches or body states. Most of us, however, can imagine ourselves to be free, and we can and do experience freedom. Sometimes this means that we can imagine ourselves thinking, experiencing, perceiving, or acting. Moreover, we do have much concrete reafferent evidence. That is, we can look where we wish, reach out and touch where we wish (both, with rational restrictions, of course), and we can move physically and explore where we wish, and we can smell and taste where we wish and – but to a lesser extent because we cannot shut off our ears – we can listen how and to what we wish. And thus we can create at will, if not quite as freely as we might wish, an almost endless sequence of marvellously precise successive intrinsic models. And we can have awareness of our awareness of our awareness . . . that we are doing this.

If we cannot ourselves regenerate an arm when and where we might wish, we can, as it happens, search about in nature and, lo!, actually find creatures for which this appears almost to be so. More than this, we can imagine it to be so for ourselves, and hence work on artificial limbs and mechanical or electronic hands; and on artificial noses, mouths, breasts, arms, legs, penises, ears, eyes, skins, even brains.

With the still further and perhaps sudden evolutionary leap into a firm ego relatively apart from the senses, we can consider man without the senses, we can even consider man with many more senses than he now seems naturally to have, and we can even consider the whole vast (imaginary?) catalogue of neither sensory nor rational ways of knowing: intimation, palmistry, astrology, laughing, chiromancy, esotericism, hallucination, foresight, prescience, foreboding, angering, intuition, revelation, delusion, divination, speaking-in-tongues, prediction, foretelling, oracular interpretation, inspiration, reveries, clairvoyance, thought transference, clairaudience, telepathy, association, ectasy, premonition, omens, sanctification, appointment, benediction, demonology, obsession, fascination . . . and so forth.

FREE WILL AND SOCIAL DEMOCRACY

In sum then: the intrinsic dynamic flexibility (temporal change) and plasticity (geometric change) of the internal neural modelling capacity of the human nervous system *is* the process at the neuropsychiatric foundation of our sense of being free, and thence of all our ideas of freedom and of civil and social and political democracy. Without stressing this point here, the various forms of democracy are thus not trivial solutions to the problem of the social organization of mankind, they are the ones to which (at least my) modern understanding of intrinsic cortical neurology most naturally leads.

If this were found eventually, by others and by other means, to be correct in this sense *only* among some competing views, this alone would justify my engagement with these tasks.

13 The neural foundations of accelerated self-awareness

In examining the inherent meaning of this idea – that the self of man is aware, or can be, that it is aware that it is aware that it is aware – we must admit at the start that we have no clear idea yet as to the character of the restrictions, if any, on the successive number of these mirror reflections that might be achieved. One seems quite justified in suggesting, however, that ego-strength and intelligence are complexly related to the number of levels of remove to which this regression can be taken, before one becomes dizzy and disassociated. For example, Dostoevsky (in his *Tales from the Underground*) displays an absolute wizardry in his mastery of these reverberations. This is surely one reason why Freud called him the greatest psychologist.

THE SINGLE BRAIN CELL WITH MULTIPLE SYNAPSES MAKES MIRROR MODELS OF ITSELF

But let us now turn to neurophysiology. There are single brain cells in the higher cortex of man that are well-known to contain 10,000 synapses. Even assuming that only 1 per cent of these synapses are functional at some given moment (i.e. 100), this still leaves us with an absolutely extraordinary number of alternatives that the patterns of excitations in a single cortical cell may assume: 2^{100}. This is a number rivalling the number of molecules in the whole human body and vastly greater than computer modellers or even sophisticated theoretical neurologists ever seem to think about.[1] Clearly, however, even from the point of view of a theoretical neuroscience, that number is probably too large for one to deal with concretely in terms of synaptic transmitters and the like. But, none the less, it must have at least this concrete consequence: that the neural variance-modelling capacity of even a single brain cell in man (and perhaps in many higher animals as well) is certainly sufficient to take account of all the intimacies and intricacies and nuances and subtleties and variances

---

1 This number is: 2^{100}(1,267, 650, 600, 228, 229, 401, 496, 703, 205, 376), computed for me by Harold Shore.

and tiny differences that may appear in any psychological present no matter how numerous. Could a single cell take on all these alternatives distinctively (leaving specifications of 'distinctiveness' aside for the moment), it would have all the capacity that we would ever need to model the individuality of present psychological reality. This means that a single cell could quite adequately model (by destructive and constructive interference) all the historical (psychoanalytical) and situational (gestalt) influences that might bear on the current lifespace. Herein, at the intra-cellular multi-synaptic level, the Young experiment has all it needs to take place. And structure has all it needs to occur within turbulence, and coalescence to occur far-from-equilibrium, and order to emerge three levels out of disorder, and self-awareness to burst forth like Zeus. Another cell might do this for some next moment, and so forth. The whole brain, as some hypothetical gestalt volume conductor, need not be involved at all, when one single cell only can do all this. This, indeed, is finally Sir Charles Sherrington's 'pontifical cell; the one that processes the whole of the momentary present, the Now, come to full fruition'.[2]

THE EXPERIENCE OF AN ACCELERATED AWARENESS OF SELF

If we grant this to be so – and I do not now see serious objections to this notion (even as we also, no doubt, model 'objections' somewhere in that very same cell) – then what follows from the retention of the neuro-plastic capacity of the brain cells to divide or to self-modify is this:

> The highest form of cell division is that which, in the energy–energy interactions that constitute mind, reproduces cell excitation-arousal geometries which are models of themselves. Such mirror-image cell geometries, then, are or evoke the quality of being conscious of themselves. Thus: multiple regressive accelerated self-awareness develops in the ego as a natural envelope of all the minute cortical brain cells which, in their 2^{100} states, model themselves and know that they do so.

Of course I am aware that I am aware that I am aware ... that this says quite a bit more than I can simply demonstrate, and that its entertainment requires some elements of willingness to suspend momentary disbelief: fantasy. But that is just how good ideas start in science. And more serious arguments can be developed. One hopes that others who think it worthy may now be drawn to this task.

------

2 Sherrington, C. (1906) *The Integrative Action of the Nervous System*, New York: Scribner's Sons.

14 Crucial concepts for pedagogy and child development

Reason is experimental intelligence.

John Dewey[1]

All these arguments have the important consequence of giving a sound and genuinely scientific meaning to the heretofore wholly diffuse concept of mental nourishment. For generations actually, since the Greeks – there has been an emphasis on 'training the mind', 'exercising the intellect', because of a concept of mind as virtual muscle. It was widely said that struggling in school with problems gives one the ability later on to struggle in reality better with other real but related problems, and so forth. Probably this idea reached its zenith during the late nineteenth century in American and European pedagogy, where the ideas of the importance of drill and repetition in reading, writing, and arithmetic were developed as ways to prepare the child for the real world. Sparing rods and loosening discipline spoiled the child, and so all 'progressive' Rousseauistic education was anathema. And there is a kernel of truth in those old ideas.

MULTIPLICITY INGESTION AND VARIANCE PRODUCTION IN AN ECOLOGICALLY SOUND ENVIRONMENT

As we can now understand, sensory experiences are essential for the maintenance of the healthy singular modes. Similarly, bio-psychological arousal events involving *intersensory* processing are also crucial. Singing, rocking, caressing, warming, nuzzling, cooing to, and embracing infants, in short good mothering, is essential to sound neurological development and ego integrity. As is good fathering, in similar form. These, critically, constitute vestibular, tactile, and somaesthetic arousals, as well as visual and aural and self-body reinforcements generally. Once we reach intersensory processing we reach the mind. The key aspect that the old pedagogues missed, however, was *variance*. Repeating the exact same perfect blue

---

1 Dewey, J. (1920) *Reconstruction in Philosophy*, New York: Holt, p. 89.

over and over again may do for the *eye* but not for the *vision*. What they emphasized by 'copying what's on the board' and by repeating endlessly the same maths problems and the same vocabulary drill was the more peripheral aspects of mental function which are, in fact, the least trainable, in the sense of not being generalizable, though they readily enter memory as specifics. Rather, by experiencing many blues and many copyings and all sorts of maths problems, and producing them as well, they would have addressed the more crucial issue of the malleable mind.

It is not fanciful or a mere convenience to speak of great art or great music or great theatre or great dance as uplifting, as inspiring, as enriching, as nourishing. They are nourishing, in ways very similar to the ways in which food and water and air are nourishing. As the great utopian socialists Pierre Proudhon, François Fourier, and Claude Saint–Simon emphasized: 'you become what you eat.' They meant by this catch-phrase (used first in about 1825 by J.A. Brillat-Savarin) that the intake of specific nourishment goes directly into the formation of muscles and blood and sinews and glands and secretions and bones and nails and hair, so that the body reflects in many ways the nutritional opportunities of childhood. The aim of their idea, of course, was to show how the lack of proper nourishment for certain peoples was an unfair detriment to their physical well-being.

In my sense, since information is also nourishment, it also follows that you become what you experience. And this catch-phrase has a closely analogous if perhaps not quite so stern a meaning. If one has no opportunities to think-experience liberty, that indeed will be one inalienable right that one will not be able to formulate well or to comprehend. And that is a great impoverishment indeed. Who can say when bread is really more important?

It happens that the gestalt psychologists highlighted the argument against this concept, that repeated sensory experience would facilitate one's later processing of similar sensations. They were trying to establish the true limits of the excessively rigid Pavlovian and Germanic pedagogy prominent in the years before World War I and claimed strongly that the primary organizational processes of perception were largely independent of conditioning and ritual repetition. In particular, in many classical studies, they showed that repeated experience with and repeated solving of puzzle pictures (such as to find the *bowl* hidden in some complex pattern of overlaid line-texture figures) did not really increase one's efficiency, the next time, in solving puzzles embedded in just slightly different patterns (e.g. a cup hidden in just slightly different line-texture figures). And so on. To some quite large degree, they are correct. Conditioning and repetition in pattern perception tasks, which model many learning drills, are very limited teaching methods, especially when there is no understanding of the importance of minimal clues and organization. Moreover, intelligence as a process of sensory-rational analysis does not change in any simplistic way with experience or training (see Shipley 1990; Bouchard *et al.* 1990).[2]

But the gestaltists did not then know of the importance of direct sense nourishment for the actual development and survival of sense anatomy and function. And they also did not fully appreciate the exquisite importance of variance processing. So the extremes of their argument are false. Lack of sensory experience does directly diminish the prowess of that particular modality. Moreover, it directly diminishes the contribution that that mode may make to the processing of intersensory information. And so, finally, to *that* extent, the lack of any sensory experience directly diminishes mind.

What this means for pedagogy and child development is that the growing emphasis on multisensory stimulation is entirely correct. (It seems this is particularly advanced in some Latin American countries, and in France and Switzerland, under the all-important influence of Piaget.) Children should be given the fullest possible opportunity successfully and joyfully to experience as wide as possible a variance of single and multimodal events. And they should be encouraged to develop novel and complex integrations of those experiences into new mental realities: little mechanical inventions (a plate that doesn't hold spinach) and new musics (a melody for elephants) and novel dances (how would a worm dance with a butterfly) and alternative paintings (finger or tongue) and unheard words (secret sounds or passwords).

In this way, the early childhood years in particular, but also all the developmental years and even education through college (and through life?) should involve the greatest possible variance processing and the greatest opportunity for enriched, nourished, healthful development of single sensory and sense rational intersensory function. This, then, all other social factors being in balance, leads to a healthy mind. That this strongly supports certain progressive educational philosophies of the John Deweyan species, and not others, is clear. But this follows as a natural consequence of modern insights into sensory and mental function and so is of major importance. It is no longer merely a hypothesis, but reflects the fundamental insight (to which much of my work is devoted) that there are many genuine nutritional parallels between sense-information ingestion and the ingestion of good food and clean air and fresh water, and (relatively speaking) noise-free environments.

---

2 Shipley, T. (1990) *The Theory of Intelligence: A Sensory-Rational View*, Springfield, Illinois: Thomas. The recent report of work on monozygotic twins reared apart strongly supports the idea of a large, ca. 70 per cent heritability coefficient for human intelligence. It is essential to note, however, that this work quite rightly leaves untouched the crucial issue of the role of pedagogy in the social expression of that intelligence. See Bouchard, T.J., Lykken, D.T., McGue, M., Segal, N., and Tellegen, A. (1990) 'Sources of human psychological differences: the Minnesota study of twins reared apart', *Science* 250: 223–8.

Of course these are ideal conditions, but they are the only ones worth striving for. And the ecological implications are also clear. Neuroscience is absolutely not indifferent on that score.

15 Afterword

MYTHOPOETRY'S SECOND SENSE REJECTION

A great many religions, for some reasons that are really not obvious, have taught us that the world of the senses is misleading and at best a route to short-lived enticements and illusions upon which no rich and full or moral life should be constructed. And, while it is now clear that the co-ordination of the senses is precisely what has brought the conscious mind into some state that we may call being, much of philosophy and of science, because of its abstract nature, deliberately strives to leave the senses behind, although not in some moral fashion. Mathematics also leaves the senses behind, and leaps. That is its nature. And often the poets teach us similar caution lest we trust too deeply what we appear to see or to hear or to touch:

> There are in our existence spots of time,
> Which with distinct pre-eminence retain
> A renovating Virtue, whence, depress'd
> By false opinion and contentious thought,
> Or aught of heavier or more deadly weight
> In trivial occupations, and the round
> Of ordinary intercourse, our minds
> Are nourish'd and invisibly repair'd,
> A virtue by which pleasure is enhanced
> That penetrates, enables us to mount
> When high, more high, and lifts us up when fallen.
> This efficacious spirit chiefly lurks
> Among those passages of life in which
> We have had deepest feeling that the mind
> Is lord and master, and that outward sense

---

1 William Wordsworth, 'The prelude, Concerning the Growth and History of his own mind.' Cited in Reed, M.L. (ed.) (1992) *The 13-Book Prelude*, Ithaca, NY: Cornell University Press. This poem is one of the longest and is widely considered to be among the finest in the English language. This two-volume work by Reed is now also considered the definitive reprinting and analysis of this great work.

Is but the obedient servant of her will.
Such moments, worthy of all gratitude,
Are scatter'd everywhere, taking their date
From our first childhood; in our childhood even
Perhaps are most conspicuous.[1]

SCIENTIFIC RESTORATION OF THE SENSES

This book has tried to demonstrate that the origin of the mind has come
from the integration of multisensory coherent and, especially multisensory incoherent messages, but that this 'come from' has within it perhaps
the greatest discontinuity found in human bio-psychology. As the new
understanding of even simple unimodal and often unidimensional perception and comprehension already requires acceptance of discontinuities and
cusps, especially in all the rates of change of the rates of change of human
experience and thought and expression, so we must recognize that the
emergent leap that mind then took from sensory integration into imagination and memory and confabulation and fantasy and mythopoesis and
ethics and art and law and language remains fully to be described in terms
communicable outside or beyond direct personal experience. No one
person can achieve this, though many of our greatest artists and writers
exactly illustrate it. And also the best of our religious inventors and our
scientists and ethicists.

That extraordinary transition is now the directly focused task of the
science of psychology. And it is mine as well.

A COMMENT ON INFORMATION THEORY

Those impressed by information theory, as giving us a fundamentally novel
and fruitful approach to *all* of human thinking, are reminded that George
Boole himself, originator of information theory in the mid-nineteenth
century in his book *The Laws of Thought*, clearly stated that his binary
model of 0 and 1 applied only to certain quite restricted aspects of human
thought. And so they should give some attention to supra-binary or N-
ary modelling of all those other highly enriched mental acts left out of
the exclusionary middle. Non-Aristotelian multi-valued logic comes immediately to mind.

WHAT THE SENSES TEACH

The senses teach us to interpolate (this red belongs between these two
other reds) and to extrapolate (this pitch comes after that); and then to
encourage us when we reason in these same processes: interpolation
(this punishment fits that crime) and extrapolation (this good deed is
worth more dispensations than that). In my analysis of sensory-rational

intelligence (*op. cit.*) I have shown how simple linear interpolations and extrapolations along sensory dimensions lift up into the core of intellectual and abstract mental processes. In this present work, I have tried to show that this lifting up is an enduring process, taking complex intersensory co-ordinations into mathematical reasoning and artistic and ethical reasoning as well.

One of the finest conceptions of such a lifting up – and I cite this often – comes from the brilliant Scottish philosopher David Hume, who suggested that our notion of the divine *is* the extrapolation without limit of our ideas of goodness and beauty. In my view, it is that 'without limit' which is the key. Though in mathematics such extrapolations can be and usually are continuous, in cognitive thought (the way the mind goes) they are not. There is, so to say, no nearest neighbour to God. The point is that in these sorts of non-mathematical extrapolations, discontinuities abound. And they emerge in virtually all the lesser everyday mental extrapolations as well. Which is why discontinuous functions hold the key to our understanding of all the unpredictable acts of conscious and unconscious mental life.

BIG-ENDERS VS. LITTLE-ENDERS IN SCIENCE

There seem, actually, to be three sorts of people in science or in life, not two. Perhaps the eggs can be broken in the middle.

There are those who must go down to lower and lower levels to explain the one that they are on; there are those who prefer to model on the same plane; and there are those who model from higher levels downwards, as when God is used to explain human free will.

In a full picture of human psychology – while I myself make my choice in the middle level-to-level approach – I do not think that either reduction to subatomic particles or elevation to the divine is absurd.

Each of the three approaches can be useful, and certainly is to different individual scientists. Three of the greatest, for example, Galileo, Newton, and Einstein, clearly reasoned from the top downwards; experimentalists today tend, more usually, to reason from the bottom up. The only danger is when either approach becomes so vibrant and enthralling that it encourages its followers into the arrogance of absolute knowledge, either of facts or of methods. Humanity has suffered much from both species of excess.

Those of us willing to contend with the reality of human consciousness, as bearing that qualia of experience no less vigorously than it bears the qualia of blue or of outside or of 'a lion stands there', cannot on principle, it seems to me, limit the granting of reality by others to genuine transcendental processes. In a valid pre-mathematical sense, consciousness is a qualia that is 'as close as you wish to the transcendent' but is not yet quite there. Who can say that other men and women, equally earnest and of goodwill ought not or cannot take the next step? Since there is a leap involved in the first, why not retain an element of credence concerning a further leap? Indeed, it is the essence of the scientific attitude that it allows for that. Humility is the core of science, even as it attains knowledge for all times.

Similarly, when colleagues assert the attractions of reductionism – and there are many – they cannot in principle do so and wholly deny the usefulness or validity of other approaches; nor can they maintain in any valid scientific posture that only their level of reduction counts. It is common, for example, for many in the neuro-bio-science modelling activity, to note that reduction to the level of molecular charge or atomic valence is sufficient, because the interactions at this level explain or can be used to model well and communicably almost all the higher events of neuronal function. But this ignores entirely the importance of molecular shape or geometry, which is an absolutely key issue in all of biology, as a mere reference to stereo-isomerism immediately shows. One amino acid, as we have noted here, that is exactly the same chemical formula as another but which rotates the polarization of light to the left instead of to the right because it has a different shape, becomes a poison instead of an element crucial to life.

In psychology and psychophysics, reductionism has been no less attractive. Threshold studies are one way in which to come just about as close as you wish to the physiology but not yet quite be there so as to retain at least a faint aura of being mental. But human purpose does not come from physiology nor, arguably, by integrating up from thresholds.

And let us recall that Gustave Fechner, a major figure in the history of psychophysics, if not its founder, was a spiritualist and a mystic.[2] He determined, so he then thought, that all just-noticeable differences in the intensity or brightness or loudness of some sensation were equal, within the dimension. That is: a change in brightness, for example, that was just perceptible over absolute threshold was *perceptually equivalent* to a change in brightness that was just perceptible at virtually all brightness levels, even at some several log units above threshold. This led him to believe that he could create a firm scientific model of supra-threshold experience, by simply integrating up from threshold to the levels of everyday experience, over however many just-noticeable differences (or JNDs) that would occur along the way. For him, this was a virtual solution to the mind–body problem and was, ultimately, a way of refuting Descartes and giving a spirit to body and a body to spirit.

---

2 Fechner, G. (1860) *Elemente der Psychophysik*, Leipzig: Breitkopf and Hartel. Much of the early history and controversy about these methods is given in the two excellent, if early, books by E.G. Boring: (1929) *A History of Experimental Psychology*, New York: Appleton-Century; (1942) *Sensation and Perception in the History of Experimental Psychology*, New York: Appleton Century. As an aside, few books since, in the history of our field, have matched Boring's in either their precision and care or their fine humanistic conception of the history of science.

The field since, though very active, has dropped the mind–body implications, yet even the powerful and relatively new methods of signal detection and decision theory keep us largely at threshold levels in modern psychophysics, so the physiology remains always just in sight.[3] In these methods, for example, we obtain an index of how often, in some measurement run, a subject reports that a stimulus set well above his/her average threshold is, none the less, below it, and we can compare this to how often this subject reports that a stimulus well below his/her threshold is none the less above it. In this way, we close in from both sides on the probability that, indeed, some perceptual event is or is not, to such and such a probability, over threshold. These methods, thus, give a certain dynamism to that otherwise somewhat static concept.

Building naturally upon some older traditions, it is to the great credit of S.S. Stevens of Harvard that he perfected methods in psychophysics that have all the usual attractions of reliability and communicability, but which now permit us to study supra-threshold experiences directly.[4] His methods are called magnitude estimation and ratio estimation or comparison, and have applicability to single dimensionalities (set this brightness to half that of the other) and to intersensory co-ordinations in particular (squeeze this, grip as loud as is that sound). And despite the initially odd-sounding nature of the tasks, they have proven of great reliability and applicability, in bright and retarded children and adults, and to issues in cognitive psychology concerning such complex matters as racial relations and attitudes towards war (how strongly do you hold that view?) as well as in everyday phenomenal experience (how big really is that pain?) As such, they aid us in scientifically modelling the leap to consciousness that, hitherto, only poets could tell. Combining these new methods, with an acceptance of the processes, of insight and other consequent and independent discontinuities, will, in the hands of future consciousness experimenters, give genuine conviction and veracity to models of that leap.

BIOCHEMICAL REDUCTION

The best case to date for reductionism is not made via computers or via neurons or via neural networks, i.e. not yet by any biophysical or physiological model, but by the biochemical route. This is not to say that our knowledge is profound, it is not. But it is to say that the accumulated experience suggests as strongly as for any reductionist level that this may work well.

---

3 See, for example, Green, D.M. and Swets, J.A. (1988) *Signal Detection Theory and Psychophysics*, Los Altos, Calif.: Peninsula.

4 Stevens, S.S. (1961) 'To honor Fechner and repeal his law', *Science*, 133: 80–6. And, for a more recent review, Bolanowski, S.J. and Gescheider, G.A. (eds) (1991) *Ratio Scaling of Psychological Magnitude*, Hillsdale, NJ: Erlbaum.

One reason why I state that our knowledge is not profound is this. Aspirin, for example, salicylic acid, is the longest known and most widely used psychoactive drug, accounting for probably some millions of uses each day, the world over. Yet we still do not know the fundamental neuronal action of aspirin.

During the early days of the French Revolution, Philippe Pinel became a physician and administrator of the prison hospital in Paris known as Bicêtre. At the beginning of his tenure, and amid the throes of political insights as to the nature of man and the meaning of democracy, he made the secular medical decision to consider the 'inmates' of the Bicêtre as ill in a mental sense and not as evil or stubborn or merely obtuse and deliberately violent or obscene. Only a few years later on, in the first years of the nineteenth century, the members of the Religious Society of Friends (or Quakers) in York, England, made a similar but now religious medical decision that, because there was that of God in every man, these people deserved care and not punishment, and they established the first mental hospital, known as the York Retreat, for the gentle and loving treatment of the mentally ill.

It is entirely due, in our history, to these initial efforts, that today, certainly in all of western culture, the treatment of the mentally ill has been wholly separated from the treatment of the physically ill and – if treatment it can be called – of the criminal as well.

That the concept of 'illness' is used may not be altogether to the good, because of the biochemical implications of this term, and I prefer the term 'mental distress' for at least some of what passes as the psychiatric nosology, but that is not a fundamental objection to the fact that, under this aegis of 'illness', enormous progress has been made in the chemical control of psychiatric symptoms.

In the current handbook or *Diagnostic and Statistical Manual (DSM#)*, the number depending upon the edition), certain American mental health workers have in hand an absolutely fine parametric description of virtually all possible unified sets of the symptoms of mental illness that they may encounter. Although the motivations for constructing such a guide have been in part economic (the medical insurance companies needed to have some sort of diagnosis in order to know what they were being billed for), none the less, for all mental health workers the world over who operate under the influence of Pinel and the Quakers and the concept of mental illness now prevalent in the west, this has become of enormous applied value. For one thing, it also gives to the patient some confidence that his/her symptoms have been recognized and may be understood and that, despite the awful loneliness of mental distress, she/he is not alone. That the insurance companies now know, sort of, what they are being asked to pay for is also salutary, so long as it keeps them out of the task of diagnosing and prognosing (managing) mental illness.

The reason that this issue concerns us is the reductionist fact that close to 30 per cent, some would say 50 per cent or more, of the symptoms, and the classes of symptoms in general, of mental illness can now, since the last two or three decades of the many discoveries of 'psychoactive' drugs, be controlled and even ameliorated by biochemical means. Since the Quakers and Pinel began to give such patients special diets, the ingestion of various potions and poultices and gruels has been a key component of psychiatric treatment modalities; also, certainly since the York Retreat, talking and caring cures.

Be this as it may, and despite the daily use around the world of literally millions of psychoactive drugs, we do not yet fully comprehend the action of any one of them. We may know that some affect synapses more than neuronal cell membranes, or the nodes of Ranvier more than the dendrites, and we may know that some have action in one gross region of the central nervous system more than in another. But in no instance do we yet have specific knowledge that this drug is acting just here, within this cortical column or module, or in this sub-set of pyramidal cells and not that. We cannot restrict the drug's action even to one hemisphere of the brain, much less to one lobe, say frontal only or parietal. Or to one region: the thalamus. We may well be able to do something like this some day, by specially preparing some cells (activating them by injection or radiation exposure or, with the advent of the PET scan and SPEC and other such metabolic monitors, activating them with special mental processes such as listening to music instead of to speech), so that they become more receptive to drug infiltration, the way we already do for many physical illnesses.

But, even then, would we know precisely in which cortical column or module they were acting, and precisely how they were acting? Perhaps, but would that then be enough for a full reduction: the experience of this hallucination is 'nothing but' an imbalance in or too much of or a lack of this or that biochemical molecule?

Most hallucinations in mental illnesses such as schizophrenia are auditory. So, presumably, this means that we are looking for chemicals that might affect, more than other regions of the CNS, the tympanic membrane, the oval window, the basilar membrane, the eighth cranial nerve, the temporal lobe. And, were we to find such a chemical that we knew acted at some specific locus along this orthodromic route, would we then have the true reduction? The answer still is no, we would not.

Although we may control symptoms, that is not the same as explaining their origin, even in biochemical or neurophysiological terms, nor is it the same as 'understanding the symptoms'.

The vast majority of care of the mentally ill in the United States is undertaken by trained social workers and psychologists, with psychiatrists doing most of the biochemical management. This is certainly correct, because the former are not well trained in biochemistry or psychopharmacology, and the latter are not well trained in any of the Quaker species of nurturing cures. It is absolutely clear to me, as a teacher of physicians in the US for some thirty years, that medical education as it is done today is strongly anti-psychiatric and there can be little doubt about the fact that Freud was entirely correct in his assertion that psychoanalysis certainly, but also, in my opinion, all of the talking cures, are as well if not better done by people who are not trained in either the neuro-physiological or biochemical biases that medical education in the United States encourages.

On the other hand, the very existence of the *Diagnostic and Statistical Manual* has, in recent years, given the whole profession of mental health care a defence not only against medical insurance companies but against medically trained colleagues who have heretofore often been scornful of what it is, actually, that mental health care is all about.

Despite the great success of modern psychopharmacology, it is more directly to our concept of the mind that this new nosology has mostly been addressed. But tempting as this success may be to a full theoretical and applied reduction, it would be entirely false to take it in this way. Biochemicals are not symptoms of mental distress, nor will they ever be; nor, likewise, are quirks in neural networks symptoms, or over-excitabilities in synapses or excesses in the permeabilities of axonal membranes or distortions in cortical columns or vastly spreading losses through horizontal cross-modular connections of neural inhibitions. Symptoms of mental distress are as strongly level restricted as any phenomenal experience, and ultimately must be dealt with in their own right. Which is why the directions that Pinel and the Quakers pointed out so long ago are still the proper way: phenomenology addressing phenomenology.

A case in point: considering the three major modalities, vision, audition, and touch, can we, using the level analysis, begin to approach some answer as to why most hallucinations are auditory? Recalling some of the insights from the chart in Chapter 9, we may add a few more. Vision is the major sense mode that keeps us in distant contact with the 'real' world. Consequently, were visual hallucinations to occur *in daytime while awake*, the mind would be constantly exposed to conflicting information within the same mode that something was not correct. That is, daylight vision has within it an inherently corrective or anti-hallucinatory process. On the other hand, visual hallucinations at night are fine, indeed, quite normal: we all do regularly dream, though perhaps fewer of our dreams are night-mares than are those of the mentally distressed.

As for hallucinations in the tactual mode, these are so very distressing that they simply cannot be tolerated. Were one unable to escape the feeling of bugs crawling on one's skin or animals gnawing at one's body or of being tickled mercilessly, one could not really handle that well, despite the negative visual feedback that there is nothing there. Moreover, in the natural use of the tactile-somatosensory mode, we often have experiences for which there are no direct visual confirmations or denials (muscle cramps), so the intersensory conflict (touch vs. vision) is, in itself, not controlling. The tactual experience, on its own, the touch of the imagination trying to survive that sort of compelling hallucinatory input, must suppress the hallucination, or find itself wholly unable to cope.

As it happens, many natural auditory events in the real world often seem to 'occur within the head', so that there is less of a disablement (inability to cope) when some voices or sounds are heard within the head that do not also there and then have intersensory confirmation.

FACILITATED COMMUNICATION AND SENSORY IRRATIONALISM: A CONCRETE APPLICATION

Since we have noted that autistic children have difficulty shielding themselves from excessive intersensory arousals,[5] we may conclude that neural inhibitory losses, probably throughout the cortex, are likely somehow at issue. In addition, it may be useful to the field for me to comment, from the point of view of intersensory rationalism, on the widespread use of communicative 'facilitators' in the United States to help parents and others to communicate with their autistic children.[6] There are close to 500,000 autistic people identified in the US, so that, while this is a method apparently begun in Australia, it is understandable that it has been pursued here with particular zeal. This has created considerable controversy, so some clarification may help.

The method (deemed suitable, perhaps, with autistic children of 8 or more years old) requires a highly trained facilitator who works in a one-to-one relationship with the child, and presumably helps that child to control the motion of his or her hands or fingers as they move onto a keyboard to spell out letters and words in answer to questions or in the actual creative act of writing poems or stories or short autobiographies. The keyboard is usually something like the conventional typewriter or

---

5 The now famous veterinarian, Dr Temple Grandlin (PhD in Animal Science, now a Professor at Colorado State, Boulder), herself a high functional autistic, comments widely that as a child she always had intersensory difficulties: 'the sound of a foghorn actually hurt'; 'petticoats felt like sandpaper'; 'a hug was an overwhelming tidal-wave of stimulation'; and so on.

6 The method of facilitated communication grew up in strong contrast to the more widespread methods of aversive conditioning, openly behaviourist approaches that, despite some good results, have received considerable criticism on their own. The bibliography on facilitated communication is now too large to give the reader anything but a few sample citations: Eberlin, M., McConnachie, G., Ibel, S., and Volpe, L. (1993) 'Facilitated communication: a failure to replicate the phenomenon', *J. autistic & develop. disord.* 23: 507–30; Szempruch, J. and Jacobson, J.W. (1993) 'Evaluating facilitated communications with people with developmental disabilities', *Res. in devel. disabil.* 14: 253–64; Wheeler, D.L., Jacobson, J.W., Paglier, R.A., and Schwartz, A.A. 'An experimental study of facilitated communication', *Mental retardation* 31: 49–59.

computer keyboard, and the child and facilitator sit in front of it, with the facilitator guiding the child's arm, so that finger by finger (or fist by fist, as the case may be) the proper letters to make words are spelled out.

The context becomes clearer when one realizes that a great many of these children have virtually never spoken before and then only poorly (some 40 per cent of autistic people never speak), and that very few show signs of having studied and learned to spell or to read.[7] None the less, placed this way in the facilitating posture before an alphabet on a keyboard, they are, or so it seems, now able to produce sometimes quite remarkably complex answers to complex questions. Some have been 'seen' to begin to have success almost at grade level in school work to which, in fact, they have not previously been exposed. Many dedicated psychologists and researchers are intensely involved in this work, in testing it and in devising methods for display and in training facilitators, so that the number presently involved is well into the hundreds. Autism is a desperately distressing difficulty, and one can only commend the researchers and facilitators, who are trained now almost like nurses/teachers, and sympathize with the parents wishing to try anything to increase their communication with their child.

But the evidence that has been emerging argues strongly that something else entirely is occurring. For example, in virtually all the actual experimental studies thus far, the results have been disappointing. When the child is shown visually one object and the facilitator is shown visually another object, and then the child is asked to 'name' the object, close to 100 per cent of the time the child 'identifies' the object seen by the facilitator.

Perhaps more disturbing than this is the fact that occasionally, when the children have been asked to tell little stories about their childhood, there have appeared tales of infant and child abuse. Often these have been believed, with disastrous legal consequences. In some instances, the children have actually been removed from parental custody because of these stories, only to have them be proven manifestly false at some later date and the children returned home after this familiarly devastating accusation and separation.

But, in addition to such problems, some frank intersensory methodological concerns must be raised. These children are confronted with a tiny typewriter keyboard having the usual half-inch-or-less-sized letters, when it is not even sure that these children have been examined previously by physicians to ascertain that they have the requisite visual acuity to resolve that keyboard. Further, kinaesthetically (in terms of

---

7 There are, increasingly, many highly adaptive and socially competent autistics now surfacing around the world. See Williams, D. (1994) *Somebody Somewhere: Breaking Free from the World of Autism*, New York: Times Books/Random House.

eye–hand motor control), the keys are much too close together for any such child to direct his/her gaze properly and in sequence onto separate letters. Further, there is no evidence presented that these children have as yet a true concept of the alphabet or of spelling or of words as written, although no doubt people have been reading to them in the past. Finally, it is not at all sure – and, in fact, there is considerable doubt – that these children have any clear idea as to what this 'game' is about.

While it is natural to think that the close, warm, and friendly contact with the facilitator can only be a positive experience for these children, there is some body of evidence showing that many autistic children do not like to be touched or to have any close intimate contact with people. (Hence the often quite positive results with aversive conditioning methods.) It is well-known that many autistic children display strongly aversive hyperaesthetic responses, and that they often do much better with pets than with humans, yet these facts seem not to have been fully considered when developing these methods.

If one were actually expecting largely non-verbal and largely linguistically untrained children to be able, suddenly or with only modest training, to be able to single out (by memory-matching, after all) individual letters on a keyboard, one should devise one that has raised letters about 2 inches in size and which says each letter out loud as it is hit, to underscore the auditory aspects of early speech/spelling learning; and also arrange to have the children's heads and bodies supported appropriately so that one might justly surmise that some actual successive visual scanning is taking place. It is known, for example, that eye-movement control in these children is poor, so considerable attention must be given merely to that. It is not only finger and hand and arm and gross motor control which is defective. Eye–hand co-ordination is a complex subject, and has been studied for at least fifty years or more, and deficits in dyslexic and other abnormal readers are well documented in hundreds of research papers. On the other hand, there exist eye-movement monitors these days that are sufficiently easy to use and sufficiently accurate as to tell us precisely where these children are looking when they 'choose' this or that letter to spell out this or that word. But, to my knowledge, no one has yet done this test. In films of some of these sessions, the children often appear to be looking anywhere but at the keyboard. Consequently, given that the use of the senses is to encourage rational-intersensory communicative processes, there are just too many unanswered questions about this work for it to be accepted. Many of these controls are not difficult, but they must be done. Keyboards made up of large pictures of pets and waterfalls and trees and mountain scenes and exotic animals and favourite ice-creams and snow and houses, and other such unambiguously recognizable entities that do not require precise eye-movements and fixation for their recognition, would seem to offer a better and more rational first step in trying to communicate with these children than do alphabetic keyboards. Since the earliest writing systems in human culture were iconic, for sound socio-psychological reasons, it would seem most reasonable to start this way with these children.

Lastly, one must add this note: the facts are that the facilitators are themselves, in so far as the accounts go, highly motivated and keenly convinced teachers. They are on average firmly convinced that what they do is genuine, and that the written product is really 'from the child' and not from them. However, some of those 'producing' the subsequently disproven tales of infant abuse have themselves become deeply distressed by that event and have given up being facilitators.

As examples of the power of hysteria, and of similar self-delusional processes, in precisely the now classical sense that Freud uncovered, these genuinely tragic events are hard to surpass.

With cerebral palsied children, however, this would be an entirely different affair. Such devices, with wide keys and easy handling, are in wide and successful use, since these children do not have any specific cognitive difficulty with communicative acts, however mechanically hindered they may be, nor do they have difficulty with intersensory co-ordination or with hyperaesthesias.

Indeed, for autistic children, there remain many untried approaches that are much sounder from the intersensory-rational point of view. These children are being tested in open classrooms, when facilitation should be tried with the child and the facilitator alone in a single quiet chamber. Further, since these children have difficulty with the multisensory world all about them, it would be useful to introduce some sort of specially comfortable brace or even *full body swaddling* so that the children are 'gentled' down in the way that horses are sometimes 'gentled' down after races, or normal children after frights or temper tantrums. The original reasons for swaddling in various human cultures are not precisely known, but it is reasonable to suppose that both portability and emotional security were factors. It is known that some highly functional autistic adults find such swaddling comforting. Dr Grandlin, whom we have already quoted (see footnote 5 to this chapter), actually invented and had built a hugging machine or 'huggy' just for this purpose, into which she crawls daily to give herself comfort and intersensory quiescence. A more direct use of swaddling could hardly be found, but very clearly without any actual human contact; that is crucial. Why this is not being more widely tried with these children, I do not know. But the intersensory-rational view shows that swaddling would remove the disturbing influence of multisensory stimuli, kinaesthetic and tactile and vestibular and, to some degree, somaesthetic noises and uncertainties among them, and possibly, for the first time, permit these children to concentrate, to the extent that they can, on the communicative games at hand. Swaddle the child, and then monitor eye movements onto a giant iconographic keyboard placed in front of him or her, and start the communicative process in that way. The child looks at or touches the large kitten-button, so produce a giant kitten on a screen in front of the child, or a real kitten (having this ready), and also say 'kitten' out loud. This sort of controlled but directed intersensory cueing plays a quite different role, neurologically and psychologically, in the communicative process than do random intersensory noises. The child looks at a ball, so produce a ball and let the child reach to touch it (do not so much touch it to the child) and say 'ball'. And so forth.

On a more fundamental level still, efforts must be made to develop methods on which the children can be tested and encouraged to explore the fundamental dimensions of basic sensory reality: up, upper, uppermost; big, bigger, biggest; blue, bluer, bluest. And so forth. Elsewhere I have shown[8] that there is a direct intersensory-rational contribution to what we term intelligence, so that in commencing the difficult task of communicating with these children, it is wholly reasonable to begin with a deliberate and then move to a voluntary exploration of the unitary sensory dimensions that form the foundation for all later and more abstract intellectual processing.

Furthermore, no one has explored with these children the ranges of their form-processing capacity, and that must be done before we could assert that, when looking at a letter 'g' on the typewriter, they do indeed have the capacity to recognize it as a member of the set 'g'. This method, first used by me many years ago with the brain injured,[9] was called psychomorphometry: the psychophysical capacity to recognize familiar forms when systematically distorted in shape or in size or in colour, and so on. Before we can be sure that these children can recognize some given letter, much less word, and much less still sentence, we need to know not only the fundamental character of their processing skills of motions along single and unitary sense-quality dimensions, but also that of their multi-sensory shape and form processing as well. Show them a picture of their puppy, for example, or their sister, or their favourite ice-cream, and then systematically change the picture in visually controlled ways until the recognition ceases. Would their puppy be recognized if it were upside down, for example, or of a different colour; would their sister be recognized in a strange hair style or as very small; would they recognize the taste (switching modalities to illustrate the generality) of their favourite ice-cream if it were served in an unusual dish? And so on. Are such capacities within their normal range of communication, if not the normal range for their age? If so, one can build up communicative bases from there. Try a picture of themselves: when does the self-image mature sufficiently in them so that they know what they look like, as in a mirror. The now

---

8 Shipley, T. (1990) *The Theory of Intelligence*, Springfield, Illinois: Thomas.

9 Shipley, T. (1964) 'Quantitative psychophysical methods applied to the neuropsychiatric examination of the visual agnosic', *Neuropsychologica* 2: 145–52.

rather famous mirror test is this: one surreptitiously puts a smudge on the nose of a child and has him/her look into a large mirror standing directly in front. A normal child of just under 22 months, on average, reaches out to touch the smudge on the nose in the mirror. A normal child of 24 months or older, on average, reaches to its own nose.[10] But the evidence thus far with autistic children suggests that they would fail to point to their own noses, generally even up into their teen years. Since they fail to give any concrete evidence of self-recognition, should we not then be somewhat cautious in expecting or asserting that they would recognize something or some process as letters, which is of so much lesser significance?

Mostly, these children do not even regularly sit up well, nor show many aspects of a focused attention, though they do display characteristic signs of sensory arousal, sometimes becoming alert when a light suddenly goes on or when one claps one's hands. In the more objective evoked brain potential, they do not show signs of being able to deal at all well with even just two simple and short sensory messages at once.[11] Moreover, on average, they do not eat all that well or control their bowels that well, so that our rational anticipation of successful communication with them ought not to be unduly elevated to the level of highly complex alphabetical interchange, no matter how well the keyboard is laid out and the writing gestures facilitated. As far as I know, prior to all of this work with facilitative communication, there was nothing to indicate that these children possessed any reading or spelling skills at all, nor even any kinaesthetic pointing or eye-aiming skills ... or sufficient ego-strength to form the intent to communicate, much less to spell.

I do not mean to imply that, from the sensory-rational point of view, no means can ever be found to help parents find the soul of their child behind that awe-fully dark autistic shade,[12] but only to caution that the approach must be simpler in all the visual and auditory and vestibular and somaesthetic and kinaesthetic and cognitive methods that are employed, and more coherent with the children's obviously reduced ego-strength and communicative capacity. Since our aim, as it always is in interpersonal and cognitive communication, is to attempt a transformation from an extrinsic mental geometry into an intrinsic one, we must

---

10 For example, Shipley, V. (1986) 'The development of the sense of self in children', PhD thesis, Miami, Florida: Barry University.

11 Shipley, T. (1980) *Sensory Integration in Children*, Springfield, Illinois: Thomas.

12 In an astute aside, the physicist, Freeman Dyson, gives a fine image of what he calls an 'alien intelligence'. He describes the response of a 10-year-old autistic girl who had just received a letter from another autistic child that consisted of a whole page of numbers. The little girl 'read' the letter rapidly, and then suddenly started to shout out repeatedly: 'Mistake, mistake!' It appears that the letter consisted entirely of prime numbers, except for one that was in error. Cited in Horgan (1993) *J. Sci. Amer.* August: 27.

carefully seek to establish this special conformability by going from the simplest upwards, and not the reverse.

With children who have great difficulty in adequately and without considerable parental empathy communicating how sleepy they are or that they are hungry for this food and not for that, or that they are upset for this reason and not for that, the emotional pressures are certainly strong on all of us to find coherent ways back into the geometry of that weak and fuzzy intrinsic ego structure. And it is clearly important that I should not be taken as discouraging the facilitator approaches. I am only trying to urge them towards approaches that are more solidly scientific and intersensorily controlled.

Clearly, much needs to be done. And perhaps the proper use of principles of intersensory–rational psychology may give some guidance to those active in this field.

SIMPLE IN MIND AND IN MATHEMATICS: A CAUTIONARY TALE

It is pretty much of an accepted principle of language communication theory that, if one truly does have a thought clearly in mind, it can be expressed simply. Actually, according to Wittgenstein, the philosopher of language, it can *only* be said simply, or not at all. Obfuscation is the damnedest intellectual sin. But it is a widespread sin, also, in experimental neuronalism and in mathematical biology. As one can pretty nearly always find in nature some creature odd enough to illustrate any theory of the true 'origin' or 'nature' of life; so, in neuronalism, there is almost no limit as to the sort of neurons that one can devise to find somewhere. And in mathematics, as both its strength and its temptation, one can fit pretty nearly any observation and experimental result 'as close as you wish' with any fancy equation; the mere multiplication of variables is almost always enough. Or one can add another constant or another negative exponent.

But, for communication and the getting across of scientific meaning, one's neurons ought also to be simple and direct, as, presumably, are one's thoughts about neurons, and so also one's mathematics.

In science, as in carpentry and agriculture, from which applied science came, one always searches for processes that proceed in orderly ways, the simplest of which is linear. This means that we can model them with a straight line, as in analytic geometry, using an equation of the species:

$$y = ax + b.$$

A buttress is a fine example of such an event, in all these fields. But there is an infinite number of linear equations, so that that restriction is good only if we take it seriously and do not hedge. Perhaps there is a second-degree variable hidden inside one of the constants . . . will we ever know?

Secondly, after the linear, we hope that simple and regular and possibly repeating non-linear equations may well enough describe what is happening. Say we use a sinewave equation:

$$y = a \sin \theta + b,$$

or something similar to this, and hope that this gives an idea as close as we wish to the reality. Ocean waves, for example, may occasionally be acceptibly sine-like in form, but generally they are not. Wind patterns are too variable. Dampened sinewaves do come radially out from the skip of the pebble on the pond, provided there are no water-lilies or frogs. But electro-magnetic waves are most often veridically sinelike over large regions of cosmic space-time: X-rays and radio-waves and light. Musical notes, as they travel in the relatively homogeneous air, can also be very closely modelled as sinewaves, with some variations for overtones and the special timbre of different voices and instruments.

But it is the bane of editors of science publications and readers of science articles that the authors sometimes present equations that are more precise than their measurements, more complex than the reality that they seek to describe and which, in the event, include so many wholly hidden assumptions and collapsed variables that, when these are discovered, the reader is tempted to throw the whole thing out. When such obtuseness occurs, it is quite likely that, despite the symbolic elegance, the neurono-matho-scientist does not have a clear idea in mind as to what he or she is actually trying to describe. One can scribble in mathematics almost as easily as one can in alphabetics and musics.

Further, that we, all of us in all fields of both science and the humanities, find widely skewed processes best modelled by cusps and sudden flexes (though these are newly coming into their own, with catastrophe theory and chaos theory in physics and weather predicting) is natural enough, because these are so difficult to think clearly about. Hence the mathematics becomes clumsy. We need a calculus of disappearing intersections and of collapsing gaps, as we already have one of vanishing quantities.

The mind is 'like that' . . . why, precisely, we have not the slightest communicable idea. But the mind does like things in their proper places and it does like changes to be gradual along clear and unambiguous sensory and cognitive dimensions, but not so gradual that directions cannot be well and precisely determined. And it does not like too many directions all at once, and it hates most of all the fact that too many variables are always nagging at one's ear, racing about the lab like so many unruly urchins.

And, mostly, mostly (to use a Boolean conundrum), the mind dislikes processes which have gaps in them, in which, so to say, in just this space here, there is . . . no space. Or in just that time there . . . no time. Or in just this anything, any process, any quality . . . no thing, no process, no quality.

Do all scientists, men and women, hate gaps because they are bad; or because God had a prior hatred for gaps? Could we not now imagine, in the maturity if not the twilight of our evolution, a Creator who liked discontinuities and emptinesses, and so incarnated in us an affection for them as well?

'Discontinuity-loving, non-entropic psycho-neurons.' How much more absurd can one get than that ... but is this crazy enough?

Psyche's dance eludes and ever she flits away. And it seems to me that no future psychology can attain solid scientific status or attract a serious audience that does not, henceforth, give due attention to the prevalence of intersensory non-linearities and emergences and discontinuities in our mental life, and either show that in the current instance they can be discarded as insignificant or artifactitious, or confront them directly as essential to the pirouettes, postures, leaps, and twirls that Psyche gives to her so especially attractive dance.

Appendix: a short listing of some influential works

It is clear that the full bibliography of long-standing serious work on the anatomy of the human brain and the co-ordination of this with perceptual and cognitive and in-depth psychological processes is now well into the thousands. An exacting review of this important history is clearly overdue. In my opinion, the history of ideas in science is not less important than is the thrusting ahead with what one hopes, perhaps somewhat vaingloriously, may be new ideas in science. The latter only seems more intellectually vigorous. It is my earnest hope that, in the next few years, someone may choose to develop a definitive treatise on this so important history. One awaits a giant like Stephan Polyak.[1] Perhaps, in some ways, my small effort will be helpful to those wishing to undertake this broader and more profound task, without which the meaning of our present debates may remain obscure.

Without being exhaustive, since this work is not a history, but to give the reader some sense of the vigour and productivity of this field, I list here just a few of the more pertinent recent books that have come to my attention and that have, to various degrees, influenced some of my own thoughts, but are not otherwise cited in the text. Specific points are, of course, carefully referenced when noted. Some books cited present views quite contrary to my own, some others seem to me in many ways patently absurd, but they all deserve mention because the issues are by no means closed. A useful and readily available debate on some of these issues between J.R. Searle and the Churchlands appears in a *Scientific American* (1990) 262: 26–37. See also:

Boden, M.A. (1989) *Computer Models of Mind: Computational Approaches in Theoretical Psychology*, New York: Cambridge University Press.
Brown, H.I. (1988) *Rationality*, New York: Routledge.

---

1 As in his unexcelled classic (1957) *The Vertebrate Visual System*, Chicago University Press; also *The Retina*, Chicago University Press, in the corrected 1948 edition.
  A recent book, just come to my attention, deserves special mention in this regard: Finger, S. (1994) *Origins of Neuroscience*, New York: Oxford University Press.

Chaisson, E. (1981) *Cosmic Dawn: The Origins of Matter and Life*, New York: Norton.
Changeux, J.P. (1986) *Neuronal Man: The Biology of Mind*, New York: Oxford University Press.
Chomsky, N. (1988) *Language and Problems of Knowledge*, Cambridge, Massachusetts: MIT Press.
Churchland, P.M. (1979) *Scientific Realism and the Plasticity of mind*, New York: Cambridge University Press.
Churchland, P.M. (1984) *Matter and Consciousness: A Contemporary Introduction to the Philosophy of Mind*, Cambridge, Massachusetts: MIT Press.
Churchland, P.M. (1990) *A Neurocomputational Perspective: The Nature of Mind and the Structure of Science*, Cambridge, Massachusetts: MIT Press.
Churchland, P.S. (1986) *Neurophilosophy: Toward a Unified Science of the Mindbrain*, Cambridge, Massachusetts: MIT Press.
Cottingham, J. (1988) *Rationalism*, London: Aladdin.
Dennett, D.C. (1984) *Elbow Room: The Varieties of Free Will Worth Wanting*, Cambridge Massachusetts: MIT Press.
Dennett, D.C. (1991) *Consciousness Explained*, Boston, Massachusetts: Little, Brown.
Diamond, M. (1988) *Enriching Heredity: The Impact of the Environment on the Anatomy of the Brain*, New York: The Free Press.
Evans, P. and Deehan, G. (1990) *The Descent of Mind: The Nature and Purpose of Intelligence*, London: Grafton.
Fodor, J. (1983) *The Modularity of Mind*, Cambridge, Massachusetts: MIT Press.
Franklin, J. (1987) *Molecules of the Mind: The Brave New Science of Molecular Psychology*, New York: Atheneum.
Gazzaniga, M.S. (1988) *Mind Matters: How Mind and Brain Interact to Create our Conscious Lives*, Boston, Massachusetts: Houghton–Mifflin.
George, A. (ed.) (1989) *Reflections on Chomsky*, Oxford: Blackwell.
Glees, P. (1988) *The Human Brain*, New York: Cambridge University Press.
Goody, W. (1989) *Time and the Nervous System*, Westport, Connecticut: Greenwood.
Gregory, R. (1974) *Concepts and Mechanisms of Perception*, London: Duckworth.
Gregory, R. (1981) *Mind in Science*, London: Weidenfeld & Nicolson.
Humphrey, N. (1992) *A History of the Mind: Evolution and the Birth of Consciousness*, New York: Simon & Schuster.
Hundert, E.M. (1989) *Philosophy, Psychiatry and Neuroscience: Three Approaches to Mind*, Oxford: Clarendon Press.
Klivington, K. (1990) *The Science of Mind*, Cambridge, Massachusetts: MIT Press.
MacDonald, C. (1990) *Mind-Body Identity Theories*, London: Routledge.
Minsky, M. (1987) *The Society of Mind*, New York: Simon & Schuster.
Norwich, K.H. (1993) *Information, Sensation and Perception*, Orlando, Florida: Academic Press.
Popper, K. and Eccles, J. (1977) *The Self and its Brain*, Berlin: Springer.
Pribram, K.H. (1990) *Brain and Perception: Holonomy and Structure in Figural Processing*, Hillsdale, NJ: Erlbaum.
Purves, D. (1988) *Body and Brian: A Trophic Theory of Neural Connections*, Cambridge, Massachusetts: Harvard University Press.
Pylyshyn, Z.W. (1984) *Computation and Cognition: Towards a Foundation for Cognitive Science*, Cambridge, Massachusetts: MIT Press.
Richards, R.J. (1988) *Darwin and the Emergence of Evolutionary Theories of Mind and Behavior*, Chicago: University of Chicago Press.
Rollins, B.E. (1989) *The Unheeded Cry: Animal Consciousness, Animal Pain and Science*, New York: Oxford University Press.

Sanford, A.J. (1988) *The Mind of man: Models of Human Understanding*, New Haven, Connecticut: Yale University Press.

Searle, J.R. (1984) *Minds, Brains and Science*, Cambridge, Massachusetts: Harvard University Press.

Shallice, T. (1988) *From Neuropsychology to Mental Structure*, New York: Cambridge University Press.

Sorabji, R. (1988) *Matter, Space and Notion: Theories in Antiquity and their Sequel*, Ithaca, N.Y.: Cornell University Press.

Star, S.L. (1989) *Regions of the Mind: Brain Research and the Quest for Scientific Certainty*, Stanford, California: Stanford University Press.

Whitrow, G.J. (1989) *Time in History: The Evolution of our General Awareness of Time and Temporal Perspective*, Oxford: Oxford University Press.

Wylie, R.C. (1989) *Measures of Self-Concept*, Lincoln, Nebraska: Nebraska University Press.

Yoder, J.G. (1989) *Unrolling Time: Christian Huygens and the Mathematization of Time*, New York: Cambridge University Press.

Young, J.Z. (1987) *Philosophy and the Brain*, New York: Oxford University Press.

Zohar, D. (1988) *The Quantum Self: A Revolutionary View of Human Nature and Consciousness Rooted in the New Physics*, London: Bloomsbury.

Index

Groce, N.E. 203–4

hallucinations 232, 233–4
havings 147–9
Head, Henry 59–60, 61
hearing: auditory cliffs 33; aural
symmetry 163; extrinsic and intrinsic
geometries 9–10; hallucinations 232,
233, 234; loss of variance-processing
capacity 202
Hécaen, Henri 14–15
heraldic neurology 173–5, 218
holography 172
Hume, David 118–19, 228
humour 6–7, 136–7
hysteria 16, 61–2, 237

ideas 117, 118–37; innate 109, 167–9,
170–1; and objects 138–56; unverbalizable 6–8
illusions: sensory 216–17
imagination 60, 75; and creativity
39–41; senses in 3–4
inclusion 161, 165
indirect routes 74–6
infants: intersensory conflict 31–2, 33;
search for nipple 20–3
infinite routes 85–9
intellectual destiny 82–3
intelligence: and autism 238; innate
167–9; location of 36–41; and loss of
variance-processing capacity 200–3;
mental routes 83–6
interaction of senses: and autism
234–40; and child development
222–5; and conflict 17–20, 33, 54,
171–2; contribution to cognitive
processes 157–75; dynamics of 23–4,
55–6; and free will 206–19; and
ideas 118–37; innate 20–3; and
objects 138–56; and reason 34–6;
and reductionism 228–34; relation
with mind 52–68; routes 69–92;
single brain cells 67–8; and space
108–17; and time 93–107
interference: of ideas 121–2
internal milieu 53–4
introspection 120
isomorphism 173–5

James, William 140
jokes 6–7, 136–7
Joyce, James 86, 128
Jung, Carl Gustav 168

kinaesthesis 34–5; symmetry 163
Köhler, Wolfgang 27
language 94; as approach to mind
13–16; autantonyms 127–32; after
brain injury 13–15; as expressions of
order 177–8; limitations in 147–8;
litotes 132; and loss of variance-
processing capacity 202;
onomatopoesis 134–5; oxymorons
133–4; of physical dimensions 107;
unverbalizable 6–8; *Urworten* 126;
and vision 13
languages: learning multiple 14; sign
158, 203–4
leaf-room: Ames' 29–30, 31
learning: one-trial 198–9; importance
of variance in 222–5
Leibnitz, Gottfried 168, 171
light 116–17, 122–3
linear equations 240
linearity 189–91; Pythagoras' theorem
76–82
litotes 132
lobectomies 62
lobotomies 62
local signatures 18–19, 53, 117
location 18–19; of intelligence 36–41;
of mind 5; of pain 117; sensory
interaction 35, 53–4
logic 82–3, 90, 161; Lewis Carroll
sorite 84–5

machines: relationship to mind 144–6,
179–85
magnitude estimation 230
Martha's Vineyard, USA 203–5
mathematics 14, 55; linear and non-
linear equations 240–2; Pythagoras'
theorem 76–82; and sensory
dimensionalities 125–6
mazes 74
meaning: and motion 28
memory 22–3, 36, 113
mental illness 5, 8; and sense of
freedom 216; treatment 231–4
mental self: geometric 8–9
meta-ideas 138–56
metalanguage 94
metaphors: machines as 179–85
Michotte, A. 141–2
migrations: animal 94, 110–13
mind: approaches to 12–41; compa-
risons with 176–91; contribution of
senses to 157–75; and machines